CDM Regulations 2015 Explained

ice
Institution of Civil Engineers
publishing

CDM Regulations 2015 Explained

Raymond Joyce BSc, MSc, LLB, CEng, FICE
Freeths LLP, UK

Published by ICE Publishing, One Great George Street, Westminster, London SW1P 3AA.

Full details of ICE Publishing sales representatives and distributors can be found at:
www.icevirtuallibrary.com/info/printbooksales

Other titles by ICE Publishing:

Practical Guide to Using the CDM Regulations 2015.
Tony Putsman and Paul McArthur. ISBN 978-0-7277-5990-0
CDM 2015 Questions and Answers. Pat Perry. ISBN 978-0-7277-6032-6
ICE Manual of Health and Safety in Construction, 2nd edition.
Ciaran McAleenan and David Oloke (eds.). ISBN 978-0-7277-6010-4

The CDM Regulations Explained, published in 1995.
ISBN 978-0-7277-2034-4
The CDM Regulations Explained, 2nd edition, published in 2001.
ISBN 978-0-7277-3036-7
CDM Regulations 2007 Explained, published in 2007.
ISBN 978-0-7277-3496-9
This edition, *CDM Regulations 2015 Explained*, published in 2015

www.icevirtuallibrary.com

A catalogue record for this book is available from the British Library

ISBN 978-0-7277-6009-8

Commissioning Editor: Amber Thomas
Production Editor: Rebecca Taylor
Market Development Executive: Elizabeth Hobson

Typeset by Academic + Technical, Bristol
Index created by Indexing Specialists (UK) Ltd, Hove, East Sussex
Printed and bound by Ashford Colour Press, Gosport

Contents

Preface

We in the construction industry have lived with the Construction (Design and Management) Regulations – commonly referred to as the CDM Regulations – for over 20 years and, as if to avoid complacency, a new version of the Regulations came into force on 6 April 2015.

The changes in the 2015 Regulations are the result of a hard pruning that has reduced the word count, put more responsibility on the client, changed the arrangements for domestic work and introduced a new role, referred to as the principal designer. This book is therefore entirely different from my earlier books on the 1994 and 2007 Regulations.

The changes ensure that the CDM Regulations remain centre stage for legislation that affects the construction industry. In their third version, it is questionable whether the latest revision to the Regulations represents a triumph of European jurisdiction over UK sovereignty, the lobbying of business interests of those within the construction industry and its clients, or a straightforward response to continue to improve the health and safety record of the construction industry, or all three!

The CDM Regulations represent the latest initiative to improve the health and safety record of the construction industry by influencing the design, management and construction processes. For most readers of this book, it will be important to them to have an authoritative explanation of the Regulations and insight as to how they are likely to affect their own professional and business interests. The Regulations establish principles to improve health and safety management and avoid an easy prescriptive approach, which requires designers and clients to exercise judgement. The onus on designers to avoid hazards or mitigate risks to health and safety should stimulate innovative design solutions. I am in no doubt that the Regulations will continue to be a controversial source of debate and a subject of lobbying, partly encouraged by the Secretary of

State's obligation to carry out a review of the Regulations every 5 years. In the meantime, the 2015 Regulations present many challenges, which I hope will be faced and overcome with the help of this book. The new Regulations also coincide with the digital revolution in the construction industry that makes possible the Building Information Modelling (BIM) initiative. The application of the Regulations will be made easier by BIM, to the benefit of design-driven improvements in health and safety management.

I owe a debt of gratitude to many colleagues and clients, too many to mention, who have ensured that the CDM Regulations have never been far from my work as a construction solicitor. My gratitude to Yvonne, my wife, represents the largest debt because it is she who has lived through the CDM story and this latest chapter with patience and good humour!

About the author

Raymond Joyce BSc, MSc, LLB, CEng, FICE has over 35 years' experience in the construction industry as a chartered civil engineer and a solicitor. He is also an accredited adjudicator and mediator. His first book on the 1994 CDM Regulations established his reputation as an authority on construction health and safety in addition to his reputation for assisting his clients safely through the maze of construction law.

Raymond is a member of the ICE Legal Affairs Panel and Chairman of the Dispute Resolution Panel and has been a member of several British Standards committees and a European Working Group.

Table of cases

Table of UK statutes

Table of statutory instruments

Abbreviations

1994 Regulations	Construction (Design and Management) Regulations 1994
2007 Regulations	Construction (Design and Management) Regulations 2007
2015 Regulations	Construction (Design and Management) Regulations 2015
ACOP	Approved Code of Practice
ALARP	as low as reasonably practicable
BIM	Building Information Modelling
CDM Regulations	Construction (Design and Management) Regulations
Commission	Health and Safety Commission
EU	European Union
Executive	Health and Safety Executive
Framework Directive	Council Directive of 12 June 1989 on the introduction of measures to encourage improvements in the safety and health of workers at work (89/391/EEC)
Management Regulations	Management of Health and Safety at Work Regulations 1999
HASWA 1974	Health and Safety at Work etc. Act 1974
SFAIRP	so far as is reasonably practicable
SPV	special-purpose vehicle
TMCSD	Temporary or Mobile Construction Sites Directive. The Council Directive of 25 June 1992 on the implementation of minimum safety and health requirements at temporary or mobile construction sites (92/57/EEC)

CDM Regulations 2015 Explained
ISBN 978-0-7277-6009-8

http://dx.doi.org/10.1680/cdmre.60098.001

Chapter 1
Introduction

- **Have the CDM Regulations improved the health and safety record?**
- **The origin and evolution of the CDM Regulations**

Have the CDM Regulations improved the health and safety record?

The statistics produced by the Health and Safety Executive ('the Executive') for fatalities and serious injuries in the construction industry have shown a downward trend since 1974. In the last 20 years there has been a significant reduction in the number and rates of injury in the construction industry, which just happens to coincide with the introduction of the 1994 Construction (Design and Management) Regulations – the 'CDM Regulations'.

In the 10 years following the introduction of the 1994 Regulations, the improvement in the annual statistics for fatalities was from 5 to 3.5 per 100 000 workers, representing an improvement of 30%. There had been some upward blips in the 10 years after the introduction of the 1994 Regulations but the trend was undeniably downward. In the last 5 years the trend has continued, with an average rate of fatal injury of 2.1 per 100 000 workers, and in 2013/14 there were 2.0 fatal injuries per 100 000 workers (HSE, 2014).

The construction industry remains one of the high-risk industries, which is underlined by the fact that it represented 31% of the fatal injuries and 10% of the reported major injuries/incidents in 2013/2014 for only 5% of all employees in the workforce. But fatalities are only one indicator, because the Executive has estimated that for the same period there were 76 000 total cases of work-related ill health. Injuries accounted for 592 000 lost working days, and ill health for 1.7 million days (HSE, 2014).

Can the general downward trend in the construction industry be attributable to the 1994 Regulations or did the legislation, in fact, make no difference at all to the statistics?

The difficulty with analysing statistics that are either expressed as an absolute number of deaths or a number of deaths per 100 000 workers is the extent to which they can be distorted by one or two significant accidents or incidents within the relevant year and by the complex interdependencies of many disparate contributory factors. Without the CDM Regulations it is arguable that the construction industry would still have benefited from a continuing improvement in the statistics for fatalities.

Improvements would have been likely to come about as a result of the following

- society's expectation to see improvements in the working environment
- continued improvements in the construction techniques
- increased investment by the construction industry in health and safety management
- compliance with other relevant health and safety regulations.

Thus, it is impossible to say that the CDM Regulations have been a success in improving the health and safety record of the construction industry. Although compliance with the CDM Regulations will have been a contributory factor, no one can know with any certainty to what extent lives were saved.

The CDM Regulations have made a significant difference in one very important regard, and that was their contribution to improving the awareness of health and safety risks in the construction industry and in promoting communication and coordination between the parties on projects.

There is one factor that has emerged from all the statistics, which the 2015 CDM Regulations seek to address, notably the fact that serious and fatal injuries have shifted in the past 10–15 years from large sites to small sites where there are fewer than 15 workers. This is unsurprising because the large sites where larger contractors are working have invested in health and safety management commensurate with a business climate that has promoted the Considerate Constructors Scheme, improved corporate governance, trade union representation and employer–employee relationships generally.

The origin and evolution of the CDM Regulations

The health and safety record of the construction industry in the 1980s was such that the Health and Safety Commission ('the Commission') planned to introduce far-reaching legislation targeted at the management of construction projects. However, these plans were overtaken by the Temporary or Mobile Construction Sites Directive (TMCSD), which would achieve a very similar result when incorporated into domestic law.

The preamble to the TMCSD on the implementation of minimum health and safety requirements on temporary or mobile construction sites underlined the importance of the pre-construction phase as a cause of accidents across the European Union as follows:

> unsatisfactory and/or organisational options or poor planning of the works at the project preparation stage have played a role in more than half of the occupational accidents occurring on construction sites in the Community.

Therefore, the 1994 CDM Regulations came into being for the purposes of implementing the TMCSD, but there is no doubt that similar legislation would have come into being in any event. The implementation of the TMCSD through the introduction of the 1994 Regulations represented a major change by putting the design and management arrangements at the centre of the initiative to improve the record for health and safety in the construction industry. So, the 1994 Regulations came into force on the back of high expectations that they could contribute to a significant improvement in health and safety management. The 1994 Regulations challenged the construction industry because they created specified duties for named duty holders and demanded judgement as opposed to following the prescriptive requirements for physical safeguards in the Factories Act.

The uncertainty as to how the 1994 Regulations should be adopted and how they might be enforced caused duty holders to document each detail without any thought about the essence of identifying hazards. Suddenly the construction industry had to accommodate a new professional role – named in the 1994 Regulations as the planning supervisor – together with a deluge of additional documents, which led to serious criticism of the effectiveness of the 1994 Regulations. The debate about their effectiveness and the unnecessary bureaucracy was never off the agenda within the construction industry. After the Executive issued a discussion document, *Revitalising Health and Safety in Construction* (HSE, 2002), the main areas of criticism were

- inadequate client focus
- complexity of the Regulations and their structure
- the failure of the planning supervisor role
- bureaucracy.

The Executive realised that the 1994 Regulations needed to be revised, and the 2007 CDM Regulations – which were influenced by the consultation process – addressed the main areas of criticism. The 2007 Regulations, which came into force on 6 April 2007, were significantly different in emphasis. The 2007 Regulations had been developed in line with Better Regulation principles, and were intended to reduce bureaucracy and to improve the commercial and business management of construction projects. The Executive also put greater focus on the client, who was the party in a project team that had most influence over the allocation of resources: time, people and money. The 2007 Regulations therefore attempted to

- be clearer – making it easier for duty holders to know what is expected of them
- be flexible and to accommodate a wide range of contractual arrangements
- emphasise the need to plan and manage work, rather than treating the paperwork as an end in itself
- emphasise the communication and coordination advantages of duty holders working in integrated teams
- simplify the way that duty holders assessed competence.

Despite wide consultation, it was inevitable that the 2007 Regulations were not without their detractors. At the eleventh hour, within days of the 2007 Regulations coming into force, the opposition party tabled an Early Day Motion in Parliament. The opposition had been lobbied by the various client organisations on the basis that clients were at an unfair risk of prosecution. The Early Day Motion was a means of requesting a Parliamentary debate that the 2007 Regulations should be annulled. The client's role under the 2007 Regulations was undoubtedly more onerous than it had been under the 1994 Regulations. Very few persons would deny that clients have a significant influence over health and safety on a project, and for many the additional responsibility was welcome. The debate took place on 10 May 2007, and the Early Day Motion was defeated by the government, thus leaving the 2007 Regulations in place and without amendment. There was an important concession by the government that it would carry out an early review of the 2007 Regulations.

There were those who complained at the time that the attempt to reduce the bureaucracy and the costs to the construction industry would fail because of the increased need to comply with the assessment of competence and the Commission's optimistic assumptions as to improvements in the future health and safety statistics. In fact, the results of external research published in 2012 and other channels of evaluation suggested that the 2007 Regulations had moved only a small step forward. In particular, the conclusions were that

- the 2007 Regulations were viewed more positively by duty holders than the 1994 Regulations
- their broad structure was fit for purpose
- problems generally arose through mis- and over-interpretation
- significant concerns remained, which included
  - the 2007 Regulations had not reduced bureaucracy as hoped
  - the industry approach to the assessment of competence was heavy handed and created another contribution to bureaucracy

– the coordination function in the pre-construction phase was not generally well embedded.

The conclusions of the evaluation process of the 2007 Regulations were then subject to further scrutiny by reference to the Löfstedt Review of health and safety legislation, which meant that any revision had to take into account

- the extent to which these regulations have led to positive health and safety outcomes and the extent to which they have created significant economic costs for businesses of all sizes
- whether the requirements of EU directives are being unnecessarily enhanced ('gold plated') when transposed into UK regulation
- any evidence or examples of where health and safety regulations have led to unreasonable outcomes, or inappropriate litigation and compensation.

In July 2011, health and safety legislation was subjected to scrutiny as part of the Red Tape Challenge, which led to a number of comments being made on the 2007 Regulations.

So, the drafting of the 2015 CDM Regulations, further refined after going out to consultation in 2014, is the result of the concerns of the construction industry following the evaluation process and government initiatives. The government had published its strategy for the construction industry in July 2013 (HM Government, 2013), which included

- improved coordination
- better value for money
- improved efficiency and procurement
- use of technology improvements, including Building Information Modelling.

The 2015 Regulations have therefore also been drafted to support the government's strategic objectives.

The final result is another radical revision of the CDM Regulations. The new 2015 Regulations put the client at the centre of a project, and refocuses on the design and construction process by increased reliance upon the professionalism of designers and contractors to give due consideration to recognising hazards and managing risks to health and safety. There are fewer words than before and the language is more direct, using plain English, which will hopefully improve the accessibility and interpretation of the 2015 Regulations.

CDM Regulations 2015 Explained
ISBN 978-0-7277-6009-8

http://dx.doi.org/10.1680/cdmre.60098.007

Chapter 2
Framework of health and safety law

- **Introduction**
- **Common law**
- **UK legislation**
- **European health and safety initiative**

Introduction
The CDM Regulations are a small part of a very much larger legal framework of law in the UK and the European Union (EU) that addresses matters of health and safety.

The CDM Regulations, except for some amendments to associated legislation referred to in regulation 38 and set out in Schedule 5, do not change the general principles of health and safety law. They are, however, a comprehensive implementation of the EU's Temporary or Mobile Construction Sites Directive (see Appendix 3) and a continuing development of the widely accepted need to influence and regulate management practices to improve health and safety in the construction industry.

Common law
Common law is often referred to as that part of English law which cannot be found in acts of Parliament but in the decisions of the courts and other tribunals. Common law principles change and develop with the decisions of the courts. Conversely, acts of Parliament can abolish well-established rules of common law.

The importance of common law in health and safety matters has diminished considerably with the increased amount of legislation. Statute law will always prevail whenever there is a conflict with the common law, thus upholding the legislative supremacy of Parliament. However, despite the extensive statutory legislation that affects matters of health and safety, common law principles coexist with statutory provisions. For example, there is implied in every contract of employment a term that the employer will provide safe plant and premises, a safe system of work and reasonably competent fellow workers.

The common law, insofar as it is based on decisions of the courts, also serves to give effect to the intentions of Parliament in the interpretation of statutes.

Reasonably practicable

Where an employer's obligation is qualified by the test of 'so far as is reasonably practicable', commonly referred to as SFAIRP, the employer can escape liability if they can show they has taken sufficient care and implemented the necessary measures to avoid risks to the health and safety of workers. The leading case that established the guiding principle as to the interpretation of 'reasonably practicable' is *Edwards* v. *National Coal Board* [1949] All ER 743(CA). Asquith LJ stated that

> 'Reasonably practicable' is a narrower term than 'physically possible' and seems to me to imply that a computation must be made by the owner in which the quantum of risk is placed on one scale and the sacrifice involved in the measures necessary for averting the risk (whether in money, time or trouble) is placed in the other, and that, if it is shown that there is a gross disproportion between them – the risk being insignificant in relation to the sacrifice – the defence has discharged the onus on them. Moreover, this computation falls to be made by the owner at a point in time and anterior to the accident. The questions he has to answer are:
> (a) What measures are necessary and sufficient to prevent any breach ...?; and
> (b) are these measures reasonably practicable?

However, SFAIRP was not accepted as a lawful principle by the EU prior to June 2007 on the basis that the Framework Directive should impose strict liability on employers for any circumstances that are a risk to the health and safety of its works, thus depriving an employer of a defence that the costs of prevention would have been grossly disproportionate. UK employers' obligations were therefore inconsistent with those of employers throughout the EU, and bestowed an unfair cost advantage.

The only exceptions to escape strict liability in the European Commission's view were 'unusual and unforeseeable circumstances, beyond the employers' control, or to exceptional events, the consequences of which could not have been avoided despite the exercise of all due care' (Article 5(4) of the Framework Directive).

SFAIRP was challenged by the European Commission on the basis that it qualifies UK employers' obligations in a way that is inconsistent with the Framework Directive. In June 2007 the European Court of Justice ruled that SFAIRP is not unlawful, meaning that measures to reduce risks do not have to be grossly disproportionate. Therefore, the approach adopted by the courts since 1949, and recently endorsed by the European Court, is one of proportionality.

To determine what is reasonably practicable, a cost–benefit analysis is required that takes into account actual costs and indirect costs of supervision and other measures that would need to be implemented that cannot be easily be costed. The cost–benefit analysis is not a finely balanced calculation but requires professional judgement to identify whether the costs of prevention are grossly disproportionate. If the risk is insignificant in relation to the sacrifice that would be incurred by the employer, it is not reasonably practicable to take steps necessary to control a hazard.

The Health and Safety Executive ('the Executive') has recently issued guidance to its own employees to explain the concept of 'reasonably practicable' (HSE, 2014; see http://www.hse.gov.uk/risk/theory/alarpglance.htm). The Executive asserts that the test of 'as low as reasonably practicable' – abbreviated to ALARP – is synonymous with SFAIRP. The significance of this guidance is that the Executive uses the ALARP test because it describes the level to which the Executive expects to see workplace risks controlled. Thus, it assists duty holders in identifying goals and the means to achieve them. From a legal point of view, the terminology used in the CDM Regulations is SFAIRP. An example used by the Executive is to consider the costs that would be reasonable for an employer to incur to mitigate the risk of bruised knees.

Thus, an employer or duty holder who conducts a cost–benefit analysis and concludes that the costs of implementing health and safety procedures outweigh the benefit is, in theory, not obliged to take any further action. But a word of warning: as a basis for a defence, such arguments are not convincing except in the most compelling of circumstances.

The distinction between SFAIRP and a duty to take 'all practicable steps' highlights that where such a duty is imposed (see regulations 19 ('Stability of structures') and 22 ('Excavations')), the costs that an employer would incur are not a factor to be taken into account.

UK legislation

Numerous acts of Parliament and statutory instruments have come into force with the intention of regulating the improving health and safety management in the construction industry. The legislation which laid the foundation for the revolution in health and safety management is the Health and Safety at Work etc. Act (HASWA) 1974. The far-reaching consequences of the HASWA 1974 cannot be overestimated.

The HASWA 1974 established the Health and Safety Commission ('the Commission'), and gave it the power to propose health and safety regulations and approve codes of practice. It also set up the Executive with responsibility for enforcing health and safety laws.

The radical difference between the HASWA 1974 and all preceding health and safety legislation was the emphasis on individuals and their duties as compared with premises. Rather than a prescriptive approach, the HASWA 1974 is based on principles designed to bring about a greater awareness of the problems associated with health and safety issues. The legislation imposes duties on all businesses in all sectors and includes employers and employees. The Corporate Manslaughter and Corporate Homicide Act 2007 is a legislative landmark because it can hold companies and other organisations accountable for the results of a serious failure in management systems, which amount to a gross breach of the duty of care. This act does not create any additional accountability for individuals that was not already in existence, but it is an important step to bring health and safety issues to the main boards of companies as part of the improvement of corporate governance in the UK.

As the primary safety legislation in the UK, the HASWA 1974 is the act under which virtually all subsequent health and safety regulations have been made. All the regulations which implement the EU directives referred to below were made under the powers granted by the HASWA 1974.

The Management of Health and Safety at Work Regulations are one of the most important regulations, and cover all areas of work, except sea transport, and apply to all businesses regardless of size. However, the nature, extent and cost of the measures that need to be taken to ensure compliance will vary, depending on the nature of the hazards and the level of risks associated with different industries.

The three main requirements of the Management Regulations concern

- risk assessment
- arrangements for protective and preventative measures
- the appointment of competent persons to assist with protective and preventative measures.

They require an employer and self-employed employer to implement any preventative and protective measures on the basis of the following principles, set out in Schedule 1 to the Management Regulations, which apply equally to construction sites:

(a) avoiding risks;
(b) evaluating the risks which cannot be avoided;
(c) combating the risks at source;
(d) adapting the work to the individual, especially as regards the design of workplaces, the choice of work equipment and the choice of working and production methods, with a view, in particular, to alleviating monotonous

work and work at a predetermined work-rate and to reducing their effect on health;

(e) adapting to technical progress;
(f) replacing the dangerous by the non-dangerous or the less dangerous;
(g) developing a coherent overall prevention policy that covers technology, organisation of work, working conditions, social relationships and the influence of factors relating to the working environment;
(h) giving collective protective measures priority over individual protective measures; and
(i) giving appropriate instructions to employees.

European health and safety initiative

The European Communities Act 1972, which came into effect on 1 January 1973, incorporated the treaties constituting the European Economic Community, now called the EU, into UK legislation. EU law, which includes directives, is implemented as a domestic law in the UK by legislation passed or approved by Parliament either by acts or by statutory instruments.

The Single European Act (enacted as the European Communities (Amendment) Act 1986) introduced Article 118A into the Treaty of Rome, which obliges the EU member states to 'pay particular attention to encouraging improvements, especially in the working environment, as regards the health and safety of workers'. Article 118A also provides that the health and safety policy would be introduced, by the adoption of directives on working conditions and technical standards, on the basis of majority voting in the EU Council of Ministers. The directives adopted under Article 118A are intended to avoid, as far as possible, imposing administrative, financial and legal constraints that would 'hold back the creation and development of small and medium-sized undertakings'. The directives are only intended to establish minimum standards. EU member states are not prevented from maintaining or introducing more stringent measures, provided that the measures do not interfere with other objectives of the Treaty of Rome, including measures that would have an anti-competitive influence on the open market. To a greater or lesser extent, all the directives adopted under Article 118A and the regulations that implement them have an impact on the construction industry, and share the same overall strategic objective with the CDM Regulations that form the subject matter of this book: to improve the health and safety of workers.

The directives that have been adopted under Article 118A include the following:

(a) The Council Directive of 12 June 1989 on the introduction of measures to encourage improvements in the safety and health of workers at work (89/391/EEC) (the Framework Directive). The Framework Directive is so called because it created the framework for further directives. By creating broad and general duties on employers, employees and the self-employed, the need for dealing with specific hazards and work situations was dealt with in subsequent directives. This directive has been implemented by the Management of Health and Safety at Work Regulations 1999.

(b) The Council Directive of 30 November 1989 concerning the minimum safety and health requirements for the workplace (the first individual directive within the meaning of Article 16(1) of Directive 89/391/EEC)(89/654/EEC). This directive has been implemented by the Workplace (Health, Safety and Welfare) Regulations 1992 (as amended).

(c) The Council Directive of 30 November 1989 concerning the minimum safety and health requirements for the use of work equipment by workers at work (the second individual directive within the meaning of Article 16(1) of Directive 89/391/EEC)(89/655/EEC). This directive has been implemented as the Provision and Use of Work Equipment Regulations 1998 (as amended).

(d) The Council Directive of 30 November 1989 on the minimum health and safety requirements for the use by workers of personal protective equipment at the workplace (the third individual directive within the meaning of Article 16(1) of Directive 89/391/EEC)(89/656/EEC). This directive has been implemented as the Personal Protective Equipment at Work Regulations 1992.

(e) The Council Directive of 29 May 1990 on the minimum health and safety requirements for the manual handling of loads where there is a risk particularly of back injury to workers (the fourth individual directive within the meaning of Article 16(1) of Directive 89/391/EEC)(90/269/EEC). This directive has been implemented as the Manual Handling Operations Regulations 1992 (as amended).

(f) The Council Directive of 29 May 1990 on the minimum safety and health requirements for work with display screen equipment (the fifth individual directive within the meaning of Article 16(1) of Directive 89/391/EEC)(90/270/EEC). This directive has been implemented as the Health and Safety (Display Screen Equipment) Regulations 1992 (as amended).

(g) The Council Directive of 24 June 1992 on the implementation of minimum safety and health requirements at temporary or mobile construction sites (the eighth individual directive within the meaning of Article 16(1) of Directive 89/391/EEC)(92/57/EEC). This is the directive that has now been implemented by the Construction (Design and Management) Regulations 2015.

The regulations referred to in paragraphs (b), (c), (e) and (f) above were amended by the Health and Safety (Miscellaneous Amendments) Regulations 2002.

CDM Regulations 2015 Explained
ISBN 978-0-7277-6009-8

http://dx.doi.org/10.1680/cdmre.60098.013

Chapter 3
An overview of the Regulations

- **Introduction**
- **Application of the Regulations**
- **Notification**
- **Duty holders**
- **Construction phase plan**
- **Health and safety file**
- **Revocations and amendments**
- **Periodic review of the Regulations**
- **Published guidance**

Introduction

CDM Regulation 1 provides:

> These Regulations may be cited as the Construction (Design and Management) Regulations 2015 and come into force on 6th April 2015 immediately after the Mines Regulations 2014.

The Regulations give complete effect to Council Directive 92/57/EEC on the implementation of minimum safety and health requirements at temporary or mobile construction sites (the Temporary or Mobile Construction Sites Directive). The Regulations are organised into five parts:

1 Introduction
2 Client duties
3 Health and safety duties and roles
4 General requirements for all construction sites
5 General.

All the parts apply to all projects that include construction work.

Application of the Regulations

The Regulations apply throughout Great Britain as provided for in regulation 3:

> These Regulations apply—
> (a) in Great Britain; and
> (b) to premises and activities outside Great Britain to which sections 1 to 59 and 80 to 82 of the 1974 Act apply by virtue of articles 9 and 11(1)(a) of the Health and Safety at Work etc. Act 1974 (Application outside Great Britain) Order 2013.

Article 11(1)(a) of the Health and Safety at Work etc. Act 1974 (Application outside Great Britain) Order 2013 applies to the following activities, or preparation for such activities, within the territorial sea, which has the meaning given to it in the Territorial Sea Act 1987 (as amended): construction, reconstruction, alteration, repair, maintenance, cleaning, demolition and dismantling of any building or other structure not being a vessel.

Article 9 of the Health and Safety at Work etc. Act 1974 (Application outside Great Britain) Order 2013 applies to the production of energy from wind or water within the territorial sea or a renewable energy zone, which has the meaning given to it in section 84(4) of the Energy Act 2004.

The Regulations apply to all construction projects in Great Britain, from initial design through to completion of the construction work. There is no *de minimus* level or intensity of construction activity such that the Regulations would not apply.

A project is defined in regulation 2(1), which states:

> a project which includes or is intended to include construction work and includes all planning, design, management or other work involved in a project until the end of the construction phase.

It is apparent that a project comes into being at the very early stages of planning and design, which has implications for the appointment of construction professionals as discussed in more detail in later chapters in this book. The Regulations are specifically drafted to influence the processes of design to avoid or mitigate the hazards and commensurate risks during the construction phase.

Construction work

It is vital to appreciate the definition of construction work, because any activity that is not within the definition of 'construction work' is not subject to the Regulations. Construction work in regulation 2(1) is defined as meaning

> the carrying out of any building, civil engineering or engineering construction work and includes—
>
> (a) the construction, alteration, conversion, fitting out, commissioning, renovation, repair, upkeep, redecoration or other maintenance (including cleaning which involves the use of water or an abrasive at high pressure, or the use of corrosive or toxic substances), de-commissioning, demolition or dismantling of a structure;
>
> (b) the preparation for an intended structure, including site clearance, exploration, investigation (but not site survey) and excavation (but not pre-construction archaeological investigations), and the clearance or preparation of the site or structure for use or occupation at its conclusion;
>
> (c) the assembly on site of prefabricated elements to form a structure or the disassembly on site of the prefabricated elements which, immediately before such disassembly, formed a structure;
>
> (d) the removal of a structure, or of any product or waste resulting from demolition or dismantling of a structure, or from disassembly of prefabricated elements which immediately before such disassembly formed a structure;
>
> (e) the installation, commissioning, maintenance, repair or removal of mechanical, electrical, gas, compressed air, hydraulic, telecommunications, computer or similar services which are normally fixed within or to a structure.

The degree of fixity in paragraph (e) is not described or elaborated upon in the Regulations. Although a free-standing item (e.g. a generator) may be considered unfixed if it is fixed by its own weight, it will be relevant to ascertain the degree of connectivity by cables and pipes to other plant and equipment.

Construction work does not include the work associated with mineral exploration or extraction, as provided for at the end of the definition of construction work as follows:

> but does not include the exploration for, or extraction of, mineral resources, or preparatory activities carried out at a place where such exploration or extraction is carried out.

Thus, all work concerned directly with mineral exploration or extraction, including deep and opencast coalmining, clay pits, sand, stone and aggregate extraction, is expressly excluded, and with the expectation that the extraction of oil and gas will become a feature of the landscape as a result of fracking, the associated construction operations will also be excluded from the scope of the Regulations. It will be a matter of fact whether building, civil engineering or engineering construction work at quarries, mines or fracking sites is actually associated with exploration or extraction. The 2007 Approved

Code of Practice published for the 2007 CDM Regulations listed a number of other activities that do not come within the definition of construction work. The straightforward activities include

- putting up and taking down fabric structures, including marquees and tents
- soft landscaping comprising planting and general horticultural work
- the erection, reposition and moving of light-weight panels forming office dividers or stands and displays at exhibitions
- topographical surveys and the examination of structures
- work to or on marine vessels, including ships and mobile offshore drilling rigs
- the offsite manufacture or prefabrication of products for use in construction work, including concrete panels and roof trusses
- the manufacture or fabrication of components that will form part of offshore installations and the construction of fixed oil and gas offshore installations.

The general maintenance of fixed plant will often be excluded from construction work, except where it involves the erection of temporary structures for access to or dismantling or modification of plant that is more than would be expected for maintenance. This is a matter for consideration and the exercise of judgement in light of all the circumstances. Key factors would be indicated by an appropriate risk assessment, including, for example, the need for ancillary plant, lifting equipment and the time allocated for the task.

Each paragraph of the definition of construction work refers to a structure, and therefore cannot be appreciated fully without understanding the definition of a structure in regulation 2(1), which provides:

> (a) any building, timber, masonry, metal or reinforced concrete structure, railway line or siding, tramway line, dock, harbour, inland navigation, tunnel, shaft, bridge, viaduct, waterworks, reservoir, pipe or pipeline, cable, aqueduct, sewer, sewage works, gasholder, road, airfield, sea defence works, river works, drainage works, earthworks, lagoon, dam, wall, caisson, mast, tower, pylon, underground tank, earth retaining structure, or structure designed to preserve or alter any natural feature, and fixed plant;
> (b) any structure similar to anything specified in paragraph (a);
> (c) any formwork, falsework, scaffold or other structure designed or used to provide support or means of access during construction work,
>
> and any reference to a structure includes a part of a structure.

The types of structure described in paragraph (c) are only those used in connection with construction work and excludes grandstands and other temporary platform arrangements used by the entertainment industry.

Notification

In contrast to the previous 1994 and 2007 Regulations the requirement for the notification of a project no longer changes the scope or nature of the duties imposed on any of the duty holders of a project.

The requirements for notification of a project are provided for in regulation 6:

> (1) A project is notifiable if the construction work on a construction site is scheduled to—
> (a) last longer than 30 working days and have more than 20 workers working simultaneously at any point in the project; or
> (b) exceed 500 person days.

If a project does not fulfil the criteria in regulation 6(1), it is not notifiable.

Therefore, a project may involve many months of planning and design, but if the construction phase is planned to be less than 30 working days or is likely to involve less than 500 person days, the project is not notifiable. Moreover, in circumstances where the project is scheduled to have fewer than 20 workers on site at the same time, the project can be scheduled to last longer than 30 working days without the need for notification. The reference to working days confirms the approach to counting days by clarifying that only those days where there is work on site will count towards the totals, thus disregarding the status of any particular days as bank holidays or weekends. In the past, the need to be cautious about ascertaining the duration of construction work on site would have had a financial consequence to comply with additional requirements if a project was notifiable. However, the burden of notification in the Regulations amounts to no more than a straightforward administrative task, the purpose of which is simply to put the Health and Safety Executive ('the Executive') on notice of a project that has a duration and intensity of construction work that is less likely to be minor works.

The requirements of the notice are set out in paragraphs (2) and (3) of regulation 6:

> (2) Where a project is notifiable, the client must give notice in writing to the Executive as soon as is practicable before the construction phase begins.
> (3) The notice must—
> (a) contain the particulars specified in Schedule 1;
> (b) be clearly displayed in the construction site office in a comprehensible form where it can be read by any worker engaged in the construction work; and
> (c) if necessary, be periodically updated.

The notice must be given before the construction phase begins, but the exact point in a project when it should be given, referred to as 'soon as is practicable', will depend upon the scope and complexity of the project. If all the particulars listed in Schedule 1 are known to the client, notably that

- the principal designer and principal contractor have been appointed, and
- the construction phase programme and allocation of resources are known, together with
- a planned date for commencement of construction work on site, and
- all the conditions have been fulfilled that would enable the client to provide all the particulars specified in Schedule 1

the giving of the notice should not be delayed.

The notice must be displayed on the construction site in a comprehensible form so that it can be read by any construction worker. Thus, the notice should be posted in all the site offices and ideally in the accommodation for the welfare facilities. Although it is the client's duty to give the notice to the Executive, the principal contractor, if appropriate, and all other contractors should arrange for the display of the notice as part of the general duty to manage the project even if there is no express duty to post the notice to comply with paragraph 6(3)(b).

On construction sites where it is known that one or more of the construction workers cannot read English, the notice should be translated into the native languages of such construction workers.

On projects that include construction work in the railway sector, the client has to give the notice to the Office of Rail Regulation in accordance with paragraph 6(4), which provides:

> Where a project includes construction work of a description for which the Office of Rail Regulation is the enforcing authority by virtue of regulation 3 of the Health and Safety (Enforcing Authority for Railways and Other Guided Transport Systems) Regulations 2006, the client must give notice to the Office of Rail Regulation instead of the Executive.

The plans for building the first nuclear power station since Sizewell B as part of a programme of nuclear energy development has prompted the inclusion of notification of such projects to the Office for Nuclear Regulation in regulation 6(5) as follows:

> Where a project includes construction work on premises which are or are on—
> (a) a GB nuclear site (within the meaning given in section 68 of the Energy Act 2013);

(b) an authorised defence site (within the meaning given in regulation 2(1) or the Health and Safety (Enforcing Authority) Regulations 1998); or
(c) a new nuclear build site (within the meaning given in regulation 2A of those Regulations),

the client must give notice to the Office for Nuclear Regulation instead of the Executive.

Duty holders

The Regulations bring health and safety management, on an obligatory basis, into the planning and design of construction work, of all projects. No projects are exempted, although the duration and resourcing of a project will determine whether it will be notifiable to the Executive. The Regulations direct how the parties to a project will contribute to health and safety management from the outset of planning a project through to completion of construction. The key roles in a project are discharged by duty holders, and are named as follows.

The client

The client has a mandatory duty in respect of their project to make arrangements for the management of the project to ensure that construction work will be carried out, so far as is reasonably practicable, without risk to the health and safety of any person. Ancillary to the construction work, the client has also to ensure that there are suitable welfare arrangements for the workers and that a structure to be used as a workplace after construction complies with the Workplace (Health, Safety and Welfare) Regulations 1992.

All projects will need design input, thus there will always be a designer. The non-domestic client is not under a primary obligation to appoint a designer or contractor, but a non-domestic client must ensure that each designer and each contractor is given all the pre-construction information in the client's possession that will have a bearing on the planning and management of the project and health and safety management in particular.

The client is able to agree in writing, where there is more than one client in relation to a project, which client is to be subject to the Regulations.

Domestic clients are not exempt from the Regulations, in the same manner as they were in the 1994 and 2007 Regulations. The inclusion of domestic clients' duties, albeit that such duties are deemed to be delegated to the other duty holders, was necessary to comply with the European directive. The Regulations have imposed upon the contractor or as appropriate the designer the responsibilities that are placed upon the non-domestic clients within the Regulations, thus relieving the domestic client of any liability under the Regulations.

The principal designer

A principal designer is only appointed where there is more than one contractor or if it is reasonably foreseeable that there will be more than one contractor. There is not an express requirement to appoint a principal designer if there is more than one designer, unless the designer is also a contractor.

The principal designer is a new role introduced by the 2015 Regulations, which replaces the coordinator role that was established by the 2007 Regulations. The role of the principal designer is to control the pre-construction phase of the project. The creation of the role of principal designer recognises the need to embed risk management throughout the pre-construction phase. The principal designer's duties mirror those of the principal contractor, which are to plan, manage, monitor and coordinate the pre-construction phase of a project.

The Regulations require the principal designer to take into account the general principles of prevention. There are no prescriptive requirements to have regard to a list of specific risks that covers the full life cycle of a project, including building and operational use, thus covering initial construction, maintenance, cleaning and risks in use to persons using the structure as a workplace.

The need to plan, manage, monitor and coordinate the work involved in the pre-construction phase of a project are the keystones against which the principal designer will be judged.

The designer

A designer must not start or become involved in design work if they are not satisfied that the client is aware of the Regulations and the duties of a client.

A designer must take the general principles of prevention into account when preparing or modifying a design, so far as is reasonable practicable, to eliminate or reduce the foreseeable risks to any person who is involved in the construction work, maintaining or cleaning the structure, or using the structure as a workplace.

The principal contractor

The role of the principal contractor arises where there is more than one contractor or if it is reasonably foreseeable that there will be more than one contractor.

The principal contractor has the same keystone responsibilities to plan, manage, monitor and coordinate as the principal designer but in respect of the construction phase. The principal contractor is also required to take account of the general principles of prevention, thus providing a seamless thread of responsibility between the principal designer and the principal contractor for the health and safety management of a project.

The construction phase plan is the responsibility of the principal contractor prior to setting up a construction site. Once construction work has commenced, the principal contractor has a duty to oversee the health, safety and wellbeing of all other contractors and workers on site by establishing site rules, consulting with and disseminating information to all the construction workers, and ensuring that the welfare facilities comply with the Regulations.

Other contractors

Sole contractors or contractors working under or alongside a principal contractor do not have a requirement to coordinate either because there is no other contractor with which to interface or because they are required to cooperate with the principal contractor. Contractors still have duties to plan, manage and monitor their own construction work and workers.

Where a contractor is working on a site managed by a principal contractor, compliance with directions and site rules given by the principal contractor are express obligations. Contractors also have to provide the principal contractor with details on the management and prevention of health and safety risks created by the contractors' work on site. Contractors contribute to the management of health and safety on site by the provision of other information to the principal contractor and employees.

Construction phase plan

During the pre-construction phase, the construction phase plan is drawn up by the principal contractor, or sole contractor as appropriate, based on all aspects of the construction work such that the construction work can be carried out without risk to safety and health, so far as is reasonable practicable. The construction phase plan must be completed prior to setting up the construction site. The construction phase plan is a dynamic document that should be subject to continuous review and amendment, thus flagging up unplanned risk assessments, promoting coordination and encouraging cooperation, as construction progresses.

Health and safety file

On the completion of a construction project, the principal designer is required to prepare a health and safety file. The health and safety file is an important record document, and should be revised from time to time and made easily available to any other person who may need it to comply with the relevant legal requirements that will arise from later construction work associated with the structure or its maintenance, repair, renovation or demolition.

Revocations and amendments

The Regulations do not change the Health and Safety at Work etc. Act 1974 or repeal any part of it. However, the Regulations revoke the 2007 Regulations and amend a number of related statutory instruments in accordance with regulation 38. The instruments that are amended are dealt with in Schedule 5.

Periodic review of the Regulations

The Secretary of State with the responsibility for health and safety legislation at the appropriate time has a mandatory duty imposed by regulation 39 to review regulations 1 to 36 from time to time and to publish a report with conclusions. Regulation 39 does not affect the application of the Regulations while they remain in force, but it is a clear indication that in the future the Regulations will change as the construction industry adapts to new technology, methodologies and the demands of clients.

Published guidance

Industry guidance is drafted with the intention of providing examples and principles that will assist the relevant duty holders in complying with the Regulations. Industry guidance does not have the status of an approved code of practice for the purposes of providing a defence. Simply complying with published guidance is not a defence to a breach of the Regulations. Paradoxically, the failure to comply with industry guidance is more likely to result in an increased risk of civil proceedings for negligence.

It is uncertain if there is going to be an approved code of practice. A failure to comply with a code of practice is not in itself an offence, although such failure may be taken by a court in criminal proceedings as proof that a person has contravened the Regulations. The onus is on a person to satisfy the court that they have complied with the Regulations in some other way.

CDM Regulations 2015 Explained
ISBN 978-0-7277-6009-8

http://dx.doi.org/10.1680/cdmre.60098.023

Chapter 4
General duties and principles

- Introduction
- Appointing a contractor
- Cooperation
- Duty to warn
- Prevention
- Communication and documentation

Introduction

Failures in communication more than any other failure in project management will create or exacerbate risks to health and safety and more certainly undermine the considerable efforts in planning and managing construction work. This is supported by the judicial observation of Rose J in his judgment on the Abbeystead case involving an explosion in a waterworks valve house in which 16 persons were killed (*TE Eckersley and Others* v. *Binnie & Partners and Others* [1988] CILL 388) in which he said:

> In my judgement the most striking feature is the clear lack of liaison within and between the defendants in relation to matters of safety. This is in no way inconsistent with the existence of an undoubtedly close working relationship.

Compliance with the CDM Regulations for the purposes of improving health and safety management demands effective communication. Although there is no express general principle or duty to communicate, communication is at the heart of the keystone principles to plan, manage, monitor and coordinate together with express concomitant duties to consult, provide information, display notices, give directions, report and so on.

Appointing a contractor

Persons appointed as designers (including a principal designer) and contractors (including a principal contractor) must fulfil the requirements of regulation 8(1), which states that

> A designer (including a principal designer) or contractor (including a principal contractor) appointed to work on a project must have the skills, knowledge and

> experience, and, if they are an organisation, the organisational capability, necessary to fulfil the role that they are appointed to undertake, in a manner that secures the health and safety of any person affected by the project.

Regulation 8(1) declares a fundamental principle that is essential to managing health and safety successfully: there is no exception or test of reasonableness. The success of ensuring that designers and contractors fulfil the requirements of paragraph (1) relies on the appointer and the appointee each taking responsibility to be diligent and honest. The 2015 Regulations have replaced the requirement for competence, which was the means by which the 2007 Regulations sought to ensure that appointed duty holders were capable of designing and constructing a project without risk to the health and safety of any person, with the new tests of skills, knowledge and experience. Competence is the summation of skill, knowledge and experience, and, in the case of an organisation, the organisational ability. The intention of the Health and Safety Executive ('the Executive') to reduce the bureaucratic approach to the selection of designers and contractors is likely to be forlorn in view of regulation 8(3), which requires

> A person who is responsible for appointing a designer or contractor to carry out work on a project must take reasonable steps to satisfy themselves that the designer or contractor fulfils the conditions in paragraph (1).

The reasonable steps to be taken by a client, being the first appointer on a project, and all subsequent appointers, should take into account the complexity of the project and the attendant hazards and risks. The request for evidence of the skills, knowledge and experience and the task of comparing and auditing results from potential appointees will generate paperwork. In the case of organisations, the evidence of organisational ability will also be tested by questionnaires that will focus on health and safety policies, systems, records of reportable incidents, notices received from the Executive and penalties. The Executive has indicated that the questions that are incorporated in Publicly Available Specification 91 (PAS 91:2013), 'Construction prequalification questionnaires', will be a 'useful aid'. In theory, the appointer is assisted from making an inappropriate appointment by the honesty and integrity of the potential appointee as required by regulation 8(2), which states that

> A designer or contractor must not accept an appointment to a project unless they fulfil the conditions in paragraph (1).

A designer or contractor cannot delegate their responsibility for the assessment of their capability (competence) to a third party, which is not uncommon. It may be a defence that a third party has assessed their organisational capability, but a third party does not 'know' if the organisation should or should not accept an appointment. The temptation for a designer or contractor to win work, and gain new experience, has all the potential to leave the appointer as the enforcer of regulation 8(1).

Cooperation

The duty to cooperate is imposed on every person who has a duty in a project by virtue of the Regulations, as set out in regulation 8(4) as follows:

> A person with a duty or function under these Regulations must cooperate with any other person working on or in relation to a project, at the same or an adjoining construction site, to the extent necessary to enable any person with a duty or function to fulfil that duty or function.

Thus, the duty to cooperate is imposed upon the client, designers, contractors, the principal designer and the principal contractor.

The duty to cooperate is without any qualification when approached by a client who is fulfilling their duty under regulation 4(1) or any other duty holder under the Regulations. The person seeking cooperation does not have to be involved in the same project as the person providing the cooperation. Such a person may be involved in a different project on the same site or an adjoining site. It is also possible that the person seeking cooperation of the other may be involved in construction work that is neither concurrent nor sequential to the construction work in which the other person is either involved or has been involved. Thus, the duty to cooperate can apply to a person who is under a duty by virtue of regulation 8(4) but has no active involvement in the site or an adjoining site.

Duty to warn

In addition, other persons working under the control of any of those persons under a duty to cooperate are also subject to a duty to report as referred to in regulation 8(5) as follows:

> A person working on a project under the control of another must report to that person anything they are aware of in relation to the project which is likely to endanger their own health or safety or safety or that of others.

Therefore, persons who are working on a project – not necessarily in construction work – not only have a duty to cooperate: regulation 8(5) imposes a duty to report 'anything' to the person under whose control they are working that is likely to cause harm. Such persons, including employees and the self-employed, might typically include administrators, suppliers, off-site inspectors, quality assurance auditors, plant hire providers and even information technology suppliers in the wake of the Building Information Modelling (BIM) initiative. By this means, the Regulations impose a duty on anybody who might conceivably be working on a project. This raises a particular challenge. What is the threshold at which point a person can be said to be 'working on a project'? How can such persons with diverse roles and contributions all be made aware of the Regulations? Bringing to the attention of such persons the duty with which they are fixed is a significant challenge for the duty holders under the Regulations. Regulation 8(5) creates an offence out of the omission of failing to report circumstances that are a health and safety hazard.

At the pre-construction phase, clients have a duty to provide pre-construction information that will entail communicating and consulting with their employees and suppliers as part of the information gathering. Do the employees and suppliers have a duty, by virtue of regulation 8(5), to bring to the client's attention any circumstances that they know may endanger the health and safety of others?

Cooperation can be encouraged by regular multi-disciplinary and multi-organisational meetings and establishing lines of communication that are seen to be effective. The problems associated with the more rigid contractual lines of communication are a real threat to cooperation if a 'claims climate' is prevalent. The contribution by the client pursuant to regulation 4(1) to have ensured that there is sufficient time and other resources allocated to the project will hopefully enhance the spirit of cooperation on a project.

On domestic projects the domestic client is relieved of the duties in paragraphs (3), (4) and (6) of regulation 8 as provided for by paragraph (7):

> To the extent that they are applicable to a domestic client, the duties in paragraphs (3), (4) and (6) must be carried out by the person specified in regulation 7(1).

The domestic client is not relieved of the duty to warn as provided for in paragraph (5).

Prevention

The general principles of prevention are defined in regulation 2(1) as meaning

> the general principles of prevention specified in Schedule 1 to the [Management of Health and Safety at Work Regulations 1999].

Schedule 1 to the Management Regulations lists the principles of prevention as follows:

(a) avoiding risks;
(b) evaluating the risks which cannot be avoided;
(c) combating the risks at source;

(d) adapting the work to the individual, especially as regards the design of workplaces, the choice of work equipment and the choice of working and production methods, with a view, in particular, to alleviating monotonous work and work at a predetermined work-rate and to reducing their effect on health;
(e) adapting to technical progress;
(f) replacing the dangerous by the non-dangerous or the less dangerous;
(g) developing a coherent overall prevention policy which covers technology, organisation or work, working conditions, social relationships and the influence of factors relating to the working environment;
(h) giving collective protective measures priority over individual protective measures; and
(i) giving appropriate instructions to employees.

The importance of the Management Regulations and the general principles of prevention are imported into the CDM Regulations and reinforced by regulations 9 and 11 in respect of the pre-construction phase and regulation 13 in respect of the construction phase.

The principal designer has an overriding duty imposed by regulation 11(1), which states that

> The principal designer must plan, manage and monitor the pre-construction phase and coordinate matters relating to health and safety during the pre construction phase to ensure that, so far as is reasonably practicable, the project is carried out without risks to health or safety.

The principal designer is directed in regulation 11(2) to take into account the general principles of prevention as follows:

> In fulfilling the duties in paragraph (1), . . . the principal designer must take into account the general principles of prevention and, where relevant, the content of any construction phase plan and any health and safety file.

The principal designer's attention is also drawn in paragraphs (a) and (b) to particular tasks and activities, which are not exhaustive, as follows:

(a) design, technical and organisational aspects are being decided in order to plan the various items or stages of work which are to take place simultaneously or in succession; and
(b) estimating the period of time required to complete such work or work stages.

The principal contractor's overriding duty in regulation 13(1) for the construction phase is identical to the principal designer's duty for the pre-construction phase in regulation 11(1). However, in fulfilling the principal contractor's duties in regulation 13(2), which requires the taking into account of the general principles of prevention in similar terms to the principal designer's duties, there is no requirement to take the health and safety file or the construction phase plan into account as follows:

> In fulfilling the duties in paragraph (1) … the principal contractor must take into account the general principles of prevention.

The apparent omission of the health and safety file and construction phase plan is unsurprising since the principal contractor never has possession of the health and safety file, unless the principal designer's appointment is terminated before the end of the construction phase as provided for in regulation 12(8), in which case the principal contractor becomes responsible for the construction phase plan.

If there is only one contractor, regulation 15(4) imposes the same obligation as applies to a principal contractor in regulation 13(2) as follows:

> If there is only one contractor working on the project, the contractor must take account of the general principles of prevention when—
> (a) design, technical and organisational aspects are being decided in order to plan the various items or stages of work which are to take place simultaneously or in succession; and
> (b) estimating the period of time required to complete the work or work stages.

Communication and documentation

There is no longer a definition of writing but there are references to writing in regulations 4(8), 5(1), 6(2) and 7(1).

An agreement pursuant to regulation 4(8) is expressed as an agreement, regulations 5(1) and 7(1) are expressed as appointments, and regulation 6(2) is a notice. None of these species of documents comes within the meaning if regulation 2(2), which states that

> Any reference in these Regulations to a plan, rule, document, report or copy includes a copy or electronic version which is—
> (a) capable of being retrieved or reproduced when required; and
> (b) secure from loss or unauthorised interference.

Thus, the appointments, agreement and notice do not need to be capable of being reproduced as a printed copy or secure from loss or unauthorised interference. There are also frequent references to notices and signs that do not come within regulation 2(2). In any event, all projects generate substantial numbers of documents that are often essential as a means for communication, including the necessary cooperation and coordination. The advent of BIM, which involves the management of the digital records for the plan, rules and other documents, will ensure that all documents relevant to design and construction can be expected to be stored electronically as a matter of course.

The importance of the management of documents, including their creation, storage, distribution, retrieval and archiving, to implement BIM and compliance with the obligation to maintain the health and safety file indefinitely cannot be over-stated.

CDM Regulations 2015 Explained
ISBN 978-0-7277-6009-8

http://dx.doi.org/10.1680/cdmre.60098.031

Chapter 5
Provisions for the welfare of workers

- Introduction
- Duties
- Sanitary conveniences
- Washing facilities
- Drinking water
- Changing rooms and lockers
- Facilities for rest
- First aid
- Concluding remarks

Introduction

Schedule 2 to the Regulations sets out the requirements for the provision of welfare facilities to be provided for persons carrying out construction work. The inclusion of welfare facilities within the Regulations recognises that the health and safety of workers is directly affected by their personal welfare.

The provision of a good standard of welfare promotes recruitment, good morale and employee retention, which should be sufficient commercial justification for the investment in welfare facilities. Workers who are variously cold, overheated, dirty, dehydrated or generally uncomfortable are not going to be efficient and effective, and, more importantly, are also likely to be unsafe to themselves and their fellow workers.

Duties

The client, principal contractor and contractors all have direct duties to provide welfare facilities for persons working on site.

The client has a direct responsibility that extends to ensuring that welfare facilities are provided for any person carrying out construction work as set out in regulations 4(1) and 4(2)(b) as follows:

(1) A client must make suitable arrangements for managing a project, including the allocation of sufficient time and other resources.

> (2) Arrangements are suitable if they ensure that … the facilities required by Schedule 2 are provided in respect of any person carrying out construction work.

A prudent client would request and retain evidence from the principal contractor of their past record in the planning, provision and management of welfare facilities, including the provision for cleaning and maintenance. Such steps at the selection stage of a contractor would demonstrate the client's own commitment to influencing effective health and safety management on their projects.

The client will discharge their express duty if in the process of making arrangements for managing a project they obligate the principal contractor and other contractors directly engaged by them to provide welfare facilities that comply with Schedule 2. To ensure that sufficient time and other resourees are allocated by the principal contractor, the client should be satisfied, before awarding a contract, that there is a demonstrable commitment to sufficient planning and design of the welfare facilities and arrangements for cleaning and maintenance by the principal contractor and other contractors before work on site commences.

The client should be aware that the cost of welfare facilities can represent a disproportionate cost when compared with the cost of the construction works for small projects. The client should take due account of the fact that a contractor has allocated sufficient resources for welfare facilities or has taken steps to make arrangements with the client or adjacent land owners or others for use of other organisations' welfare facilities.

The client's duties before the start of the construction phase are in fact a continuing duty by virtue of regulation 4(3), which states that

> A client must ensure that these arrangements are maintained and reviewed throughout the project.

A principal contractor has a direct and wide-ranging duty in respect of all the welfare facilities on their site for the duration of the construction works in regulation 13(4)(c) as follows:

> The principal contractor must ensure that—
> (c) facilities that comply with the requirements of Schedule 2 are provided throughout the construction phase

A contractor's duty under regulation 15(11) is as follows:

> A contractor must ensure, so far as reasonably practicable, that the requirements of Schedule 2 are complied with so far as they affect the contractor or any worker under that contractor's control.

The regulations are not prescriptive as to identifying which of the parties with a duty to ensure compliance with Schedule 2 must provide the welfare facilities. Primarily for this reason the client should enquire of the principal contractor who will provide the welfare facilities. On many projects, the client will provide facilities for the contractors.

Where there is a principal contractor, or client, who has failed to provide adequate welfare facilities in accordance with Schedule 2, the contractor's duty is to provide such facilities for their own employees and sub-contractors. The qualification to the contractor's duty of ensuring 'so far as is reasonably practicable' that the welfare facilities are available in circumstances where there is a failure of others to comply with Schedule 2 will not, except where Schedule 2 recognises it may not always be reasonable practicable to make full provision, provide the contractor with a defence if they fail to provide such facilities for their own workforce.

Inevitably, the duty holders have to apply a degree of judgement in complying with Schedule 2 because it only provides an outline specification for the welfare facilities. The number, dimensions and location of facilities and other details are not specified. Where there is a judgement that leads to underprovision or otherwise inadequate welfare facilities, the client should make enquiries and be satisfied that the welfare facilities are either compliant with Schedule 2 under all the circumstances or require the principal contractor to make further or improved provision.

Sanitary conveniences

Schedule 2 includes a requirement that construction sites are provided with appropriate sanitary conveniences in paragraph 1 as follows:

> (1) Suitable and sufficient sanitary conveniences must be provided or made available at readily accessible places.
> (2) So far as is reasonably practicable, rooms containing sanitary conveniences must be adequately ventilated and lit.
> (3) So far as is reasonably practicable, sanitary conveniences and the rooms containing them must be kept in a clean and orderly condition.
> (4) Separate rooms containing sanitary conveniences must be provided for men and women, except where and so far as each convenience is in a separate room, the door of which is capable of being secured from the inside.

The provision of sanitary conveniences prevents a public health risk and also preserves the modesty of both men and women.

The sanitary conveniences should be readily accessible and not involve a person having to walk or take other transport for a journey of an unreasonable duration. Construction sites should be planned so that the locations for sanitary conveniences are established at the outset.

The sanitary conveniences should be adequately ventilated and lit, which is particularly relevant if the construction work is taking place during hours of darkness.

Sanitary conveniences that are not kept in a clean and orderly condition are likely to present a health hazard.

The workforce on a construction site is now almost certainly no longer entirely made up of men, and therefore men and women should be catered for separately unless that is not reasonably practicable, in which case the doors should be capable of being locked from the inside.

Washing facilities

The washing facilities that are required to be provided by a contractor are set out in Schedule 2 paragraph 2 as follows:

(1) Suitable and sufficient washing facilities, including showers if required by the nature of the work or for health reasons, must, so far as is reasonably practicable, be provided or made available at readily accessible places.
(2) Washing facilities must be provided—
  (a) in the immediate vicinity of every sanitary convenience, whether or not also provided elsewhere; and
  (b) in the vicinity of any changing rooms required by paragraph 4, whether or not provided elsewhere.
(3) Washing facilities must include—
  (a) a supply of clean hot and cold, or warm, water (which must be running water so far as is reasonably practicable);
  (b) soap or other suitable means of cleaning; and
  (c) towels or other suitable means of drying.
(4) Rooms containing washing facilities must be sufficiently ventilated and lit.
(5) Washing facilities and the rooms containing them must be kept in a clean and orderly condition.
(6) Subject to paragraph (7), separate washing facilities must be provided for men and women, except where they are provided in a room the door of which is

capable of being secured from inside and the facilities in each room are intended to be used by only one person at a time.

(7) Sub-paragraph (6) does not apply to facilities which are provided for washing hands, forearms and the face only.

In planning for washing facilities, the contractor should take account of the nature of the construction work being undertaken by the workers, particularly activities that cover workers in mud and dust. The Regulations recognise that washing facilities may only be necessary for washing the hands, forearms and face only. In those circumstances it is not necessary to provide separate washing facilities for men and women. Where, however, washing facilities are necessary for washing other parts of the body or showering, separate facilities for men and women should be provided.

When planning the layout for sanitary conveniences, due account should be taken of the provision of washing facilities.

Drinking water

The requirements for drinking water set out in Schedule 2 paragraph 3 are as follows:

(1) An adequate supply of wholesome drinking water must be provided or made available at readily accessible and suitable places.

(2) Where necessary for reasons of health or safety, every supply of drinking water must be conspicuously marked by an appropriate sign.

(3) Where a supply of drinking water is provided, a sufficient number of suitable cups or other drinking vessels must also be provided, unless the supply of drinking water is in a jet from which persons can drink easily.

The water must be safe to drink and made available at readily accessible and suitable places on the construction site. On some construction sites, where water is recycled for use in the sanitary conveniences and washing, it is important that water that is safe to drink is clearly identified.

The contractor is required to provide drinking vessels for the workers unless the water is under pressure and can be drunk from a jet.

The need to provide water for drinking facilities may be a particular challenge for remote construction sites. Drinking water can be supplied in bowsers, in which case the contractor should ensure that there is an adequate supply based on the proper estimates of quantities that will be consumed. The Food Standards Agency recommends at least 1.2 litres of fluids each day for normal conditions. Fluid requirements will increase as the ambient temperature increases and as the physical effort expended by workers increases.

Changing rooms and lockers

Construction workers need facilities to change into appropriate clothing for the work to be undertaken, and Schedule 2 paragraph 4 requires changing rooms and lockers to be provided as follows:

(1) Suitable and sufficient changing rooms must be provided or made available at readily accessible places if a worker—
  (a) has to wear special clothing for the purposes of construction work; and
  (b) cannot, for reasons of health or propriety, be expected to change elsewhere;
(2) Where necessary for reasons of propriety, there must be separate changing rooms for, or separate use of rooms by, men and women.
(3) Changing rooms must—
  (a) be provided with seating; and
  (b) include, where necessary, facilities to enable a person to dry any special clothing and any personal clothing or effects.
(4) Suitable and sufficient facilities must, where necessary, be provided or made available at readily accessible places to enable persons to lock away—
  (a) any such special clothing which is not taken home;
  (b) their own clothing which is not worn during working hours; and
  (c) their personal effects.

The requirement to provide changing rooms and lockers may be a significant expense for small projects. However, the need for workers to have somewhere secure to store their clothing and other personal belongings and dry work clothes should not be overlooked or underestimated.

Facilities for rest

Workers are entitled to breaks during the working day for taking refreshment or for receiving medical assistance. The facilities for rest are set out in Schedule 2 paragraph 5 as follows:

(1) Suitable and sufficient rest rooms or rest areas must be provided or made available at readily accessible places.
(2) Rest rooms and rest areas must—
  (a) be equipped with an adequate number of tables and adequate seating with backs for the number of persons at work likely to use them at any one time;
  (b) where necessary, include suitable facilities for any woman at work who is pregnant or who is a nursing mother to rest lying down;

(c) include suitable arrangements to ensure that meals can be prepared and eaten;
(d) include the means for boiling water; and
(e) be maintained at an appropriate temperature.

The Regulations state specifically that the rest facilities should provide the opportunity for workers to eat meals and have access to boiling water. The rest facilities are also required to be maintained at an appropriate temperature, which may mean air-conditioning or fan-assisted air circulation in extreme hot conditions in addition to the normal requirement for heating.

First aid

First aid facilities are not specifically referred to in the 2015 Regulations, although the Approved Code of Practice for the 2007 Regulations referred to first aid together with the welfare facilities in the contents for the construction phase plan. The welfare facilities are, at the very least, required to have suitable facilities for a pregnant woman or a nursing mother, in which case the extension to first aid facilities generally is logical.

Concluding remarks

The welfare facilities are an essential part of planning and managing construction work, underlined by the fact that the client has a specific duty to ensure the welfare facilities are adequately and properly provided for. Welfare facilities should be available at the outset of construction work, and the client should take steps to ensure that welfare facilities are provided to an acceptable level capable of delivering appropriate facilities for the nature of the construction work.

The principal contractor and other contractors should take account of the provision and installation of welfare facilities as part of the project's resourcing and overall programme of construction works. Contractors should also make provision for the cleaning and maintenance of welfare facilities throughout the entire duration of the construction work.

CDM Regulations 2015 Explained
ISBN 978-0-7277-6009-8

http://dx.doi.org/10.1680/cdmre.60098.039

Chapter 6
Consideration for hazardous operations

- **Introduction**
- **Duties relating to health and safety on construction sites**
- **Safe places of construction work**
- **Site movement**
- **Site environment**
- **Construction of structures**
- **Specific hazards**

Introduction

Part 4 of the CDM Regulations has direct relevance to working on a construction site and the identification of specific hazards as opposed to the administration and management of health and safety.

An important and overlooked benefit of Part 4 is the very fact that it provides a checklist against which a designer and a contractor can assess the inherent risks in the project and its design and construction relative to each of the regulations 17 to 35 inclusive.

Duties relating to health and safety on construction sites

The duties on domestic clients and contractors, to ensure that all the hazards and activities in regulations 17 to 35 are taken account of, are described in regulation 16, which establishes the application of regulations 17 to 35 in the following terms:

(1) This Part applies only to a construction site.
(2) A contractor carrying out construction work must comply with the requirements of this Part so far as they affect the contractor or any worker under the control of the contractor or relate to matters within the contractor's control.
(3) A domestic client who controls the way in which any construction work is carried out by a person at work must comply with the requirements of this Part so far as they relate to matters within the client's control.

A domestic client's liability is considerably increased by paragraph (3) to the extent to which a domestic client 'controls the way in which any construction work is carried out'. In many small domestic projects the contractor will be self-employed or a very small business, and in reality unlikely to be familiar with the Regulations. In those circumstances and without a professional designer having been appointed, the domestic client is likely to become involved in control of the construction work and to assume the responsibilities, in whole or part, of applying regulations 17 to 35. In an ideal situation, the contractor should advise the domestic client of their liabilities under Part 4, although in practice this is unlikely to be common practice.

By virtue of regulation 16 it follows that it is imperative that every domestic client and contractor who exercises any control over the manner in which persons undertake any tasks on a construction site must be familiar with regulations 17 to 35. The subject matter of regulations 17 to 35 provides the ideal checklist for the identification of risks and the basis for a training programme for all persons immediately prior to working on a site.

A person, who is an employee, carrying out construction work on a construction site has a general duty to themselves and every other person on site, underlined by section 7 of the Health and Safety at Work etc. Act 1974, which states that

> It shall be the duty of every employee while at work—
> (a) to take reasonable care for the health and safety of himself and of other persons who may be affected by his acts or omissions at work; and
> (b) as regards any duty or requirement imposed on his employer or any other person by or under any of the relevant statutory provisions, to cooperate with him so far as is necessary to enable that duty or requirement to be performed or complied with.

Except to the extent provided by section 7, a person is not under a further positive duty to report any defect of which they may be aware that could cause a danger. A person cannot be expected to recognise certain types or specific defects as likely to be dangerous without appropriate training.

Safe places of construction work

The fundamental principle in relation to safe places of work as found in regulation 17(2) is put as simply as

> A construction site must be, so far as is reasonably practicable, made and kept safe for, and without risks to, the health of a person at work there.

A place of work is defined in regulation 2(1) as meaning

> any place which is used by any person at work for the purposes of construction work or for the purposes of any activity arising out of or in connection with construction work.

The definition is more comprehensive than might be understood by many to be a construction site, which is defined in regulation 2(1) as including

> any place where construction work is being carried out or to which the workers have access, but does not include a workplace within it which is set aside for purposes other than construction work.

While the place of work will mean a construction site, it also denotes a specific place where a person works (e.g. within a cofferdam), or off site where prefabrication or precasting yards are supplying the construction site. Crucially, the place of work, as referred to in regulation 17(2), will change in material respects with time as the construction work proceeds. It is vital that the changing situation at a place of work is recognised as a hazard in itself and therefore requires that places of work need to be monitored for changing risks and hazards. To summarise the effect of regulation 17, it deals with

- safe access and egress
- keeping the workplace safe, including the provision of adequate working space.

In complying with regulation 17, it is virtually impossible not to have regard to regulations 18 to 23 and 25 to 35, which all contribute to providing a safe place of work. There are broad categories of compliance that can be subdivided as in Table 6.1.

The regulations collected together under the above categories have only been grouped for convenience and as an aid to the planning of the construction phase. There is no intention

Table 6.1 Categories of compliance (regulations in parentheses)

Site movement	Traffic routes (27), vehicles (28), emergency procedures (30), emergency routes and exits (31), lighting (35)
Construction of structures	Stability of structures (19), excavations (22), cofferdams and caissons (23)
Site environment	Good order and site security (18), fresh air (33), temperature and weather protection (34), lighting (35)
Specific hazards	Good order and site security (18), demolition or dismantling (20), explosives (21), energy distribution installations (25), prevention of drowning (26), prevention of risk from fire, etc. (29)

to exclude any other regulations from consideration under a category of compliance, but it makes sense of what at first appears to be a random selection and order of topics.

Site movement

The need to move to and from one place to another on a construction site without risk is a fundamental requirement. Regulation 17(1) states that

> There must, so far as is reasonably practicable, be suitable and sufficient safe access and egress from—
> (a) every construction site to every other place provided for the use of any person whilst at work; and
> (b) every place of construction work is being carried out to every other place to which workers have access within a construction site.

Always subject to the principle of so far as reasonably practicable, the reference to 'suitable and sufficient' means that the contractor or domestic client has to take account of the size, weight and frequency of usage that personnel, vehicles, equipment and materials will need for access and egress. The need to maintain safe access and egress is an express obligation, as is the need to prevent any person using unplanned access or egress, as underlined by regulation 17(3), which states that

> Action must be taken to ensure, so far as is reasonably practicable, that no person uses access to or egress from or gains access to any construction site which does not comply with the requirements of paragraph (1) or (2).

The space in which a person carries out construction work must be sufficient to accommodate a person's physical characteristics and take into account any equipment that will be needed, and this is addressed in regulation 17(4) as follows:

> A construction site must, so far as is reasonably practicable, have sufficient working space and be arranged so that it is suitable for any person who is working or who is likely to work there, taking account of any necessary work equipment likely to be used there.

Traffic routes

The Regulations recognise that access and egress and movement within a construction site require planning and that pedestrians must coexist with vehicular traffic. A traffic route is defined in regulation 2(1) as meaning

> a route for pedestrian traffic or for vehicles and includes any doorway, gateway, loading bay or ramp.

A loading bay is defined as meaning

> any facility for loading or unloading.

Regulation 27 sets out in detail an action list of 'do's' to ensure compliance with the requirements for traffic routes. The basic obligations are in regulations 27(1) and (2), which state that

> (1) A construction site must be organised in such a way that, so far as is reasonably practicable, pedestrians and vehicles can move without risks to health or safety.
> (2) Traffic routes must be suitable for the persons or vehicles using them, sufficient in number, in suitable positions and of sufficient size.

Regulation 27(3) states that paragraph (2) cannot be satisfied unless sub-paragraphs (a) to (e) are observed and/or provided as follows:

> A traffic route does not satisfy paragraph (2) unless suitable and sufficient steps are taken to ensure that—
> (a) pedestrians or vehicles may use it without causing danger to the health or safety of persons near it.

To fulfil this requirement there will need to be, at the very least, a risk assessment of the likelihood of persons being too near a traffic route such that they would be in harm's way.

Paragraph (b) addresses the visibility of vehicles:

> (b) any door or gate for pedestrians which leads onto a traffic route is sufficiently separated from that traffic route to enable pedestrians to see any approaching vehicle or plant from a place of safety.

This requires there to be a sufficient visibility splay for pedestrians to assess the distance and speed of any approaching vehicle before crossing the traffic route.

Paragraph (c) concerns the separation between vehicles and pedestrians:

> (c) there is sufficient separation between vehicles and pedestrians to ensure safety or, where this is not reasonably practicable—
> (i) other means for the protection of pedestrians are provided; and
> (ii) effective arrangements are used for warning any person liable to be crushed or trapped by any vehicle of its approach.

Sufficient separation will depend upon the size and speed of vehicles and the quality of the road surface to avoid vehicles straying onto the pedestrian routes. A risk assessment should consider splashes, spillages and jettisoning of loads that could endanger pedestrians. Effective arrangements for warning persons as required by paragraph (c)(ii) should include audible warnings and sensors that engage when the vehicle is in reverse gear.

Paragraphs (d) and (e) are self-explanatory and prescriptive as follows:

> (d) any loading bay has at least one exit for the exclusive use of pedestrians; and
> (e) where it is unsafe for pedestrians to use a gate intended primarily for vehicles, at least one door for pedestrians is provided in the immediate vicinity of the gate, is clearly marked and is kept free from obstruction.

Traffic routes have to be obvious and maintained such that they do not become health and safety hazards throughout the terms of the construction work, as required by regulation 27(4), which provides that

> (4) Each traffic route must be—
> (a) indicated by suitable signs where necessary for reasons of health or safety;
> (b) regularly checked; and
> (c) properly maintained.

The maintenance of traffic routes should involve maintaining the trafficked surface, but it also follows that traffic routes must be unobstructed and capable of being trafficked, as provided for in regulation 27(5), which states that

> (5) No vehicle is to be driven on a traffic route unless, so far as is reasonably practicable, that traffic route is free from obstruction and permits sufficient clearance.

Vehicles

Regulation 28(1) states that

> Suitable and sufficient steps must be taken to prevent or control the unintended movement of any vehicle.

A vehicle is defined in regulation 2(1) as including

> any mobile work equipment

and work equipment is defined as meaning

> any machinery, appliance, apparatus, tool or installation for use at work (whether exclusively or not).

Vehicles will include, therefore, trucks, cars, mobile cranes, excavators, drilling rigs, concrete pumps, mobile generators and fuel tenders; in fact, any item on a construction site that can be moved under its own power or towed.

The unintended movement of a vehicle needs to be considered both during intended movement and when stationary. Unintended movement when actually on the move can be caused by (*a*) ground instability, (*b*) excessive gradients, (*c*) deflection or failure of a supporting structure, (*d*) undue speed on an irregular driving surface, (*e*) punctures and (*f*) lack of competence of the driver/operator.

The risk of an unintended movement when stationary can be caused by (*a*) to (*c*) but can also be caused by vandalism or theft. The prevention or mitigation of unintended movement can be addressed by considering each of the causes and introducing appropriate measures. Drivers must have passed an appropriate test to be in control of a vehicle to comply with regulation 28(1).

There are a large number of accidents on construction sites caused by persons being knocked down or crushed by vehicles, and regulation 28(2) requires that a vehicle has a means of warning. Regulation 28(2) states that

> Where a person may be endangered by the movement of a vehicle, suitable and sufficient steps to give warning to any person who is liable to be at risk from the movement of the vehicle must be taken by either or both—
> (a) the driver or operator of the vehicle, or
> (b) where another person is directing the driver or operator because, due to the nature of the vehicle or task, the driver or operator does not have full visibility, the person providing directions.

The person who has effective control of the vehicle has the onus of warning pedestrians. In each case the responsible person in regulation 28(2) will have to decide what means would be appropriate for warning pedestrians: for example, audible and/or flashing light warnings and whether entirely manual or automatic. The duty under regulation 28(2) should be related to the measures taken to comply with regulation 27(3)(c)(ii).

A properly trained driver/plant operator is essential to ensure compliance with the requirements of regulation 28(3) as follows:

> A vehicle being used for the purposes of construction work must, when being driven, operated or towed be—
> (a) driven, operated or towed in such a manner as is safe in the circumstances; and
> (b) loaded in such a way that it can be driven, operated or towed safely.

Regulation 28(4) specifically bans unintended passengers joyriding or hanging on for a lift, which provides as follows:

> A person must not ride, or be required or permitted to ride, on any vehicle being used for the purposes of construction work otherwise than in a safe place in that vehicle provided for that purpose.

Persons who ride without permission may be risking their own safety and the safety of others, and as such should be subject to disciplinary measures.

Loading or unloading of loose materials, which include aggregates and powders, have specific hazards, and regulation 28(5) emphasises the need for a person to be in a safe place of work during such loading or unloading as follows:

> A person must not remain, or be required or permitted to remain, on any vehicle during the loading or unloading of any loose material unless a safe place of work is provided and maintained for that person.

The risks referred to in regulation 28(6) might more appropriately have been listed under regulation 27:

> Suitable and sufficient measures shall be taken to prevent a vehicle from falling into any excavation or pit, or into water, or overrunning the edge of any embankment or earthwork.

The sufficient and suitable measures will include the width of the route, an adequate slope and/or excavation, stability, kerbs and/or barriers.

Emergency procedures

Regulation 30 is concerned with emergency procedures, while Regulation 31 is concerned with emergency routes and exits. The relevant fire authority may be the enforcing authority in respect of this aspect of the works, and consulting with the relevant fire authority may be appropriate for large and complex construction sites and where there are persons carrying out non-construction activity within or adjacent to the construction site that forms part of the premises.

Regulation 30(1) creates the duty to make arrangements for emergency procedures as follows:

> Where necessary in the interests of the health or safety of a person on a construction site, suitable and sufficient arrangements for dealing with any foreseeable emergency must be made and, where necessary, implemented, and those arrangements must include procedures for any necessary evacuation of the site or any part of it.

The matters listed in regulation 30(2) are exactly the same matters that, it is suggested, should be used to assess safe access to and egress from a construction site required by regulation 17(1). These are set out as follows:

(a) the type of work for which the construction site is being used;
(b) the characteristics and size of the construction site and the number and location of the places of work on that site;
(c) the work equipment being used;
(d) the number of persons likely to be present on the site at one time; and
(e) the physical and chemical properties of any substances or materials on, or likely to be on, the site.

In making the arrangements, account should be taken of the points under regulation 30(2)(a) to (e), as above. Foreseeable emergencies will vary according to the location of the construction site and the proximity to man-made or natural hazards.

Arrangements made for emergency procedures must be communicated to the persons who will rely upon the emergency procedures being effective. The procedures should also be tested to ensure that they are effective. Regulation 30(3) creates such duties as follows:

> Where arrangements are made under paragraph (1), suitable and sufficient steps must be taken to ensure that—
> (a) each person to whom the arrangements extend is familiar with those arrangements; and
> (b) the arrangements are tested by being put into effect at suitable intervals.

Emergency routes and exits

The emergency routes and exits are an integral part of the emergency procedures. An emergency route is designed to evacuate persons at risk away from the source of danger as quickly as possible. Regulation 31(1) makes the point commensurate with the duty to provide such emergency routes as follows:

> Where necessary in the interests of the health or safety of a person on a construction site, a sufficient number of suitable emergency routes and exists must be provided to enable any person to reach a place of safety quickly in the event of danger.

The emergency routes do not have to follow the established traffic routes. However, the remainder of regulation 31 in paragraphs (2) to (5) provides rules that are an integral component of an emergency route and exit as follows:

> (2) The matters in regulation 30(2) must be taken into account when making provision under paragraph (1).
> (3) An emergency route or exit must lead as directly as possible to an identified safe area.
> (4) An emergency route or exit and any traffic route giving access to it must be kept clear and free from obstruction and, where necessary, provided with emergency lighting so that it may be used at any time.
> (5) Each emergency route or exit must be indicated by suitable signs.

Therefore, emergency routes and exits must

- be as short as possible, leading to safe areas
- be kept clear of obstructions
- be provided with emergency lighting
- take account of the matters that were assessed for the emergency procedures
- be identified by suitable signs.

Lighting

Traffic and emergency routes and movement on site can only be safe and compliant with the Regulations if visibility is clear in all situations. In hours of darkness, the need for lighting is obvious, but lighting will also be necessary when working in unlit interiors, underground, and heavy shadows during daylight hours. For this reason, regulation 35 requires the following:

> (1) Each construction site and approach and traffic route to that site must be provided with suitable and sufficient lighting, which must be, so far as is reasonably practicable, by natural light.
> (2) The colour of any artificial lighting provided must not adversely affect or change the perception of any sign or signal provided for the purposes of health or safety.

(3) Suitable and sufficient secondary lighting must be provided in any place where there would be a risk to the health and safety of a person in the event of failure of primary artificial lighting.

To ensure compliance with regulation 35, the light source should not be of a wavelength that changes the colours of or affects the ability of any person to read the signs or signals that have been provided for health and safety purposes.

The lighting will usually be powered from the mains electricity supply. However, the risk of power cuts is foreseeable, and where artificial lighting is required, especially for underground works and unlit interiors, there should be a provision for emergency generation. This requirement is a provision that should be highlighted in the construction phase plan.

Site environment

Good order and site security

The site environment includes space, tidiness, security, fresh air, general climate and visibility. All the factors that contribute to a safe environment can be planned for and provided by the design and construction planning.

Working space is important so that the workers' tasks can be carried out safely and without compromise, and permits quick avoidance of immediate danger. Regulation 17(4) requires that

> A construction site must, so far as is reasonably practicable, have sufficient working space and be arranged so that it is suitable for any person who is working or who is likely to work there, taking account of any necessary work equipment likely to be used there.

Regulation 17(4) draws attention to the fact that the work equipment will also be taking up space. This may include hand tools in addition to freestanding equipment. Importantly, the equipment should not prevent free movement or access to or egress from the place of work.

An untidy site will invariably be a more dangerous site. One of the common injuries to workers is injuries to the foot caused by projecting nails or other sharp objects. Regulation 18(1) requires that

> Each part of a construction site must, so far as is reasonably practicable, be kept in good order and those parts in which construction work is being carried out must be kept in a reasonable state of cleanliness.

There can be no excuse for a contractor to allow a construction site to be a risk to health and safety as a result of plant, materials and debris not being kept in their proper place and/or being removed. The tidiness that exists on a construction site is a good indicator of the attitude of a contractor to health and safety and the culture that is likely to exist towards the management of health and safety generally.

The importance of preventing injuries to hands and feet primarily is highlighted by regulation 18(3) as follows:

> No timber or other material with projecting nails (or similar sharp object) must—
> (a) be used in any construction work; or
> (b) be allowed to remain in any place,
> if the nails (or similar sharp object) may be a source of danger to any person.

The principal contractor has a duty pursuant to regulation 13(4)(b) to ensure that measures have been taken to prevent unauthorised persons entering their construction site, and a contractor must not start work on a construction site unless measures have been taken to prevent unauthorised persons gaining access to the site, by virtue of regulation 15(10). Specifically, regulation 18(2) assists a contractor with guidance as to the approach to securing the perimeter of a construction site as follows:

> Where necessary in the interests of health and safety, a construction site must, so far as is reasonably practicable, and in accordance with the level of risk posed, comply with either or both of the following—
> (a) have its perimeter identified by suitable signs and be arranged so that its extent is readily identifiable; or
> (b) be fenced off.

The contractor has, therefore, to undertake a risk assessment as to the required degree of security at the perimeter. Particular external risks will include children nearby, and proximity to places of work and housing. Internal risks that would be particularly severe include dangerous plant and machinery, and access to high platforms, excavations and water. On sites where the hazards represent a severe risk to health and safety, the precautions that a contractor should take to prevent unauthorised entry might include the need to invest in high steel fencing topped with barbed wire or other means of preventing climbing over together with coverage of the perimeter by CCTV. At another extreme, on a site of low risk the security to the site might only require some signs and temporary taping.

Fresh air

Fresh air includes air that can be breathed without harm to health. Thus, fresh air will not have noxious or dangerous fumes, or a high dust load of fine particulate matter.

Regulation 33(1) requires the following steps:

> Suitable and sufficient steps must be taken to ensure, so far as is reasonably practicable, that each construction site, or approach to a construction site, has sufficient fresh or purified air to ensure that the site or approach is safe and without risks to health or safety.

The steps that can be taken to ensure that the fresh air is not polluted by noxious or dangerous fumes or airborne particulate matter include fans, air-conditioning and dust suppression. If such systems are provided, then it is important that account is taken of the consequences of any failure of such system as provided for by regulation 33(2):

> Any plant used for the purpose of complying with paragraph (1) must, where necessary for reasons of health and safety, include an effective device to give visible or audible warning of any failure of the plant.

In the event of such failure, the workers should have access to personal protective equipment, including goggles, face masks and personal breathing apparatus, especially if working underground.

Temperature and weather protection

For workers engaged in construction activities indoors, they should not be exposed to excessive heat or cold. Regulation 34(1) requires that

> Suitable and sufficient steps must be taken to ensure, so far as is reasonably practicable, that during working hours the temperature at a construction site that is indoors is reasonable having regard to the purpose for which that place is used.

In undertaking a risk assessment of the temperature range likely to be experienced indoors and the wellbeing of workers, account should be taken of the nature of the construction activities. Where heavy physical work is needed, the maximum acceptable temperature will be lower than what might be needed for fine manual movement. Conversely, the lowest acceptable temperature may be lower. The contractor should consider heating and air-conditioning or other means of circulating air. In the event that this is not reasonably practicable, the contractor should issue appropriate personal protective equipment to the workers and also consider the maximum amount of time that any worker should be exposed to such conditions in a shift.

The external environment cannot be controlled. However, by providing shelter, which can be created by the planned sequence of construction of the permanent works, workers can be afforded some protection. To that extent, regulation 34(2) provides that

> Where necessary to ensure the health or safety of persons at work on a construction site that is outdoors, the construction site must, so far as is reasonably practicable, be arranged to provide protection from adverse weather, having regard to:
> (a) the purpose for which that place is used; and
> (b) any protective clothing or work equipment provided for the use of any person at work there.

Although the contractor can have taken such steps as are reasonably practicable in providing temporary shelter or shelter from the permanent works and having issued appropriate personal protective clothing, the adverse weather conditions might still be considered a risk to health and safety. In such circumstances, the contractor has no option other than to suspend the works until such time as the adverse weather conditions abate.

Lighting

The conditions on a construction site should be clearly visible, and this will require artificial lighting outside of daylight hours. Lighting has been discussed above, under the category of site movement.

Construction of structures

Stability of structures

'Structure' is a defined term in regulation 2(1), and comes within the scope of regulation 19.

If structures are unstable, they obviously present a risk to the health and safety of workers and other persons who may be affected by the construction work. Regulation 19, which makes provision for the stability of structures, relates to the construction phase and does not address stability post-construction.

The construction of structures should not present a risk to the health and safety of workers on the construction site. Equally, existing structures that are required to be modified should also not present any risks arising from instability. Regulation 19 creates a duty to ensure that structures are stable, as follows:

> (1) All practicable steps must be taken, where necessary to prevent danger to any person, to ensure that any new or existing structure does not collapse if, due to the carrying out of construction work, it—
> (a) may become unstable; or
> (b) is in a temporary state of weakness or instability.
> (2) Any buttress, temporary support or temporary structure must—
> (a) be of such design and installed and maintained so as to withstand any foreseeable loads which may be imposed on it; and
> (b) only be used for the purposes for which it was designed and installed and is maintained.

(3) A structure must not be so loaded as to render it unsafe to any person.

The reference to structures includes existing permanent structures, new structures under construction and structures associated with temporary works.

The role of the designer in identifying potential states of instability during construction and demolition cannot be overstated. The starting point for any risk assessment associated with transient instability or weakness is the identification of the foreseeable loads. Both the designer and the contractor should liaise to identify loads that can be created by the construction process due to plant and equipment, spoil heaps, the filling of tanks, exposure to wind loading and so on.

After establishing the necessary loading conditions, the designer should consider the condition of the structure. Existing structures may be weakened by partial demolition, materials may not have acquired full strength (particularly reinforced concrete), and assumptions should be checked that were made at the design stage about dimensions that could not be verified before construction.

In respect of temporary structures, the parties should have exchanged design information to ensure that the assumptions for loading are communicated and that appropriate steps are taken not to exceed the loading during construction.

Excavations

Regulation 2(1) defines 'excavation' as including

> any earthwork, trench, well, shaft, tunnel or underground working.

One of the areas in which clients can make a significant contribution in providing resources for improving the health and safety management of excavation operations is allocating sufficient funds for site investigation. Too often the site investigation is underfunded, if funded at all, by the client. It is incumbent upon the designers and the contractors to satisfy themselves that the information they require for design includes the ground information, so that excavations can be undertaken safely. Where there are significant excavations required as part of the project, a client should be prepared to allocate further resources for site investigation during the course of construction if the predicted soil or rock conditions, as exposed by the excavation, differ from the conditions predicted from the original site investigation.

Regulation 22 refers to the duty to prevent danger to any person from excavation by requiring all practicable steps to have been taken. These practicable steps include the site investigation.

Regulation 22(1) states that

> All practicable steps must be taken to prevent danger to any person, including, where necessary, provision of supports or battering, to ensure that—
> (a) no excavation or part of an excavation collapses;
> (b) no material forming the walls or roof of, or adjacent to, any excavation is dislodged or falls; and
> (c) no person is buried or trapped in an excavation by material which is dislodged or falls.

The design of supports or battering to an excavation should never be guesswork. The provision of supports or battering is a design process that requires knowledge of the relevant soil or rock parameters. These can only be obtained from appropriate field and laboratory testing as part of the site investigation.

The appropriate design of linings to tunnels, wells, shafts and the sides of open earthwork excavations should prevent the dislodgement or falling of material.

Open excavations are an obvious hazard to workers on a construction site. Such hazards are a particular risk to persons who obtain unauthorised entry to construction sites. Regulation 22(2) requires that

> Suitable and sufficient steps must be taken to prevent any person, work equipment, or any accumulation of material from falling into any excavation.

The steps to be taken are to prevent three occurrences. First, any person falling into an excavation, second, work equipment falling into an excavation and, finally, any spoil from the excavation falling back into the excavation. These steps will include physical barriers of appropriate strength and dimensions, and will also include restrictions on traffic and site movement adjacent to the excavations, and site planning so that stock-piling of materials or excavated spoil are sufficiently distant from the edge of the excavation.

The access of plant and equipment close to excavations cannot always be avoided, in which case the designer is required to ensure that the support to the excavation can with-stand such loading. Regulation 22(3) requires that

> Suitable and sufficient steps must be taken, where necessary, to prevent any part of an excavation or ground adjacent to it from being overloaded by work equipment or material.

If work equipment or material is needed close to the excavation, the designer will need confidence in the soil or rock properties to factor in a sufficient factor of safety in the event of inadvertent loads being placed adjacent to the excavation.

Excavations are a serious hazard for workers on construction sites. Many construction workers have been killed working in trenches that are not as deep as the height of the victim. A construction worker who goes to work in an excavation to carry out construction activity has the right to be confident that it is a safe place to work. Regulation 22(4) recognises the serious hazards associated with excavations, by requiring that excavations should be inspected by a competent person as follows:

> Construction work must not be carried out in an excavation where any supports or battering have been provided in accordance with paragraph (1) unless—
> (a) the excavation and any work equipment and materials which may affect its safety have been inspected by a competent person—
> (i) at the start of the shift in which the work is to be carried out;
> (ii) after any event likely to have affected the strength or stability of the excavation; and
> (iii) after any material unintentionally falls or is dislodged; and
> (b) the person who carried out the inspection is satisfied that construction work can be safely carried out there.

The requirement for inspection by a competent person only arises where the excavation is either supported or where the profile of the edge of excavation has been cut to a slope. The condition of the support or the angle and profile of the slope within the excavation has to be inspected. The requirements with respect to the reports of inspections are dealt with in regulation 24. However, the significance of the requirement that the inspection should be carried out by a competent person with respect to excavations is particularly difficult to assess. A person can inspect the supports or slopes and identify any movement or distortion to the profile at the beginning of the shift. Such an inspection may, of course, include monitoring of measurements to reference points, but will the same person know what to do if there is any change in the measurements? In the opinion of the author, competence cannot be achieved without the inspector having a sound grasp of geotechnical engineering. Events that are likely to affect the strength or stability of the excavation are unlikely to be known to persons who are not educated to a high level in geotechnical engineering. To identify such events requires close inspection and monitoring throughout the excavation, to the extent that a competent geotechnical engineer may have assessed a need for an in-situ monitoring system to check for pore pressures and soil movements.

Only after such checks have taken place before the start of a shift and the person referred to in regulation 22(4)(b) is satisfied that the work can proceed safely, should work proceed.

In the event that the person who has undertaken the inspection required by regulation 22(4) has any concerns, regulation 22(5) provides that

> Where the person carrying out an inspection has informed the person on whose behalf the inspection is carried out of any matter about which they are not satisfied (under regulation 24(1), construction work must not be carried out in the excavation until the matter has been satisfactorily remedied.

The person who has undertaken the inspection is likely to be aware of the commercial consequences of preventing further excavation work. For that reason, it is especially important that the competent person is properly trained in geotechnical principles, and has sufficient seniority and experience not to be unduly influenced by the commercial consequences when health and safety matters associated with excavations are at stake.

Cofferdams and caissons

Cofferdams and caissons are usually associated with heavy civil engineering works. The fundamental requirement of a cofferdam or caisson is to provide a working environment within a structure that is retaining soil or water on the outside. The design of a cofferdam or caisson requires the same extent of knowledge as required by excavations if the cofferdam or caisson is retaining soil, whereas, in the case of a cofferdam or caisson that will be retaining water to maintain a dry working environment, the designer should take account of conditions that will vary the depth of water. The consequences of a failure in a cofferdam or caisson in which workers are engaged in construction work are sufficiently serious to devote a considerable amount of time and expense in complying with regulation 23(1), which requires that

> A cofferdam or caisson must be—
> (a) of suitable design and construction;
> (b) appropriately equipped so that workers can gain shelter or escape if water or materials enter it; and
> (c) properly maintained.

Maintaining the cofferdam or caisson may involve supplementary construction work such as grouting, putting in place additional structural members, caulking or the installation of pumping to remove water.

The means of equipping the cofferdam or caisson so that workers can gain shelter or escape if the retained water or material on the outside enters the working environment will depend on a number of factors – including the depth of the excavation within the cofferdam or caisson, the mode of failure (including water bursts or overtopping) and whether soil or water is being retained.

The risk to health and safety of any persons working in a cofferdam or caisson is similar to the risk of working in excavations, such that a competent person is required to inspect the cofferdam or caisson in accordance with regulation 23(2):

> A cofferdam or caisson must not be used to carry out construction work unless—
> (a) the cofferdam or caisson and any work equipment and materials which may affect its safety have been inspected by a competent person—
> (i) at the start of the shift in which the work is to be carried out; and
> (ii) after any event likely to have affected the strength or stability of the cofferdam or caisson; and
> (b) the person who carried out the inspection is satisfied that construction work can be safely carried out there.

The extent and scope of the inspection is very similar to the requirements for inspection for excavations. If a cofferdam or caisson is within soil, the competent person should be qualified similarly to the competent person to inspect excavations. In respect of cofferdams or caissons that are in water, the competent person will be a civil engineer with experience of the design and construction of cofferdams and caissons in such circumstances. Regulation 23(3) is in the same terms as regulation 22(5) for excavations, such that if the competent person is not satisfied that the cofferdam or caisson can provide a safe place of work, then work should not be carried out within the cofferdam or caisson.

Reports of inspections

The importance of ensuring the integrity of excavations, cofferdams and caissons, pursuant to regulations 22 and 23, respectively, is such that the regulations require a competent person to make inspections at the start of every shift. Regulation 24 provides the regulatory requirements for the inspection procedure.

Reports will be the evidence that the regulations have been followed, and, moreover, they will also be the evidence needed to investigate the cause of any failures in excavations, cofferdams or caissons. Although the competent person is required to inspect the excavation, cofferdam or caisson at the start of every shift, only one report needs to be completed every 7 days, as required by regulation 24(4):

> This regulation does not require the preparation of more than one report where more than one inspection is carried out under regulation 21(4)(a)(i) or 22(2)(a)(i) within a 7 day period.

Regulation 24(1) is primarily addressed to the person who carries out the inspection, and provides as follows:

> Where a person who carries out an inspection under regulation 22 or 23 is not satisfied that construction work can be carried out safely at the place inspected, that person must—
>
> (a) inform the person on whose behalf the inspection was carried out, before the end of the shift within which the inspection is completed, of the matters that could give rise to a risk to the safety of any person.

In the event that the inspector is not satisfied that construction work can be carried out safely, they should draw this to the attention of the person for whom the inspection is carried out without delay and before the end of the shift within which the inspection was completed. In any event, the inspector is required to prepare a report to include the particulars in regulation 24(1)(b), which are to

> prepare a report, which must include—
>
> (i) the name and address of the person on whose behalf the inspection was carried out;
> (ii) the location of the place of construction work inspected;
> (iii) a description of the place of construction work or part of that place inspected (including any work equipment and materials);
> (iv) the date and time of inspection;
> (v) the details of any matter identified that could give rise to a risk to the safety of any person;
> (vi) details of any action taken as a result of any matter identified in sub-paragraph (v);
> (vii) details of any further action considered necessary; and
> (viii) the name and position of the person making the report.

The report has to be provided within 24 h of the inspection and given to the person who was required to obtain the inspection, as required by regulation 24(1)(c) as follows:

> Where a person who carries out an inspection under regulation 22 or 23 is not satisfied that construction work can be carried out safely at the place inspected, that person must provide the report, or a copy of it, to the person on whose behalf the inspection was carried out, within 24 hours of completing the inspection to which the report relates.

The person who is required to prepare the report has only 24 h in which to provide it for projects that involve significant excavations, a cofferdam or caissons. In practice this will mean that there will be many days, weeks or even months of reporting. The requirement for a competent person to undertake the inspection should take account of cover for absence by a competent inspector.

The last report should be prepared when either the excavation is completed to its final profile without any permanent works or at such time when the permanent works are completed within the excavation. In the case of cofferdams and caissons, the last day of inspection will be on the day that the cofferdam or caisson is dismantled or incorporated into the permanent works.

The person undertaking the inspection can be an external consultant. By this means the person for whom the inspection is being carried out can ensure that the appropriate level of competence is obtained. The employer or person under whose control the inspector carries out the work is under a duty to ensure that the inspector turns up each day and carries out the inspection as required by regulation 24(2):

> Where the person who carries out an inspection works under the control of another (whether as employee or otherwise) the person in control must ensure the person who carries out the inspection complies with the requirements of paragraph (1).

The reports prepared by the inspector should be kept in accordance with regulation 24(3) as follows:

> The person on whose behalf the inspection was carried out must—
> (a) keep the report or a copy of it available for inspection by an inspector for the Executive—
>   (i) at the site where the inspection was carried out until the construction work is completed; and
>   (ii) after that for 3 months; and
> (b) send to the inspector such extracts from or copies of the report as the inspector may from time to time require.

The requirements for keeping the report are self-explanatory. However, to keep the reports for longer than 3 months after completion of the work would be prudent as part of the record of the project history that may become relevant for any later contract disputes.

Specific hazards

Demolition or dismantling

In the Regulations there is no special treatment or consideration for demolition, and as such this is treated like any other construction work and has to be assessed on its own merits for hazards and associated risks.

Regulation 20 makes provision for demolition or dismantling as part of the consideration for safety on construction sites as follows:

> (1) The demolition or dismantling of a structure must be planned and carried out in such a manner as to prevent danger or, where it is not practicable to prevent it, to reduce danger to as low a level as is reasonably practicable.
> (2) The arrangements for carrying out such demolition or dismantling must be recorded in writing before the demolition or dismantling work begins.

The requirement for recording in writing arrangements for demolition or dismantling is absolute. There is no indication as to the detail that will be required to satisfy regulation 20(2), although for all intents and purposes it will be a risk assessment and method statement.

The requirements to comply with regulation 20(2) are in addition to the requirements for a construction phase plan, but can be effectively dealt with by incorporating the written arrangements in the construction phase plan. However, there is no reason why they cannot exist as separate documents.

Explosives

Merely the storage and transport of explosives is a hazardous operation, which is recognised by regulation 21(1) as follows:

> So far as is reasonably practicable, explosives must be stored, transported and used safely and securely.

Explosives may be used in demolition, excavation or tunnelling. An excavation and a tunnel are both places of work that are required to be safe within the meaning of regulation 17. The requirement to ensure that no person is at danger of harm when explosives are detonated is set out in regulation 21(2) as follows:

> An explosive charge may be used or fired only if suitable and sufficient steps have been taken to ensure that no person is exposed to risk of injury from the explosion or from projected or flying material caused by the explosion.

As part of the planning in the use of explosives, the contractor should pay due regard to maintaining a safe place of work, emergency routes and procedures, the instability of structures caused by vibration, the views of the competent person appointed to carry out inspections of excavations, cofferdams and caissons, and the prevention of risk from fire, fire detection and fire-fighting.

Energy distribution installations

Electric power cables are a particular risk, either because of the interference of overhead power cables with on-site plant and equipment or cutting through buried cables.

The first challenge is to locate such installations as required by regulation 25(1) as follows:

> Where necessary to prevent danger, energy distribution installations must be suitably located, periodically checked and clearly indicated.

To deal specifically with the risk from electric power cables, regulation 25(2) provides that

> Where there is a risk to construction work from overhead electric power cables—
> (a) they must be directed away from the area of risk; or
> (b) the power must be isolated and, where necessary, earthed.

There will be circumstances where the directions in paragraphs (a) and (b) cannot be implemented, in which case regulation 25(3) provides that

> If it is not reasonably practicable to comply with paragraph (2)(a) or (b), suitable warning notices must be provided together with one or more of the following—
> (a) barriers suitable for excluding work equipment which is not needed;
> (b) suspended protections where vehicles need to pass beneath the cables; or
> (c) measures providing an equivalent level of safety.

The cost associated with relaying cabling or isolating power can be considerable, and should be identified as a necessary step in the project programme, thus requiring the allocation of time and other resources.

The Regulations highlight the importance of this particular hazard by virtue of regulation 25(4), which requires that

> Construction work which is liable to create a risk to health or safety from an underground service, or from damage to or disturbance of it, must not be carried out unless suitable and sufficient steps (including any steps required by this regulation) have been taken to prevent the risk, so far as is reasonably practicable.

Prevention of drowning

Construction workers who have to work over water, on the water, or below the water level are at risk of drowning if they fall into the water or the water inundates them.

Construction workers are at risk of drowning in liquids other than water. Liquids are found in the food and drink manufacturing sector and other industrial processes. The duty to prevent drowning is in regulation 26(1), which provides that

> Where, in the course of construction work, a person is at risk of falling into water or other liquid with a risk of drowning, suitable and sufficient steps must be taken to—
> (a) prevent, so far as is reasonably practicable, the person falling;
> (b) minimise the risk of drowning in the event of a fall; and
> (c) ensure that suitable rescue equipment is provided, maintained and, when necessary, used so that a person may be promptly rescued in the event of a fall.

The preventative measures that should be considered for adoption as a risk prevention measure can include barriers, non-slip surfaces, harnesses and safety nets.

Minimising the risk of drowning can include draining the water or other liquid away or to such a depth that the risk of drowning is minimised.

Equally, persons who are required to work with the risk of drowning should, under certain circumstances, be issued with personal protective equipment, including life jackets, that will ensure that they remain buoyant if they fall into the water or other liquid. Wherever water presents a hazard to construction workers or any other person, there should be suitable rescue equipment that will include buoyancy aids, resuscitation equipment, ropes and, if necessary, small rescue craft.

Where construction workers have to be transported to the construction site across water, regulation 26(2) applies as follows:

> Suitable and sufficient steps must be taken to ensure the safe transport of any person conveyed by water to or from a place of work.

The transport of workers by water should pay particular regard to the transfer from the land to the craft and from the craft onto the construction site.

A boat that is used to convey construction workers cannot be safe if it is overcrowded or overloaded as referred to in regulation 26(3), which provides that

> Any vessel used to convey any person by water to or from a place of work must not be overcrowded or overloaded.

Prevention of risk from fire, flooding or asphyxiation

Regulation 29 requires that

> Suitable and sufficient steps must be taken to prevent, so far as is reasonably practicable, the risk of injury to a person during the carrying out of construction work arising from—

(a) fire or explosion;
(b) flooding; or
(c) any substance liable to cause asphyxiation.

Apart from the obvious risk associated with the use of explosives, which is subject to regulation 21, the use of fire or any other naked flame is a potential hazard. Flooding is a hazard that should be assessed and taken into account as part of the design and construction process. Substances liable to cause asphyxiation will include gases such as carbon monoxide or methane by inhalation, or particulate materials, including powders and certain foodstuffs, due to inundation.

There is always a risk of fire, and the sooner fires are detected the better the opportunity to contain the fire and mitigate its consequences. Regulation 32(1) refers to fire-fighting equipment and fire detection as follows:

> Where necessary in the interest of the health or safety of a person on a construction site, suitable and sufficient fire-fighting equipment and fire detection and alarm systems must be provided and located in suitable places.

The enforcing authority in respect of this duty will be the relevant fire authority.

In planning for the type of fire-fighting equipment and detection systems and locations where they should be provided on a construction site, the contractor should take account of the points under regulation 30(2) as required by regulation 32(2) as follows:

> The matters in paragraph 30(2) must be taken into account when making provision under paragraph (1).

The nature and extent of the fire-fighting equipment will be dependent upon the nature of the construction site, the work equipment, the number of persons working on the construction site and the physical and chemical properties of other materials on the site. A full risk assessment will be necessary to ascertain what fire-fighting equipment will be necessary.

The fire-fighting equipment and detection systems should be regularly tested as required by regulation 32(3) as follows:

> Fire-fighting equipment or fire detection and alarm systems must be examined and tested at suitable intervals and properly maintained.

Fire-fighting equipment that is not automatic should be clearly identified and easily accessible as required by regulations 32(4) and 32(7) as follows:

(4) Fire-fighting equipment which is not designed to come into use automatically must be easily accessible.
(7) Fire-fighting equipment must be indicated by suitable signs.

Fire-fighting equipment requires training, and there may be particular construction activities that create a particular risk of fire. In these circumstances, regulations 32(5) and 32(6) provide that

(5) Each person at work on a construction site must, so far as is reasonably practicable, be instructed in the correct use of any fire-fighting equipment which it may be necessary for the person to use.
(6) Where a work activity may give rise to a particular risk of fire, a person must not carry out such work unless suitably instructed.

CDM Regulations 2015 Explained
ISBN 978-0-7277-6009-8

http://dx.doi.org/10.1680/cdmre.60098.065

Chapter 7
Suitable, sufficient and competent

Introduction

In the 1994 and 2007 CDM Regulations there was an express requirement that the duty holders (excluding the client) under the Regulations had to be competent. Demonstrating and assessing competence generated its own industry, and the Health and Safety Executive ('the Executive'), in an attempt to reduce the attendant bureaucracy, omitted from the Regulations a requirement, or threshold, for competence.

The test of suitability and competence

The test of competence that created an excessive bureaucratic response as a result of appointers checking corporate competence and the competence of individuals in the workforce has been replaced by regulation 8(1), which refers to skills, knowledge, experience and organisational capability, if relevant, in the following terms as a general duty:

> A designer (including a principal designer) or contractor (including a principal contractor) appointed to work on a project must have the skills, knowledge and experience, and, if they are an organisation, the organisational capability, necessary to fulfil the role that they are appointed to undertake, in a manner that secures the health and safety of any person affected by the project.

The general duties are discussed in regulation 4, including the duty holder's obligations to ensure that regulation 8(1) is achieved. However, the client has an overriding duty provided by regulations 4(1) and (2) to make suitable arrangements for a project:

> (1) A client must make suitable arrangements for managing a project, including the allocation of sufficient time and other resources.

(2) Arrangements are suitable if they ensure that—
  (a) the construction work can be carried out, so far as is reasonably practicable, without risks to the health or safety of any person affected by the project; and
  (b) the facilities required by Schedule 2 are provided in respect of any person carrying out construction work.

The client has to take into account the skills, knowledge and experience of a designer or contractor and organisational capability if relevant, in order to make a judgement about the suitability of the project for the duty holders they are considering to appoint. But is that enough to meet the overriding duty of a client to be satisfied that the arrangements will be suitable? The test of suitability will include an assessment of sufficiency of available time and other resources, past experience of similar projects, and the experience and qualifications of the employees. The test of suitability starts to look remarkably like a test of competence. Indeed, the *Oxford English Dictionary* (2006) definition of competent is

(1) *suitable*, appropriate;
(2) *sufficient* or adequate in amount, extent or degree;
(3) legally authorised or qualified, able to take cognizance (of a witness, evidence), eligible, admissible;
(4) having adequate skill, properly qualified, effective.

The definition identifies that competence is an alternative expression of suitability to undertake a particular project without risk to the health and safety of any persons. What this means in practice is that clients are very unlikely to modify their means of assessing the skills, knowledge and experience of potential designers and contractors when compared with the previous need to assess competence. Clients should be mindful that the need for suitability has only to extend to where the degree of competence is sufficient or adequate.

Competence for individuals

Skills and knowledge can be obtained by formal training qualifications or experience, but the standard to which the task should be performed by a competent person has only to be sufficient or adequate. The assessment of suitability should not be compared against a 'gold standard' but related to that which is necessary to achieve a satisfactory result.

The express references to competence are found in regulations 22 and 23 in respect of excavations, cofferdams and caissons, where a person is required to be competent for the purposes of inspecting excavations, cofferdams and caissons. These are examples of individual competence, but there are also requirements under related regulations, notably the

Management of Health and Safety at Work Regulations 1999 and the Electricity at Work Regulations 1989, where a competent person is required to discharge certain duties.

Decisions of the courts help to further an understanding of what is expected of a competent person.

Competence as referred to in the Construction (Working Places) Regulations 1966 was applied to persons responsible for erecting, dismantling and installing scaffolds. A competent person was required to be responsible for the inspection and supervision of competent workmen 'possessing adequate experience of such work'. In the case of *Maloney* v. *A. Cameron Ltd* [1966] 2 All ER 934, the Court of Appeal was prepared, without further comment, to recognise the competence of three painters for the purposes of erecting trestles in accordance with the Building (Safety, Health and Welfare) Regulations 1948.

The Quarries Order 1956 required the manager of a quarry to make and ensure the efficient carrying out of arrangements to secure that every inspection is carried out or done by a 'competent person'. In the absence of any definition of 'competent', Winn J in *Brazier* v. *Skipton Rock Co. Ltd* [1962] 1 All ER 955 said:

> I am not prepared to hold either that 'competent' means the most competent person available to the owners of the quarry or the manager, or that it means that he shall be so competent that he never makes a mistake. In my judgment, it means a man who, on a fair assessment of the requirements of the task, the factors involved, the problems to be studied and the degree of risk danger implicit, can fairly, as well as reasonably, be regarded by the manager, and in fact is regarded at the time by the manager, as competent to perform such an inspection.

The judge went on to say:

> experience is so often of much greater value than book-learning.

A later decision by Cantley J in *Gibson* v. *Skibs A/S Marina* [1966] 2 All ER 476 in relation to the Dock Regulations 1934 elaborated:

> Who is 'a competent person' for the purpose of such an inspection? This phrase is not defined. I think that it is obviously to be taken to have its ordinary meaning of a person who is competent for the task. I think that a competent person for this task is a person who is a practical and reasonable man, who knows what to look for and knows how to recognise it when he sees it.

Competence as a requirement for persons fulfilling roles in health and safety legislation is now well established and found in many statutory provisions, including the Management of Health and Safety at Work Regulations and the Electricity at Work Regulations.

The roles under health and safety legislation, where competence is either an express or implied requirement, have been mapped in the Executive's publication *An Outline Map on Competence, Training and Certification* 2012, prepared by the Policy Group and available on the Executive's website. In many examples to be found in health and safety legislation, competence is measured by a person having attained certain qualifications or issued with a licence to deal with a particular matter. In those circumstances it is a straightforward exercise to identify whether a person is competent merely by seeking evidence of appropriate qualifications or an appropriate licence.

For the future the Executive has decided that the construction industry's relevant professional bodies and institutions should oversee and seek to improve the competence of construction professionals. The Executive has said that it will work with the industry through non-regulatory approaches to produce a regime where the measure and attainment of competence suits the industry's needs.

CDM Regulations 2015 Explained
ISBN 978-0-7277-6009-8

http://dx.doi.org/10.1680/cdmre.60098.069

Chapter 8
The client

Introduction

It is unarguable that the role of the client is central to the procurement of construction work. This is due to the client's influence over the budget and other resources and the time frame within which the project is conceived through to completion of construction. The CDM Regulations have further increased the responsibility of the client because the client has the greatest influence on the management of a project. The Health and Safety Executive ('the Executive') expect clients to take an active role to ensure that construction work is carried out with proper attention to the risks to the health and safety of workers. The client's role is not necessarily one of management but is definitely one of leadership.

The challenge for construction industry professionals is to ensure that all clients, from sole traders to the largest multinational companies, are made aware of their general health and safety duties, such that embracing the Regulations is seen as a positive step, instead of a bureaucratic chore. Meeting the challenge should be seen as very much part of the health and safety training of construction professionals in preaching the virtues of health and safety management to the huge number of cost-conscious smaller clients, including domestic clients, whose awareness is considerably less than that of the larger corporate client organisations.

The central role of the client is emphasised by the fact that Part 2 of the Regulations is devoted to client duties, comprising regulations 4, 5, 6 and 7.

The definition of client is set out in regulation 2(1) as follows:

> "client" means any person for whom a project is carried out.

The Interpretation Act 1978 defines a 'person' to include corporations and limited companies, and partnerships as well as individuals. Therefore, any person embarking on a project that includes or is intended to include construction work which itself includes all planning, design, management or other work involved in a project until the end of the construction phase is a duty holder under the Regulations. However, identifying the client may not be without some confusion when there are landowners, investment purchasers, funders, insurers, tenants and developers. In circumstances where the identity of the client is unclear and some of the persons could be identified as clients but want to avoid the duties and obligations of the client under the Regulations, regulation 4(8)(a) allows one or more clients to make an agreement that they are to be treated as the client for the purposes of the Regulations.

A person becomes a client merely if they seek to accept the services of a designer or contractor who may be used in the carrying out of a project. Therefore, at the very outset, when inviting tenders from consultants or contractors, before there may be any settled decision to embark upon construction work, the person considering such appointments is subject to the duties of the client created by the Regulations. A client may consider carrying out part of a project themselves, particularly the initial stages of design. Even in these circumstances, the person is bound by the duties of a client pursuant to the Regulations.

Client types

Domestic clients

A domestic client as defined in regulation 2(1) means

> a client for whom a project is being carried out which is not in the course or furtherance of a business of that client.

The exceptions for domestic clients which were included in the 1994 and 2007 Regulations meant that they were not fully aligned with the Temporary or Mobile Construction Sites Directive (TMCSD) but has been finally addressed in the Regulations. A domestic client is a person not acting in the course or furtherance of a business. Construction work on domestic dwellings, where the dwelling is the principal residence of the client, will not be in the course of furtherance of a business, but if another dwelling is built within the site of the principal residence, or the family house is converted into apartments, it is likely to be in furtherance of a business. If in doubt, a reasonable test is to ascertain whether the fruits of the building activity would lead to a potential or actual tax liability on any profit, in which case the likelihood is that the domestic client has created a 'business' and therefore comes within the scope of Part 2 of the Regulations, including notification, if the project is likely to exceed 500 person days or last longer than 30 working days and have more than 20 workers on site at any one time.

Regulation 7(1) states that

> Where the client is a domestic client the duties in regulations 4(1) to (7) and 6 must be carried out by—
> (a) the contractor for project where there is only one contractor;
> (b) the principal contractor for a project where there is more than one contractor; or
> (c) the principal designer where there is a written agreement that the principal designer will fulfil those duties.

The Regulations, therefore, do absolve the domestic client from compliance with the TMCSD by using a drafting device that creates the obligation on contractors and designers working for a domestic client to carry out the client's duties. Thus, the domestic client is not required to comply with the Regulations but is deemed to have appointed the relevant duty holder. Specifically, regulation 7(3), which disapplies the default position, in the event that a client does not appoint a principal designer or principal contractor, states that

> Regulation 5(3) and (4) does not apply to a domestic client.

Where there is only one contractor carrying out the construction work for a domestic project, they are required to carry out the duties of the client by virtue of regulation 7(1)(a). In the situation where there is more than one contractor, as envisaged by regulations 7(1)(b) and (c), the question for the contractors is to decide which of them is in control of the construction phase. The contractor in control of the construction phase is deemed to fulfil the role of the principal contractor in addition to the client duties in regulation 7(2)(a), as stated in regulation 7(2)(b):

> If a domestic client fails to make the appointments required by regulation 5 the contractor in control of the construction phase of the project is the principal contractor.

A domestic client who engages a designer, often before an application for planning permission, has the option to appoint that designer to take responsibility for coordinating and managing the project. In such circumstances the designer will be the principal designer as provided for in regulation 7(1)(c) and required to carry out the duties of the client.

If the client has not made an appointment in writing of a principal designer in accordance with regulation 7(1)(c), there is a deeming provision in regulation 7(2)(a) that states that

> If a domestic client fails to make the appointments required by regulation 5 the designer in control of the pre-construction phase of the project is the principal designer.

A designer never acquires a duty to carry out the client's duties, unless they have been appointed in writing as the principal designer in accordance with regulation 7(1)(c).

The Crown as client

Her Majesty's government acts in the name of the Crown, which includes all government departments and the armed forces.

By virtue of section 48 of the Health and Safety at Work etc. Act (HASWA) 1974, the Crown is subject to the statutory duties set out in the act. However, it cannot be the subject of enforcement action by the Executive (sections 21–25), whether by way of improvement or prohibition notices or by way of prosecution (sections 33–62). Crown censures are formal recordings of a decision by the Executive that, but for Crown immunity, the evidence of a Crown body's failure to comply with health and safety law would have been sufficient to provide a realistic prospect of conviction in the courts. Accordingly, those government departments and organisations that come within the definition of the Crown have a duty to observe the provisions of the HASWA and the regulations made under it, including the CDM Regulations. This is as it should be, since the declaration by the construction minister Viscount Ullswater in 1994, in response to the publication of the Latham Report, stated that

> The government aspires to being a best practice client, and I am happy to make that declaration.
>
> (Department of Environment press release, 25 July 1994)

Employees of the Crown can, however, be prosecuted by virtue of section 48(2) of the HASWA, which is probably a sufficient incentive to ensure compliance with health and safety legislation.

In common with many other clients, the Crown is likely at times to fulfil other roles identified under the Regulations, in which case the same immunity from prosecution for the Crown and personal criminal liability of its employees will apply.

Local authorities and public bodies as clients

Local authorities, non-government organisations and health trusts within the National Health Service have no immunity from prosecution, unlike the Crown and the government departments that act in its name.

Insurance and warranty claims

Construction work that is procured as a result of a claim under an insurance policy may result in the insurance company being treated as the client. However, insurance companies are not experts in the construction process or resourced to undertake the management of construction projects. The loss adjusters that assess the need for construction work and become involved in procuring the work on behalf of an insurance company can be treated as the client. In fulfilling such a role, agents of the insurance company should ensure that their professional indemnity insurance will provide sufficient and appropriate cover.

If the insured procures the construction work on the basis that the costs of construction are to be reimbursed by the insurance company, the insured will be treated as the client.

To avoid any doubt as to who will be treated as the client, which could include the insurance company, loss adjuster or other agent and the insured, it would be prudent for the person who has the appropriate expertise or interest as the client to make the agreement in accordance with regulation 4(8).

Developers

In circumstances where a person buys a house before the construction is complete, it does not mean that the developer who has sold the land or the partially constructed house is no longer the client. The purchaser may have an interest in the property and may have specified certain features in the remainder of the construction phase, but it is still the developer who arranges for the construction work to be done, and they will be treated as the client.

Developers often fulfil numerous roles concurrently. There is no prohibition on a developer fulfilling all the roles of the duty holder as long as they take steps to ensure that they fulfil all the requirements of each type of duty holder under the Regulations.

Private finance initiative, public–private partnership and similar forms of procurement

Public projects are frequently funded by private finance or a combination of private and public funds. It is a feature of such projects that the person fulfilling the role of client will evolve to reflect the different stages in the procurement process.

The project originator, which is likely to be a public authority, will in the first instance be the client. The role of the client will move when the contract arrangements for undertaking the construction work have been resolved, which is likely to be a special-purpose vehicle (SPV). The SPV may itself comprise separate organisations responsible for the construction, whereas the other part of the SPV takes responsibility for the operational management of the project after construction. It is important for the project originator to recognise the consequences of remaining in the role of client if an SPV or other organisation has been formed, especially for the procurement of design and the execution of construction work.

The potential clients should make the decision as to which of them should make the agreement to be the client.

Agreement between clients

In the situation where there is a project with more than one party who could be reasonably considered to be a client, the parties can make an agreement, in accordance with regulation 4(8) as follows:

> Where there is more than one client in relation to a project—
> (a) one or more of the clients may agree in writing to be treated for the purposes of these Regulations as the only client or clients;
> (b) except for the duties specified in sub-paragraph (c) only the client or clients agreed in paragraph (a) are subject to the duties owed by a client under these Regulations;
> (c) the duties in the following provisions are owed by all clients—
> (i) regulation 8(4); and
> (ii) paragraph (4) and regulation 8(6) to the extent that those duties relate to information in the possession of the client.

It is often the case that a developer on behalf of a freeholder, purchaser or tenant procures the construction of a building. The definition of 'client' could include the organisation for whom the developer is procuring the construction. Quite commonly, organisations may come together on a joint venture basis to procure a project, in which case it is open to those organisations to agree one or more organisations as the client for the purposes of the Regulations. At the outset of a project, all the initial parties should be alert to the potential for all or any one of them to be treated as a client for the purposes of the Regulations.

In circumstances where an agreement has not been made in writing, the responsibility of a client under the Regulations applies with equal force to each of them. It is not specified whether the shared responsibility of the clients is joint and several or proportional based on a measured responsibility according to some measure of contribution. The difficulties of a proportional assessment would involve a detailed assessment of contribution, be it resources that might include financial, technical, manpower or legal status including 'remoteness' from the management of the construction work or legal interest in the construction site.

For an agreement to be effective it must be made in writing, although it is not a requirement of notification to the Executive. The agreement will be a simple statement within the legal documentation that will record and set out the respective roles, duties and obligations of the clients in relation to a project. However, if there is more than one party agreeing to fulfil the role of client, the Executive is likely to treat such parties as jointly and severally liable under the Regulations, to ensure that all the client duties are discharged.

An agreement, by definition, will mean that parties who have not agreed to be a client are avoiding the full effect of the Regulations except in two important respects. First, any client who has agreed not to be a client for the purposes of the Regulations is still under a duty to cooperate by reason of regulation 8(4). Second, to the extent that such a client has information in their possession that is relevant and should be included in the pre-construction information, they must comply with regulations 4(4) and 8(6) in providing the information as soon as practicable and in a comprehensible form. These exceptions ensure that an interested party who has taken the decision not be treated as a client cannot remain disinterested in a project, being subject at all times to the duty of cooperation and provision of information.

General duties

Arrangements for managing projects

The client's influence over any project is determined at the outset by the client's own commitment to taking a leadership role and allocating sufficient time and resources to discharge their duties under the Regulations. The client's decision-making, as to the scope of the project, design brief, project delivery date, project budget, choice of materials, tendering arrangements and access to site, cannot be overestimated. Regulation 4 leaves the client in no doubt as to the central role that they will fulfil at the start and for the duration of a project. Regulations 4(1) and (2) set out the client's duties in relation to arrangements for management projects as follows:

(1) A client must make suitable arrangements for managing a project, including the allocation of sufficient time and other resources.
(2) Arrangements are suitable if they ensure that—
  (a) the construction work can be carried out, so far as is reasonably practicable, without risks to the health or safety of any person affected by the project; and
  (b) the facilities required by Schedule 2 are provided in respect of any person carrying out construction work.

The client is not required to manage the project, although they may choose to do so, but must, as an absolute duty under all circumstances, make suitable arrangements to achieve the overriding objectives in regulations 4(1) and (2). Typically, the arrangements that a client might consider that affect health and safety might include

- clearing the construction of hazards ready for starting construction work
- contacting and liaising with the utility companies to make safe or secure supplies to the site

- preparing a design brief for the designers to use
- preparing an overall timetable for the project, including the date for occupation or operation of the project
- assembling the project team, including the appointment of consultants and/or contractor(s).

If the client cannot, or does not want to, undertake all the roles of the duty holders, to carry out the tasks of design and construction the client will need to make the appointments for designers and contractors as required by the Regulations. The client has the prime responsibility to ensure that such persons who are appointed have sufficient time and other resources to carry out the construction work within the client's programme for the project, without risk to health and safety to any person, and for the provision of adequate welfare facilities. The client will also need to be satisfied that the appointees are capable of performing their respective roles under the Regulations by reason of regulation 8(3), which states that

> A person who is responsible for appointing a designer or contractor to carry out work on a project must take reasonable steps to satisfy themselves that the designer or contractor fulfils the conditions in paragraph (1).

The client should not impose unrealistic constraints upon the designers and the contractors that will jeopardise effective health and safety management. In particular, the client should avoid imposing shorter timescales, undermining cooperation and coordination between the parties. Most importantly, the client should not delay in communicating the information required by regulation 4(4) which requires that

> A client must provide pre-construction information as soon as it is practicable to every designer and contractor appointed, or being considered for appointment, to the project.

Where construction work is planned to take place within existing premises that are currently being used as a workplace or on a site adjacent to the client's operations, the client should take steps to ensure that their own activities do not create any unforeseen risks.

The client should always ensure that the workers on a construction site have access to the welfare facilities, which are listed and described in Schedule 2, and are more fully discussed in Chapter 5 of this book. The client does not have to possess any particular skills and experience to ascertain whether a contractor is proceeding in compliance with Schedule 2. The client can assist contractors during the construction work in many instances by extending the use of their own welfare facilities for the use of construction workers. Indeed, this would be expected if the contractor was otherwise unable to provide such facilities when the client's own facilities are readily accessible.

As a general proposition, the client is at risk that a party to a project appointed by the client who has reasonable grounds to conclude that the client is not properly exercising their duty with respect to the arrangements for managing the project may have grounds for terminating their contract of appointment with the client.

The duration of the client's commitment and contribution to the management of a project is defined by regulation 4(3), which requires that

> A client must ensure that these arrangements are maintained and reviewed throughout the project.

The duty on the client to keep the arrangements under review and monitor their continuing suitability is not qualified by any criteria of reasonableness. It is imperative that a client should be alert to any developing shortcomings in the health and safety management by the duty holders and should have reserved rights within the contracts of appointment to deal with such circumstances.

Provision of information

Risk assessment depends upon knowing all the facts and circumstances of a situation and expertise in recognising and identifying hazards. For many projects, the hazards are not necessarily immediately apparent to experienced designers and contractors. Where hazards are intrinsically connected to the site or an existing structure, the person most likely to have the best state of knowledge will be the client. It is for this reason that the transfer of pre-construction information from the client to the designers and contractors is an important step in minimising risks during the construction phase. Regulation 4(4) requires that

> A client must provide pre-construction information as soon as is practicable to every designer and contractor appointed, or being considered for appointment, to the project.

Thus, the client is required to identify all of the designers and contractors that they have appointed or may appoint. The client should recognise that suppliers are also very often designers, and information should be provided to them. Pre-construction information should be provided promptly so that initial designs can take account of any hazards. There is an obvious commercial advantage for the client in providing such information, as it may avoid wasted design time that could result from duplication when later information comes to light.

It is unreasonable to assume that many clients will recognise particular hazards. However, the regulations do not impose a duty on the designer to draw such matters to the attention of the client, although a client should have access to a competent health and safety adviser as required by the Management of Health and Safety at Work Regulations 1999.

The scope of the pre-construction information is defined in regulation 2(1) as meaning

> information in the client's possession or which is reasonably obtainable by or on behalf of the client, which is relevant to the construction work and is of an appropriate level of detail and proportionate to the risks involved, including—
> (a) information about—
> (i) the project;
> (ii) planning and management of the project;
> (iii) health and safety hazards, including design and construction hazards and how they will be addressed; and
> (b) information in any existing health and safety file;
> "pre-construction phase" means any period of time during which design or preparatory work is carried out for a project and may continue during the construction phase.

The scope of pre-construction information and categories of information that is within the possession of a client or reasonably obtainable by the client is included in Appendix 4 of this book. The client has a judgement to make as to the extent and scope of the pre-construction information to be provided. A client is unlikely to be criticised for being conservative in identifying and providing a comprehensive body of information. The information that the client is required to produce is not just information about the site or the construction work: the pre-construction information should also include information that will affect the site. Therefore, the natural features or activities remote from the site that might create a hazard should also be identified. This might typically include flooding from a river, a delimited speed limit on the main access road to the site, or storage of hazardous chemicals on an adjacent site.

A client who is procuring the project for the purpose of building a workplace or making amendments to an existing workplace should provide pre-construction information to the designers and contractors that would be expected in any competent design brief. Perhaps not so obviously, the client should provide detailed information about the employee/visitor profiles, shift patterns, weekend working, public access and so on.

A client should allow for a reasonable period of time between providing the pre-construction information to contractors, one or more of whom will be required to start construction work by a target date. If necessary, time should be allowed for detailed investigations and surveys to verify design assumptions and to confirm design philosophies and construction methods.

The existing health and safety file is an important source of information for existing structures, and has been a mandatory requirement since the coming into force of the 1994

Regulations, and remains so for the new Regulations. Where there are gaps in the information, particularly in respect of the presence of any asbestos, the client should seek the assistance of the principal designer as to the need for undertaking or procuring specialised condition surveys.

The pre-construction information has to be provided as soon as practicable, but in practice should not be provided later than the date when the designers start the design process or contractors start to work on the tender documentation. The timing of the provision of the pre-construction information is an integral part of the client's duty to make arrangements for managing a project, but any prudent client will recognise that the early provision of pre-construction information is commercially advantageous. Unless a client is experienced and knowledgeable with respect to the information that is likely to be required by designers and contractors, the information that is provided may not meet all the relevant purposes. The designers and contractors should review the pre-construction information to satisfy themselves, at least at face value, that the information assists them in protecting construction workers, other persons who are likely to be affected by the construction work and users and occupants of the workplace. In the event that the information has any obvious gaps, the client can expect to be pressed for further information or clarification. The exchange of information and the ensuing dialogue will be a rehearsal for the cooperation that is expected from all the parties throughout the project and also of the coordination of their activities.

The approach to be adopted by the designers and contractors in reviewing the pre-construction information is to consider its completeness so that their own duties can be fulfilled under the Regulations and they can plan the construction work with the necessary allocation of sufficient time and other resources to meet the timetable for the commencement of construction work.

Duty to make appointments

A client who is under a duty to make an appointment of a principal designer and a principal contractor must take into account that the persons who are being considered as appointees are given sufficient time and such pre-construction information as is available, to enable them to take proper account of the allocation of time and other resources that they will have to provide.

Appointment of a principal designer and a principal contractor

A client's obligations in respect of the appointment of a principal designer and a principal contractor are set out in regulation 5(1) as follows:

> Where there is more than one contractor, or if it is reasonably foreseeable that more than one contractor will be working on a project at any time, the client

> must appoint in writing—
> (a) a designer with control over the pre-construction phase as principal designer; and
> (b) a contractor as principal contractor.

In making the appointments of the principal designer and principal contractor, a client has to comply with the general duty in regulation 8(3) that it has taken reasonable steps to be satisfied that the principal designer and principal contractor fulfil the conditions in regulation 8(1), which are the possession of

> the skills, knowledge and experience, and, if they are an organisation, the organisational capability, necessary to fulfil the role that they are appointed to undertake, in a manner that secures the health and safety of any person affected by the project.

The reasonable steps that a client should take are dealt with in the sections on the appointments of a principal designer and principal contractor in Chapters 9 and 11, respectively, and Chapter 4 of this book.

The appointment of a principal contractor is necessary as soon as there will be, or is likely to be, more than one contractor. Thus, if a contractor intends to use a sub-contractor at any stage in during the construction work, the appointment of a principal contractor cannot be avoided.

The principal contractor has extensive duties in relation to a project that will involve the principal contractor in the expenditure of considerable time and expenditure during the pre-construction phase. If the principal contractor is appointed at an early stage in planning a project, the client will mitigate the overall burden of costs for tendering in the construction industry that are thrown away when contractors are not appointed.

In making an appointment of a principal contractor, the client will, in many cases, have already appointed a principal designer. However, the principal designer is not expressly required to give advice on the selection of the principal contractor before appointment. It would be regrettable if a client who seeks more extensive assistance from the principal designer was to be told that there was no obligation to do so under the Regulations. A principal designer is under the general duty to cooperate in accordance with regulation 8(4), and therefore could not unreasonably refuse to cooperate. More fundamentally, the principal designer is to ensure, so far as reasonably practicable, that the project can be carried out without risks to health or safety. If the appointment of a principal contractor comes within the scope of planning, management and coordination of the pre-construction phase, the principal designer could not withhold or refuse assistance to the client without being in breach of regulation 11(1).

Timing of the appointments

The appointments have to be made as soon as possible and not later than the start of construction work as required by regulation 5(2), which states that

> The appointments must be made as soon as is practicable, and, in any event, before the construction phase begins.

The timing of the appointments in practice will be a function of the size and complexity of the project and the scope of the principal contractor's work, especially if it will involve considerable design input. The timing of the appointment of the principal designer is also linked to the reasonable foreseeability that there will be more than one contractor working on the project. Whether there is a need for more than one contractor is an objective test, although with the modern practices of construction procurement it is likely to be only the smallest or highly specialised projects that will need just one contractor. A single-contractor project does not necessarily exempt a client from the duty to notify the Executive. Once a client has foreseen that there will be, or there is likely to be, more than one contractor, the principal designer should be appointed without delay.

Duty to review the appointments

The client is not allowed to become complacent, having made the key appointments of the principal designer and principal contractor, because the client is under a duty to maintain and review the appointments they have made as required by Regulation 4(6) as follows:

> A client must take reasonable steps to ensure that—
> (a) the principal designer complies with any other principal designer duties in regulations 11 and 12; and
> (b) the principal contractor complies with any other principal contractor duties in regulations 12 to 14.

The client cannot stand by and abdicate any leadership or management role over the two key appointments. The client will need to be informed about progress, requests for information, health and safety incidents, and copies of all key health and safety documentation.

The client may have appointed a principal designer under terms of engagement to terminate before the construction phase if there is a prospect that construction work may not commence. In those circumstances, the principal designer's appointment will require renewing. The same situation may arise during the construction phase if a separate contractor is engaged to undertake site clearance and demolition work. In those circumstances, the demolition contractor will be appointed as the principal contractor, whereas the main construction contractor will be appointed later as the principal contractor. This may be the same contractor if they have been successful in winning the main works under the construction phase.

In keeping the appointments under review, the client should be alert to any failure by the appointees to maintain their skills, knowledge and experience during the project. A failure by a principal designer or principal contractor to carry out their respective duties or maintain their competence can be grounds for terminating an appointment or claiming damages for extra costs that might otherwise be incurred by the client. The duty on a client to take such steps as are reasonable to review the arrangements is only discharged at the end of the construction phase.

As an essential step in making the arrangements for a project, the client should include in the terms and engagement, for either duty holder, a procedure for transferring information to a new incoming duty holder to avoid any disruption, or vacancy, in the role.

This is of particular importance because without an appointment in writing there is no appointment for the purposes of the Regulations, and therefore the client would be in breach of regulation 5.

Duty of the client in the absence of appointments

In the event that the client does not make an appointment of the principal designer or the principal contractor, as appropriate, the client is under a duty to fulfil their roles by reason of regulations 5(3) and (4), respectively, as follows:

> (3) If the client fails to appoint a principal designer, the client must fulfil the duties of the principal designer in regulations 11 and 12.
> (4) If the client fails to appoint a principal contractor, the client must fulfil the duties of the principal contractor in regulations 12 to 14.

Thus, the client can unwittingly be subject to the duties of the principal designer and principal contractor until such time as they have been appointed. If the client intends to fulfil the role of a principal designer or principal contractor, or both, the client is not required to set out an appointment in writing, although they should record in writing an assessment of their skills, knowledge, experience and organisational capability to comply with regulation 8(2).

To avoid the possibility of a technical breach of the Regulations that would put the client at risk of assuming the duties of the principal designer and principal contractor, the client should specifically state in the written appointments that the relevant persons are appointed to the role of principal designer or principal contractor as appropriate.

The client should be particularly alert during the project to any contractual event that might terminate the appointment of the principal designer or principal contractor, so as to avoid the duties falling upon the client.

Duty to provide information

Regulation 4(4) requires the client to provide pre-construction information to each designer and contractor as soon as practicable, as follows:

> A client must provide pre-construction information as soon as practicable to every designer and contractor appointed, or being considered for appointment, to the project.

The client has to identify all those persons to whom the information should be provided, and distribute such information as appropriate.

The minimum amount of time allowed to the principal contractor between receiving the pre-construction information and drawing up the construction phase plan before the construction phase is planned to start is an important parameter for the client. The client has to make the necessary arrangements to ensure that the design is completed and the construction phase plan can be completed before construction work starts.

Commencement of the construction phase

Until the commencement of the construction phase there is no actual risk of harm to any persons. It follows, therefore, that the start of the construction phase is a critical moment in the life of the project. Regulation 4(5) requires the client to intervene at the point in the project when site work is due to start, as follows:

> A client must ensure that—
> (a) before the construction phase begins, a construction phase plan is drawn up by the contractor if there is only one contractor, or by the principal contractor.

A contractor or principal contractor must draw up a construction phase plan as required by regulation 15(5) or 12(1), respectively. The timing is expressed differently when compared with regulation 4(5) because the critical time is not the start of construction but 'setting up' the construction site. In practical terms, a client can easily cause a principal contractor to comply with this duty by giving access to the site only when there is evidence that the construction phase plan has been drawn up, or arrangements have been made that satisfy the client that construction work will not start that could cause harm in breach of regulation 12(1). This requirement on the client by virtue of regulation 4(5) offers the client an opportunity to stamp their authority on the manner in which the project will proceed. If the construction phase plan has not been drawn up by the principal contractor or the client is not satisfied that there are adequate arrangements for doing so without risk to the health and safety of any person, the client will be in breach of regulation 4(5) if they take no action.

The provision of welfare facilities that a contractor or principal contractor is bound to provide should not be overlooked by a client in the discharge of their duty in regulation 4(2)(b) as being necessary from the very start of any site operations.

Duty in relation to the health and safety file

Regulation 4(5)(b) requires the client to ensure that the principal designer prepares a health and safety file as follows:

> A client must ensure that the principal designer prepares a health and safety file for the project, which—
> (i) complies with the requirements of regulation 12(5);
> (ii) is revised from time to time as appropriate to incorporate any relevant new information; and
> (iii) is kept available for inspection by any person who may need it to comply with the relevant legal requirements.

The requirements referred to in regulation 12(5) are dealt with in detail in Chapter 14 of this book. The principal designer does not necessarily have to prepare the health and safety file, but must ensure that it is prepared and kept under review. It is the client's duty, having made the arrangements for managing the project, to ensure that the health and safety file is prepared by the principal designer or has made arrangements for it to be prepared.

The client's duty does not terminate at the end of the construction phase to the extent that they have continuing obligations in respect of the health and safety file as provided for by paragraph 5(b)(ii), to keep the health and safety file under review and revised as appropriate, and paragraph 5(b)(iii) to keep it available for inspection. The only time when a client is free of the continuing obligations is when they dispose of their entire interest in the structure or structures that are the subject of the health and safety file.

A full analysis of the requirements to comply with the preparation and custody of the health and safety file is presented in Chapter 14 of this book.

Checklist

A checklist for clients has been included in Appendix 1.

CDM Regulations 2015 Explained
ISBN 978-0-7277-6009-8

http://dx.doi.org/10.1680/cdmre.60098.085

Chapter 9
The principal designer

- **Introduction**
- **Definition**
- **Appointment of the principal designer**
- **Who can be the principal designer?**
- **Duties of the principal designer**

Introduction

During the years since the coming into force of the 1994 CDM Regulations, the Health and Safety Executive had been increasingly frustrated at the bureaucracy created by those fulfilling the role of the 'planning supervisor', later replaced by the role of the 'CDM coordinator' under the 2007 Regulations. Unwittingly the CDM Regulations had spawned a new profession for planning supervisors and, latterly, CDM coordinators. The benefits to the construction industry by introducing these new roles, with their own professional association and training courses, was far from clear. What was beyond dispute was the resultant increased costs for clients but without any evidence that the roles of the planning supervisor and the CDM coordinator contributed to a commensurate improvement in the health and safety record in the construction industry. It was finally conceded that neither the role of the CDM coordinator nor that of the planning supervisor had been as successful as hoped for in contributing to an improvement in health and safety management.

To reduce the bureaucracy and costs to the construction industry, the 2015 Regulations have revoked the role of the CDM coordinator. The role of the principal designer is not a replacement for the CDM coordinator, to the extent that the new role will be integrated with the design and project team in a way which was not achieved by the earlier roles. The earlier roles, with all the trappings of a new profession, were perceived by the construction industry as adding very little value, being no more than another person who was not embedded in the design and project team.

The Temporary or Mobile Construction Sites Directive created the roles of 'project supervisor' and 'coordinator for safety and health matters at the project preparation stage', which were combined in the CDM Regulations to create the role of the planning supervisor and, later, the role of the CDM coordinator. The project supervisor was to be a person acting on behalf of the client. In an industry where one of the many challenges is the enormous diversity of clients, the role of the project supervisor would facilitate a consistency in the application of the CDM Regulations. The role of the CDM coordinator, appointed by the client, was to provide assistance and guidance to the client. A significant difference between the principal designer and the CDM coordinator is the expectation under the Regulations that the client will be entirely responsible for making all the arrangements for procuring construction work without any assistance or guidance from any of the parties to the project, except in respect of preparing pre-construction information.

In summary, the principal designer is a new role in the 2015 Regulations, and there is some overlap with the former role of the CDM coordinator but, crucially, the appointment of the principal designer applies to all projects, irrespective of size and whether or not they are notifiable, and the principal designer's direct statutory obligations to the client are very limited.

Definition

The principal designer is defined in regulation 2(1) as meaning

> the designer appointed under regulation 5(1)(a) to perform the specified duties in regulations 11 and 12.

Appointment of the principal designer

Non-domestic clients

The appointment of a principal designer is mandatory on all projects where there is more than one contractor, or it is reasonably foreseeable that there will be more than one contractor, irrespective of the size of the project and regardless of whether the project is notifiable. The principal designer can only be a person appointed by the client by virtue of regulation 5(1)(a) as follows:

> Where there is more than one contractor, or if it is reasonably foreseeable that more than one contractor will be working on a project at any time, the client must appoint in writing a designer with control over the pre-construction phase as principal designer.

Thus, on all projects it is the client who has to appoint the principal designer in writing, and in doing so must ensure that the principal designer carries out the responsibilities in regulations 11 and 12. The preparation of the pre-construction information is a vital stage in a project, and regulation 11(6) envisages that the principal designer will be available to assist in the task. It is for this reason that regulation 5(2) requires that

> The appointments must be made as soon as is practicable, and, in any event, before the construction phase begins.

Therefore, a client would be well advised to appoint a principal designer once the collection and preparation of the pre-construction information is needed, although the client is not required to make an appointment until the construction phase is about to start.

Initial design work can span very long periods of time and include various scheme designs and the consideration of different options from economic and technical points of view. Although the construction phase may seem a long way off at the stage of considering outline schemes, it will often be the case that one scheme would be much better than another from the point of view of mitigating health and safety hazards. As an example, the initial design might include options for a bridge or tunnel for a river crossing at its earliest stage. In considering each of the options, the principal designer will be able to make use of the early possession of the pre-construction information provided by the client, for the benefit of the client and health and safety management generally. In the event that the appointment of a principal designer is delayed, the client assumes the responsibilities of the principal designer in accordance with regulation 5(3), which states that

> If the client fails to appoint a principal designer, the client must fulfil the duties of the principal designer in regulations 11 and 12.

A client who unwittingly assumes the responsibilities of the principal designer is exposing themselves to considerable commercial and health and safety management risks if they do not have the skills that would be expected of a principal designer.

During the project the client has an obligation to maintain the appointment of the principal designer and keep it under review because the appointment of the principal designer is part of the arrangements for managing a project and the client has a continuing duty to keep the arrangements under review by virtue of regulation 4(3). Once a person has been appointed to the role of the principal designer, it should remain filled until the end of the construction phase, when it is the responsibility of the client to ensure that the principal designer prepares a health and safety file as provided for by regulation 4(5)(b). The client must also take steps to ensure that the principal designer complies with their duties by reason of regulation 4(6).

Clients would be well advised to ensure that adequate provision is made in the terms of engagement of the principal designer for a smooth handover to a replacement person, particularly with regard to notice of termination or change and identification of documentation to be handed over. The client will need to ensure that the health and safety file is passed to the principal contractor if the principal designer's appointment is terminated before the end of the construction phase.

Domestic clients

A designer should be alert to the possibility, when working on a project for a domestic client, that if there is more than one contractor, or there is a reasonable likelihood that there may be more than one contractor, the designer will be treated as the principal designer as provided for in regulation 7(2)(a), which states that

> If a domestic client fails to make the appointments required by regulation 5 the designer in control of the pre-construction phase of the project is the principal designer.

The Regulations also take into account at regulation 7(1)(c) that a domestic client may have engaged a principal designer in writing, requiring the principal designer to coordinate and manage the project, in which case the principal designer must carry out the client's duties, as follows:

> Where the client is a domestic client the duties in regulations 4(1) to (7) and 6 must be carried out by the principal designer where there is a written agreement that the principal designer will fulfil those duties.

Who can be the principal designer?

There is no limitation in the Regulations as to the background or expertise of a person who may fulfil the role of the principal designer. The principal designer can be an individual, partnership, limited company, local authority or government department, subject always to demonstrating to the client that it is capable of performing their responsibilities under regulations 11 and 12 without risk to the health and safety of any persons. A person who accepts an appointment as a principal designer must comply with the general duties in regulations 8(1) and (2) as follows:

> (1) A designer (including a principal designer) … appointed to work on a project must have the skills, knowledge and experience, and, if they are an organisation, the organisational capability, necessary to fulfil the role that they are appointed to undertake, in a manner that secures the health and safety of any person affected by the project.
> (2) A designer … must not accept an appointment to a project unless they fulfil the conditions in paragraph (1).

Therefore, it is an offence for an organisation to accept the role of the principal designer if, on a self-assessment basis, it does not consider itself as possessing the necessary skills, knowledge and experience, or the organisational capability if the principal designer is not an individual.

There is no prohibition within the Regulations that prevents the role of the principal designer being combined with one of the other roles under the Regulations, the main combinations of which are set out below. The fundamental approach enshrined in the Regulations to managing health and safety risks is that avoiding the hazards and mitigating the risk should be embedded in the project team and not devolved onto one duty holder. Therefore, combining any role with the principal designer is likely to promote a more integrated and embedded philosophy in recognising that the management of health and safety risks is a project priority. The appointment of a principal designer who is independent of any other role under the Regulations is likely to be uncommon, but it can be envisaged that an organisation appointed to a project management role, with the appropriate skills and experience, could carry out the role of the principal designer. The tasks of planning, managing, monitoring and coordinating are fundamental project management skills. In fact, the role of the principal designer is a misnomer because the duties in regulations 11 and 12 do not include preparing or modifying a design.

The client as principal designer

A client can appoint themselves as the principal designer at the relevant time in accordance with regulation 5(1)(a). Indeed, the default position if no principal designer has been appointed is the deeming provision in regulation 5(3) that the client must fulfil the role of the principal designer. A client should be satisfied that in their role as the principal designer they have discharged their responsibility to have made suitable arrangements as required by regulation 5(1) and the skills, knowledge, experience and organisational capability required by regulation 8(1). There is a risk that a client will have an opinion of their attributes such that the project is suitable for their appointment as the principal designer, whereas on an objective assessment they would clearly be unsuitable. A client's self-assessment can be coloured by the cost of paying a third party to carry out the duties of the principal designer, or they may have underutilised resources. Whatever the client's reasoning might be, the principal designer's responsibilities are all encompassing and fundamental during the pre-construction phase, and should not be undertaken recklessly. Unfortunately, the Regulations do not impose on any of the duty holders, except the principal designer in respect of pre-construction information, a duty to assist or offer assistance to the client.

The principal contractor as principal designer

There is no prohibition in the Regulations that prevents the principal contractor from being appointed as the principal designer.

The principal designer has, by virtue of regulation 5(2), to be appointed by the client as soon as is practicable at the start of the pre-construction phase and not later than the start of the construction phase. A client must also appoint a principal contractor as soon as practicable, and certainly before the construction phase starts. Practically, the client will appoint a principal contractor when they know enough about the project to be able to select a suitable contractor to fill the role. The appointment of the principal contractor as the principal designer would imply that the principal contractor was expected to be involved in the pre-construction phase, which will predominately include the design process, or, alternatively, the construction work was urgent and able to proceed concurrently with design work.

If a client decides to appoint the same person to the roles of the principal designer and the principal contractor, at the outset of the project, it would suggest from a commercial point of view that the role of the principal contractor would not be subject to competitive tendering at a later date. For this reason, it is likely that clients appointing a principal contractor at the outset will be more likely to appoint design and build contractors. Commonly, a design and build contractor accepts the novation of appointments of designers, which may include the principal designer, in which event the principal contractor will acquire all the duties of the principal designer.

For large and complex projects the client should be aware of the risk that the principal contractor may lack the resources to undertake the pre-construction phase role in accordance with the Regulations from within their own resources. The client is under a responsibility to ensure that the principal contractor has the means to allocate sufficient time and other resources to carry out the pre-construction and construction phases without risk to the health and safety of any persons.

In keeping the appointments of the principal designer and the principal contractor under review, the client can take advantage of combining the roles in the same person at any stage in the pre-construction or construction phase, depending on all the circumstances.

A designer as principal designer

The roles of the designer and the principal designer share the same noun although they are distinctly different. However, the importance of the role of the designer during the pre-construction phase in identifying the hazards and mitigating the risks, such as to improve the health and safety environment for construction workers and users of a structure, is underlined by the new role of the principal designer, who is responsible for planning, managing, monitoring and coordinating the pre-construction phase. The designer has the detailed knowledge of the design process that the principal designer does not necessarily possess.

A distinct advantage of appointing a designer as the principal designer is the fact that a designer is likely to be involved at the inception of a project. This would facilitate an appropriate health and safety risk assessment to be applied to early schematic options. As noted earlier, the identification of hazards as between different options could, and perhaps should, be a significant factor in assessing the outcome of the preferred solutions at the initial design stage.

Duties of the principal designer

The duties of the principal designer are established by regulations 11 and 12. Regulation 11 sets out the general duties of the principal designer in relation to health and safety at the pre-construction phase. Regulation 12 sets out the specific duties of the principal designer in relation to the construction phase plan and the health and safety file.

Plan, manage, monitor and coordinate

Contracts of appointment between clients and principal designers will often extend the duties and obligations of the principal designer. In many situations, as described above, the principal designer will also be a designer. The principal designer should be alert to, and recognise the risk posed by, additional contractual duties and obligations that go beyond those duties in the Regulations for the principal designer. What follows is only the extent of the statutory duties for the principal designer.

The fundamental role of the principal designer is set out in regulation 11(1), which states that

> The principal designer must plan, manage and monitor the pre-construction phase and coordinate matters relating to health and safety during the pre-construction phase to ensure that, so far as is reasonably practicable, the project is carried out without risks to health or safety.

The Regulations divide projects into two phases, pre-construction and construction, which leads to two distinct roles, of which the principal designer has the overarching role for the pre-construction phase. The Regulations direct how the principal designer is expected to fulfil their duties in regulation 11(2), which leaves no doubt about the importance of the role in the following terms:

> In fulfilling the duties in paragraph (1), and in particular when—
> (a) design, technical and organisational aspects are being decided in order to plan the various items or stages of work which are to take place simultaneously or in succession; and
> (b) estimating the period of time required to complete such work or work stages,
> the principal designer must take into account the general principles of prevention

> and, where relevant, the content of any construction phase plan and health and safety file.

The principal designer has to have the skills, knowledge and experience to deal with a project's design, technical and organisational aspects as discrete activities that require planning and the allocation of time. The obligation on the principal designer to take into account the general principles of prevention is likely to mean that the principal designer is closer to the design process than might have otherwise been required by the former CDM coordinator role. It is for this reason that the person appointed as the principal designer is ideally placed to be the Building Information Modelling (BIM) manager because of the specific duties that are fundamentally project management activities before the construction phase commences.

Identification, elimination or control of foreseeable risks

The need for coordination by the principal designer of the different parties' input into the design and technical aspects in the pre-construction phase includes the identification of hazards and assessing risk. However, the principal designer has the primary role to identify the hazards and risks associated with a project as required by regulation 11(3), which states that

> In fulfilling the duties in paragraph (1), the principal designer must identify and eliminate or control, so far as is reasonably practicable, foreseeable risks to the health or safety of any person—
> (a) carrying out or liable to be affected by construction work;
> (b) maintaining or cleaning a structure; or
> (c) using a structure designed as a workplace.

The requirements of regulation 11(3) go beyond the duty of a designer in regulation 9(2) who, while taking the general principles of prevention into account, is not required to 'identify' or 'control' the foreseeable risks to the health and safety of any person.

On the assumption that the principal designer will have the primary line of communication to the client, they have the responsibility to weigh the risks to health and safety for each foreseeable risk associated with the situations in paragraphs (a) to (c) and make, as appropriate, representations to the client that changes to the construction activities and the final structure might both need revising, which in turn can affect the costs of the project.

It can only be by coordinating the work of all the designers on a project, by relying on the duty to cooperate that applies to all duty holders, as provided for in regulation 8(4), that the principal designer is expected to comply with their duties. This is recognised in regulation 11(5), where all parties of the pre-construction phase are expected to cooperate with each other as follows:

> In fulfilling the duty to coordinate health and safety matters in paragraph (1), the principal designer must ensure that all persons working in relation to the pre-construction phase cooperate with the client, the principal designer and each other.

The principal designer has no express powers to compel designers to cooperate but on the basis that the role of the principal designer is primarily one of project management, and with the adoption of BIM, the information systems introduced by the principal designer are likely to be on a shared digital platform that will promote coordination and cooperation.

The principal designer's fundamental role is discharged by ensuring that various objectives are addressed and carried out, as discussed below, and a detailed discussion of the foreseeable risks is given in Chapter 10 of this book, which considers the role of the designer.

Assistance to the client and pre-construction information

The principal designer's role in connection with the pre-construction information in regulation 11(6)(a) is limited by requiring that

> The principal designer must assist the client in the provision of the pre-construction information required by regulation 4(4).

'Pre-construction information' is defined in regulation 2(1) as follows:

> "pre-construction information" means information in the client's possession or which is reasonably obtainable by or on behalf of the client, which is relevant to the construction work and is of an appropriate level of detail and proportionate to the risks involved, including—
> (a) information about—
>   (i) the project;
>   (ii) planning and management of the project;
>   (iii) health and safety hazards, including design and construction hazards and how they will be addressed; and
> (b) information in any existing health and safety file.

The principal designer's express duty to the client is limited to assisting the client in the preparation of the pre-construction information. The extent to which the client will rely on the principal designer's knowledge and experience as to the type and nature of information comprised in the pre-construction information will depend on the client's own expertise. If the client has no prior experience of construction projects, they are not entitled to any other assistance under the Regulations from the principal designer unless the client creates such an obligation in the principal designer's terms of appointment.

As part of the assistance that the principal designer is obliged to provide, they should be alert to identifying at an early stage omissions and gaps in the pre-construction information. Although the client has a duty to provide information pursuant to regulation 4(4), the principal designer has a wider duty to identify and advise upon the preparation of the pre-construction information from all sources. The principal designer should take particular account of paragraphs (a) and (b) in the definition of pre-construction information. The situation on many projects will lead to advice that critical areas of the pre-construction information does not exist. Where the principal designer has identified gaps in the pre-construction information, they should advise the client as to how the information can be obtained. On receiving the advice of the principal designer, the client will realise that the additional work and investigations to obtain the pre-construction information will cost them additional money. If the client refuses to take the steps necessary to obtain the pre-construction information that the principal designer deems is necessary to ensure the project can be carried out without risks to health and safety, the principal designer would be in breach of regulation 11(1) if they continued to proceed in the role. The type and nature of the pre-construction information that the principal designer should take into account is listed in Appendix 4, based on the information identified in the Approved Code of Practice for the 2007 Regulations.

Distributing the pre-construction information

Once the pre-construction information is in the possession of the principal designer, they are required to ensure that the information is communicated as required by regulation 11(6)(b), which states that

> The principal designer must so far as it is within the principal designer's control, provide pre-construction information, promptly and in a convenient form, to every designer and contractor appointed, or being considered for appointment, to the project.

The pre-construction information must be provided promptly and in a convenient form. The prompt provision of the pre-construction information promotes efficiency and is generally cost-effective. The means by which the information is provided is likely to have a significant effect on the costs incurred by the receiving parties. The principal designer can have an important influence at this stage of a project in mitigating wasted costs in sorting unstructured and uncollated information.

The principal designer will have had to identify all the designers and contractors appointed by the client to ensure that the pre-construction information is received by them. In this respect it becomes apparent that the principal designer acting as the BIM manager would be promoting health and safety improvements in addition to the general benefits offered by the adoption of BIM.

Ensuring cooperation of all persons in a project

Cooperation is a general principle that underpins the philosophy of the Regulations, and the principal designer has an important duty in ensuring, not merely facilitating, cooperation of all persons working on the project as required by regulation 11(5) as referred to above.

The expression 'all persons' in regulation 11(5) includes persons other than designers, so that the principal designer needs to identify all persons who have made, or will be making, a contribution to the project that has a bearing on the risks to health and safety to all persons connected with the project. The persons whom the principal designer will need to consider taking into account, to the extent they are working on the project, include the

- client
- occupants/site users
- occupants of neighbouring sites
- utilities
- highway authority
- principal contractor
- contractors, appointed by the client and others
- suppliers.

The principal designer should establish a protocol that will encourage and promote communication between the various parties to any project during the pre-construction phase. This is a task that should be implemented as soon as possible because the planning and preparation during the pre-construction phase will have a profound effect on the management of the construction phase. To ensure that cooperation happens as a matter of fact is a challenge for the principal designer that will require close monitoring. As there are no obligations on designers or the principal contractor to comply with directions given by the principal designer, there is no coercion that can be applied through the Regulations except regulation 8(4), which imposes a general duty to cooperate.

The principal designer's challenge in monitoring communication between designers is the requirement to monitor the content, particularly needed with respect to the application of the general principles of prevention. The application of BIM will facilitate the task of monitoring the design development, otherwise the means of communication will reflect the preferences of the parties to the project and will be influenced by the proximity of the parties, the number of parties and the complexity of the issues. Sharing information is often perceived by the provider of the information as increasing the risk of criticism and loss of commercial advantage. The principal designer can overcome such a perception by adopting an even-handed approach between the parties and gain their trust so that the flow of information is open, unrestricted and transparent. The principal designer can set an example for the parties to the project by disseminating the information that they will have received from the client, and stimulating consideration of that information by making appropriate enquiries as to how the general principles of prevention are being incorporated and addressed.

Overseeing the designers

One of the key tasks of the principal designer is effectively a quality assurance role to ensure that the design development takes account of the general principles of prevention. Regulation 11(4) obliges the principal designer to monitor and check the work of other designers in the following terms:

> In fulfilling the duties in paragraph (1), the principal designer must ensure all designers comply with their duties in regulation 9.

The designers may include persons appointed by the principal designer, specialist suppliers, and the principal contractor and their contractors.

How is the principal designer to know that a designer has not complied with their duties under regulation 9? In particular, how can the principal designer ensure that designers have identified all the hazards? The pre-construction information, which will have been provided by the client, with the assistance of the principal designer, should have identified health and safety hazards associated with the site and design and construction hazards together with guidance as to how they will be addressed. While there is no express requirement for the principal designer to check the design prepared by the designer, the duty to ensure compliance by the designer must involve some degree of checking. It is not possible to check the designer's compliance with regulation 9 without having an appropriate level of skill and expertise in the particular design discipline. Without the level of skill and expertise possessed by a designer, the principal designer can still provide guidance and leadership to assist a designer to identify the foreseeable risks by careful presentation and explanation of the pre-construction information.

A principal designer should pay particular attention to the information that a designer provides with their design as required by regulation 9(4), to check that the health and safety hazards identified with the pre-construction information, and any others identified by the designer, have been addressed as part of the design. In the event that the principal designer is unable to satisfy themselves that a designer has complied with regulation 9, they should seek specialist advice, noting that there is no qualification that the steps to be taken by the principal designer are limited to what is reasonably practicable. From a commercial point of view, the warranty that a principal designer often gives to interested parties to a project in respect of performing their contractual and statutory obligations, which will include the managing and monitoring of designers' compliance with regulation 9, may extend the liability of the principal designer beyond their own design expertise.

The health and safety file

The principal designer's duties include the preparation and revision of the health and safety file. The duty created by regulation 12(5) is as follows:

> During the pre-construction phase, the principal designer must prepare a health and safety file appropriate to the characteristics of the project which must contain information relating to the project which is likely to be needed during any subsequent project to ensure the health and safety of any person.

The importance of the health and safety file is such that Chapter 14 in this book deals with the topic in detail. However, for the principal designer, the importance of the health and safety file can have far-reaching consequences. If the principal designer is negligent in creating or revising a health and safety file, either by omitting critical information or incorporating inaccuracies, this is likely to impact on those who later come to rely upon the health and safety file. The persons who rely upon the health and safety file in a later project and in so doing suffer harm, or are the cause of some other person suffering harm, may have a cause of action against the principal designer who was responsible for the health and safety file.

Liaison with the principal contractor

The principal designer's responsibilities are established by regulation 11 for the pre-construction phase, which includes the responsibility for planning, managing, monitoring and coordinating the design process: but do the principal designer's duties in respect of design suddenly stop when the construction phase commences? On projects that are complex and where the construction phase starts before the design is completed, there is an inevitable overlap of the design process between the pre-construction phase and the construction phase. The Regulations do not expressly allocate responsibilities when there is an overlap between the design process and the start of the construction phase.

The principal contractor will often be responsible for the design of structures on a project, including permanent and temporary works. Temporary works are only part of the design if they relate to a structure as referred to in the definition of design in regulation 2(1), which states:

> "design" includes drawings, design details, specifications and bills of quantities (including specification of articles or substances) relating to a structure, and calculations prepared for the purpose of a design.

The principal contractor's responsibilities in regulation 14 do not expressly refer to design, but, without any contrary indication, if design tasks fall within the construction phase the principal contractor has the responsibility to plan, manage, monitor and coordinate the design process once the construction phase starts. This interpretation is reinforced by the fact that the only reference to the principal designer in regulation 13 is the need in paragraph (5) for liaison in respect of the health and safety file and matters that may affect the planning and management of the pre-construction phase.

The transfer of responsibilities for the design process, from the principal designer to the principal contractor, at the start of the construction phase, is often managed in design and build projects by novating the designers' appointments from the client to the contractor. The benefits of BIM will ensure that storing the design information in a central digital repository will avoid any unnecessary duplication of design and provide the principal contractor with contemporary design data to facilitate seamless design development.

The onus on the principal designer to keep an accurate design record up to date will promote the avoidance or mitigation of risks to health and safety and incurring unnecessary costs.

The principal designer and the principal contractor are each required to liaise with the other throughout the duration of the project. Regulation 11(7), which is in similar terms to regulation 13(5) for the principal contractor's duty, requires that

> The principal designer must liaise with the principal contractor for the duration of the principal designer's appointment and share with the principal contractor information relevant to the planning, management and monitoring of the construction phase and the coordination of health and safety matters during the construction phase.

The principal designer's duty to liaise does not require the principal designer to advise or assist the principal contractor. However, the principal designer is obliged to provide information as required by regulation 11(6)(b) and to assist the principal contractor in preparing the construction phase plan pursuant to regulation 12(3). The duty to liaise exists for the duration of the project, which covers the construction phase, but what is comprised in a duty to liaise? Since the duty to liaise is mutual, as between the principal designer and the principal contractor, it infers a need for there to be a dialogue – not necessarily initiated by either party, but a continuing dialogue in the furtherance of a mutual goal to reduce the risks to the health and safety of any person arising from the project.

The principal designer and the principal contractor are obliged to cooperate in maintaining the duty to liaise by virtue of regulation 8(4). The best evidence of such liaison is likely to be minuted structured meetings or conference calls.

Regulation 11(7) directs the principal designer to consider relevant information for sharing with the principal contractor that they consider they may need to prepare the construction phase plan, or which may affect the planning, management and monitoring of the construction work. If the principal designer recognises that there are matters arising in the pre-construction phase that are likely to affect the construction phase plan, the principal designer is duty bound to liaise, or, in other words, advise accordingly. The principal designer must maintain their involvement in the project after the construction phase starts so that design assumptions and philosophy are compared with the actuality during construction. In circumstances where the design assumptions or philosophy are inappropriate, the principal designer should advise the principal contractor if a change is likely to be needed to the planning and management of the construction work.

Checklist

A checklist for principal designers has been included in Appendix 1.

CDM Regulations 2015 Explained
ISBN 978-0-7277-6009-8

http://dx.doi.org/10.1680/cdmre.60098.101

Chapter 10
The designer

- **Who is a designer?**
- **What is design?**
- **Selecting a designer**
- **The client as designer**
- **A contractor as designer**
- **Duties of designers**
- **Designs prepared or modified outside of Great Britain**

Who is a designer?

A designer is defined in regulation 2(1) of the CDM Regulations as meaning

> any person (including a client, contractor or other person referred to in these Regulations) who in the course or furtherance of a business—
> (a) prepares or modifies a design; or
> (b) arranges for, or instructs, any person under their control to do so,
> relating to a structure, or to a product or mechanical or electrical system intended for a particular structure, and a person is deemed to prepare a design where a design is prepared by a person under their control.

Thus, any person can be a designer. In fact, many persons contribute to design unwittingly without recognising that they are taking part in the design process.

What is design?

The definition of design in regulation 2(1) includes

> drawings, design details, specifications and bills of quantities (including specification of articles or substances) relating to a structure and calculations prepared for the purpose of a design.

It is within most people's contemplation that design would include the preparation of drawings, calculations and specifications, but note, in particular, that the preparation of bills of quantities is included within the definition of design. The inclusion of bills of quantities hints at the importance of the allocation of financial resources, although an express reference to financial resources was not included in the 1994 and 2007 Regulations nor is in the latest Regulations.

Even in the most straightforward circumstances of preparing or modifying a design, a person may not be aware that their contribution will be part of the design process. In fact, because designs are rarely finalised until the point of installation or construction, all persons involved in the decision-making up to the point of installation or construction are likely to be designers. The Approved Code of Practice (ACOP) for the 2007 Regulations recognised that the design does not have to be a neat set of written calculations or instructions but that a design can be communicated orally and therefore extends the categories of persons likely to be fulfilling the role of a designer. Although the 2007 ACOP has been withdrawn, it still assists in establishing the identity of those persons fulfilling the role of a designer as set out below:

(a) Architects, civil and structural engineers, building surveyors, landscape architects, technical consultants, manufacturers and design practices associated with the professional mentioned and contributing to, or having overall responsibility for, any part of the design.
(b) Any person who specifies or alters a design, or specifies the use of a particular method of work or material.
(c) Building service designers, engineering practices or other persons designing plant which forms part of the permanent structure.
(d) Persons purchasing materials where the choice of material has been left to the discretion of the purchaser.
(e) Contractors carrying out design work as part of their contribution to a project.
(f) Engineers designing temporary works.
(g) Interior designers, including shop fitters and associated trades who develop the design.
(h) Heritage organisations who specify materials and method statements.
(i) Persons involved in making decisions as to the refurbishment or alteration of buildings and structures.

A person who gives advice is not a designer. Also, manufacturers supplying standardised products are not considered to be designers for the purposes of the Regulations, although inevitably they will have duties under sale and purchase legislation. A person who selects a product will be deemed to be a designer and must take account of health and safety issues arising from its use in construction. If a product is made or altered for a particular project, the person who prepares the specification for the purpose-made product or alteration is a designer and so will the manufacturer who developed the detail design.

The definition of design will include, for the purposes of preparing or modifying a design, the following

- the selection of design philosophy and principles
- the specification of materials, articles and substances
- the dimensions
- the adoption of loading criteria
- method statements.

The definition of design and the role of designers are not changed in any respect according to the purpose of the design. There is no distinction between permanent works and the temporary works required for construction that will either be taken down or left within the fabric of the structure. The design 'relating to a structure' is the only test that determines the identity of the duty holders. Therefore, the client for the purpose of designing temporary works will be the contractor who needs the temporary works structure for their own purposes. A designer is subject to the same duties whether the design is for permanent structures, temporary works, modifications or maintenance works.

Arranging for or instructing persons under the designer's control

The definition in regulation 2(1) for a designer in paragraph (b) compared with the definition of a person referred to as a designer in paragraph (a) extends considerably the scope of identifying designers. It is not difficult to recognise a person who actually prepares or modifies a design if they produce drawings, design details, specifications and bills of quantities. However, the term 'designer' in paragraph (b), as applied to other persons who merely arrange for others under their control to prepare a design, is of limitless scope. The Regulations do not specify the type or nature of the required control. It cannot be assumed that the control referred to is limited to the ability or right of the arranging designer to control directly the work of preparing a design by others. Control can arise from various other situations, for example the control conferred by a majority shareholding in a subsidiary company; or contractual control (to the extent that fixing remuneration, programme and termination is not necessarily control over the design input or process); or a partner in a partnership.

The Regulations do not have a legal test for establishing if a person is arranging for or instructing others under their control to prepare or modify a design. The normal meaning of the term 'arranges for or instructs' is generally well understood, and will be interpreted as such on the facts of each case as and when the situation arises. In respect of a design prepared or modified outside of Great Britain, the test is of 'commission' and not arranging or instructing – see below.

Selecting a designer

No single person on a project is charged with the responsibility to appoint a designer. The fact that design touches most functions and disciplines involved in the construction work would mean that it would be inappropriate to have any one named person with that responsibility. On large and complex projects there may be many different organisations appointing designers.

Regulation 8(3) requires a person who is responsible for appointing a designer to take 'reasonable steps to satisfy themselves' that the designer fulfils the conditions in regulation 8(1). The conditions in paragraph (1) require the designer to have

> the skills, knowledge and experience, and, if they are an organisation, the orgainsiational capability, necessary to fulfil the role that they are appointed to undertake, in a manner that secures the health and safety of any person affected by the project.

The appointer's fundamental question is to ask what part of the design is intended to be carried out by the designer. Matters that a person making such an appointment might take into consideration include the questions that are incorporated in Publicly Available Specification 91 (PAS 91:2013), 'Construction prequalification questionnaires', which is particularly useful for organisational capability. Detailed questions about organisational capability may cover

- the information technology infrastructure
- the technical library
- laboratory services
- access to research information
- membership of professional or trade associations
- document management.

In assessing the skills and knowledge of a designer, a person should take into account the academic and professional qualifications of the key individuals as evidence of the ability to eliminate or control foreseeable risks. An appointer should make a distinction between the experience of the key persons, based on past projects, and the experience of the organisation. The competence of the individuals in a design organisation are vital, but the lack of a 'corporate memory' of an organisation's experience should not be completely overlooked.

As required by regulation 8(4), the designer is required to cooperate with the principal designer and with other parties when requested. Equally, when the designer seeks information, advice or comment from other designers or contractors, they can rely on regulation 8(4). The designer must also share the information they have, and generates, with other designers and contractors. A designer's information technology capability will become as important as their core skills and knowledge with the increasing adoption of Building Information Modelling (BIM).

The client as designer

A client is not prevented from fulfilling the role of the designer subject to being able to demonstrate that they are satisfied that their design capability, in house or otherwise, is able to comply with the duties imposed by the Regulations. In circumstances where there is an independent principal designer, it would be prudent for a client to seek their views before confirming the appointment of a designer from within their own organisation, although the principal designer is not obliged under the Regulations to provide such assistance.

In some circumstances a client may wish to impose particular design principles, standards or specifications on a designer to ensure consistency of design with other projects that the client is procuring, or has procured. While the liability for design in such situations becomes blurred, the client will be fulfilling the role of the designer under the Regulations. A client who has 'control' over the designer has to accept that they will become subject to the requirements of regulation 9 to an extent that will depend on the precise level of contribution to the design.

A contractor as designer

The Regulations have been drafted to accommodate the increasingly diverse methods of procurement now used in the construction industry, including 'design and build'. Under the forms of contract for design and build the main contractor undertakes to design the permanent and temporary works in addition to the execution of the construction phase. The exact extent of liability as to design will be subject to the agreed contract terms. The Regulations do not prohibit or discourage a design and build contractor from fulfilling both roles, as this is now a commonplace arrangement.

A contractor without any in-house design capability, whether for temporary or permanent works, will almost certainly need to appoint a designer.

Duties of designers

Client awareness

Regulation 9(1) imposes on a designer the duty not to proceed with any construction work unless they are satisfied that the client is aware of the client duties under the Regulations as follows:

> A designer must not commence work in relation to a project unless satisfied that the client is aware of the duties owed by a client under these Regulations.

The designer is not under a duty to make enquiries but merely to know that the client is aware of their duties under the Regulations. The designer does not have to be satisfied that the client is aware of the Regulations in their totality.

On a large project, where there are likely to be numerous designers, a designer can be satisfied that the client is aware of their duties if notification has been given by the client under regulation 6(2) or (4), in which case the designer should ask for a copy. On small projects, however, the situation may not be quite so obvious where the project is not notifiable. Irrespective of the contractual relationships and obligations owed by a designer to various parties, the designer should make it their business to be satisfied that the client is aware of their duties under the Regulations by making direct enquiries if necessary, of the client, which includes domestic clients. The obligation in regulation 9(1) is absolute, and the designer has no defence if they start design work without knowing that the client is aware of their duties. In making enquiries of the client the designer will have put the client on notice that they should be complying with the Regulations and can start design work without risk of being in breach of regulation 9(1).

Elimination of foreseeable risks

The duty of a designer is only related to design and does not include planning, managing, monitoring and coordinating any other activities. Regulations 9(2) and (3) succinctly set out the design objectives to achieve, what the Health and Safety Executive has referred to as 'safe by design'. The designer is instructed that they must take into account the general principles of prevention and the pre-construction information as provided for by regulation 9(2):

> When preparing, or modifying a design the designer must take into account the general principles of prevention and any pre-construction information …

The general principles of prevention are defined and listed in Schedule 1 to the Management of Health and Safety at Work Regulations 1999, and are also set out in Chapter 4 of this book. However, before the general principles of prevention can be applied, the designer has to identify the hazards associated with the site and the hazards that will arise during the construction of the project and afterwards.

The designer will be assisted by the pre-construction information that they should have received from the principal designer that will include 'health and safety hazards, including design and construction hazards and how they will be addressed'. The designer can rely on the pre-construction information, but only to the extent that if there are any omissions they identify in respect of existing hazards, or hazards that will be created during construction, they must take those into account because the hazard will present a foreseeable risk.

The remainder of regulation 9(2) then directs the designer how to use the general principles of prevention and their knowledge about the hazards connected to the project to eliminate certain risks as follows:

> ... to eliminate, so far as is reasonably practicable, foreseeable risks to the health and safety of any person—
> (a) carrying out or liable to be affected by construction work;
> (b) maintaining or cleaning a structure; or
> (c) using a structure designed as a workplace.

A foreseeable risk will be associated with a foreseeable hazard. Therefore, unless the designer has identified all the foreseeable hazards, not all the foreseeable risks will be included in the assessment. Note that foreseeability is not qualified by being 'reasonably foreseeable', which is to say that in the event of an unusual accident to a person on a project, the risk was foreseeable, however small the chances of the accident occurring. The lack of a reasonableness criterion places a very high burden of responsibility on designers. Although a designer is required to have identified all foreseeable risks, the only obligation on the designer is to incorporate the general principles of prevention to eliminate such risks. Therefore, it is not a requirement upon a designer to eliminate all foreseeable risks, which is evident by referring to regulation 9(3) with instructions on what has to be done if a risk cannot be eliminated as follows.

If it is not possible to eliminate these risks, the designer must, so far as is reasonably practicable

(a) take steps to reduce or, if that is not possible, control the risks through the subsequent design process;
(b) provide information about these risks to the principal designer; and
(c) ensure appropriate information is included in the health and safety file.

After identifying the hazards, the designer should undertake a qualitative or quantitative assessment (depending on the circumstances) of the foreseeable risks associated with each hazard because they are required to eliminate the foreseeable risks, but only so far as is reasonably practicable. The obligation to identify foreseeable risks is an onerous one. On the basis that hazards will arise during construction and be created by the physical attributes of the construction site and the construction processes, it is extremely difficult to identify what risks may not be foreseeable. A risk that is not foreseeable would mean that no person or group of persons could have foreseen such a risk even after the most comprehensive brainstorming. The test of foreseeability only provides a designer with the slimmest of defences, seeking to avoid liability on the basis that the risk was not foreseeable.

The designer is confronted with the duty to avoid foreseeable risk at the outset of a design, save for the outline design stage. Other than the outline design, which might include competition bids, applications for grants or feasibility studies, the designer has to consider risks to health and safety from the outset. Even where initial design work may be involved in feasibility studies, the health and safety aspect should not be ignored if a true comparison of the alternatives is to be undertaken. In an obvious example of comparing the options for a tunnel project, which could be carried out by compressed air tunnelling or deep open cut, the final design assessment would not be comprehensive without an appreciation of the risks to health and safety involved in compressed air tunnelling compared with working at the bottom of deep excavations.

Avoiding risks to health and safety, some designers will say, is a brake on creativity and innovation. In the case of *Independent Broadcasting Authority* v. *EMI Electronics Ltd and BICC Construction Ltd* (1980) 14 BLR 1 HL, it has been established that a designer has no defence merely because the project was innovative. The case arose from the collapse of an aerial mast 365 m high constructed on Emsley Moor in Yorkshire. It was one of the highest masts in the world. Although the House of Lords recognised that the design approach put it 'beyond the frontier of professional knowledge at that time', when balanced against the potential consequences of a collapse, a very high standard of care was required. One of the Law Lords said that 'the law requires even pioneers to be prudent', thus the case has important lessons for engineers embarking upon innovative design, especially from a health and safety perspective. Innovation is a risk that a designer should only embrace with caution.

In taking all reasonably practicable steps to eliminate risk, the designer has to take into account the likelihood of harm, the potential severity of the harm, the number of people potentially exposed to the harm and the period of duration or the turn period when the hazard would exist. Factored against those considerations are the costs, both design costs and construction costs, that would be necessary to eliminate such risks.

Construction risks

The detail and amount of time a designer will devote to a risk assessment in accordance with paragraph (a) of regulation 9(2) will depend upon the scale and complexity of the construction of a particular structure. First, the designer has to consider the effect of its design during the construction phase on any person, which includes construction workers, persons on adjacent sites and the public at large during the construction phase.

The designer may find it helpful in conducting a risk assessment exercise to break the structure down into three main sources of hazard. First, the inherent site conditions which can be modelled based on data derived from site investigation, traffic surveys, meteorological and other historic data. Second, the designer should examine methods by which the structure might be built in the context of their design options. The need to avoid risks completely, or to tackle them at source, or by reducing or controlling their effects, will impact on design decisions. Despite the need to assess the risks during the construction phase associated with the method of construction, the Regulations do not require designers to specify construction methods or to exercise a health and safety management function over contractors as they carry out construction work. In certain projects, the method of construction may be inextricably linked to the design philosophy, in which case the contractor could be contractually obliged to comply with such method of construction set out in the contract documents. Third, the designer will have responsibility for specifying substances or equipment for use during the construction work. The manufacturers of such substances and equipment are obliged, by virtue of the Health and Safety at Work etc. Act 1974, to produce product literature identifying any risks in handling or use, which should be considered by the designer. Not all hazards can be avoided, such as alkaline burns arising from skin contact with wet concrete, but prevention is easily effected provided that the information is communicated to the relevant persons.

The challenge for a designer when considering the construction phase lies in identifying and appreciating the consequences of designs undertaken by others and transient construction conditions. The designer is entitled to seek the assistance of the principal designer to ensure that there is cooperation between all the designers and other parties who will impact upon the overall design development. If the timing of activities is not identified by the designer at the outset, a low risk during the construction phase may in fact become a serious risk due to the timing of, say, deep excavations or lifting of heavy plant into place. Unless a designer can understand the manner in which a structure will be constructed, they will be unsure that the design is one that is safe. For this reason, the designer should keep their design under review during the course of construction, taking particular note of the programming of activities and considering carefully the designs of others as they also develop.

Maintenance and cleaning risks

The designer also has an obligation in paragraph (b) of regulation 9(2) to consider persons who will be engaged in maintenance and cleaning work on the structure after completion of the construction phase. The designer is forced to address the consequences of their design in use. Safe access for maintenance and cleaning requires the designer to consider the frequency of maintenance and cleaning, working at height or in confined spaces, isolation of utility supplies, visibility and exposure to adverse weather. Statistically, many deaths and injuries are due to falls during maintenance and cleaning work, which the designer could avoid typically by strengthening roof structures, and the pre-planning and design of cast-in eyebolts for the attachment of harnesses, dedicated walkways and ladders. Problems associated with the build-up of exhaust gases or other fumes can be overcome by improving ventilation in confined spaces. The examples are almost endless and are beyond the scope of this book. However, the increasing awareness of the influence of design over health and safety management of projects in use will be improved by a growing body of published literature and statistics.

A designer should be able to demonstrate as part of the design process that consideration has been given to maintenance and cleaning, either of which activity may become incorporated in the design or the basis of a recommended procedure to the client once the structure is in use.

Workplace considerations

The designer's duties go beyond considering factors such as appearance, maintenance, buildability and costs, to include the positive obligation in paragraph (c) of regulation 9(2) to consider how risks to workers in a workplace can be eliminated or reduced. Workplaces include any place where workers can be found working.

Regulation 2(1) of the Workplace (Health, Safety and Welfare) Regulations 1992 provides the definition of 'workplace':

> any premises or part of premises which are not domestic premises and are made available to any person as a place of work, and includes:
> (a) any place within the premises to which such person has access while at work; and
> (b) any room, lobby, corridor, staircase, road or other place used as a means of access to or egress from that place of work or where facilities are provided for use in connection with the place of work other than a public road;
> but shall not include the modification, an extension or a conversion of any of the above until such modification, extension or conversion is completed.

The designer therefore has to take account of the risks related to the proposed occupational use of the structure. The definition of workplace includes access and egress, and therefore the designer should take account of external works including traffic and pedestrian routes. The designer should also consider the health and safety of the workers during any activities of cleaning and maintaining the permanent fixtures and fittings.

In designing so that the risks to the users and occupants of a structure can be eliminated or minimised to acceptable levels, the designer should ideally consult with the principal designer or client to ensure that they have adequate information about the use and occupancy of the building, which might be provided as part of the pre-construction information.

Mitigating foreseeable risks

It is often not possible for a designer to eliminate risks to health and safety, in which circumstances regulation 9(3) provides further instruction as follows:

> If it is not possible to eliminate these risks, the designer must, so far as is reasonably practicable—
> (a) take steps to reduce or, if that is not possible, control the risks through the subsequent design process;
> (b) provide information about those risks to the principal designer; and
> (c) ensure appropriate information is included in the health and safety file.

If a designer recognises there is a foreseeable risk that can only be reduced or controlled, there is a duty to take the steps that will reduce or control the risks so far as reasonably practicable, which means balancing the cost and effort of implementing such measures against the potential harm.

The designer must inform the principal designer and provide the relevant design information that can be communicated to all the other designers and other parties at the pre-construction phase. Paragraph (b) does not indicate when the principal designer should be provided with the information, but any delay would potentially adversely affect the cost and progress of the project. Where BIM has been adopted, the communication to all the parties of information on risks to health and safety that cannot be eliminated would assist in avoiding unnecessary disproportionate adverse costs and delays.

The foreseeable risks that could not be eliminated for any future works on the project, maintenance and cleaning or the use and operation of the structure as a workplace or otherwise should be included in the health and safety file. It is the principal designer's obligation to prepare the health and safety file, but the designer will not have discharged their responsibility unless they satisfy themselves that the information has been included.

Provision of sufficient information

Any design has to be communicated if it is to be implemented. The Regulations also recognise that cooperation and coordination of all activities, including design, are vital to reducing risks. The designer's duty to communicate is set out in regulation 9(4) as follows:

> A designer must take all reasonable steps to provide, with the design, sufficient information about the design, construction or maintenance of the structure, to adequately assist the client, other designers and contractors to comply with their duties under these Regulations.

The other duty holders involved in a project need to know that their own proposals for designs and execution of the construction work are not going to be adversely affected by a component of the design that does not obviously create other inadvertent risks. The designer has to provide sufficient information such that those who need the information, and who may not be of the same professional discipline, can easily understand how the design may impact on their own contribution to the project. The information should include

- identified hazards
- foreseeable risks
- design assumptions and philosophy
- specification of materials
- dimensions
- the adoption of loading criteria
- conditions of temporary instability
- method statements.

The designer's information about aspects of the structure, including the design assumptions and philosophy, are particularly significant. The design assumptions and philosophy are likely to have a bearing on the construction, particularly with regard to requirements for temporary works designed to overcome potential instability during construction. Issues that arise from maintenance of the structure, to the extent that the design has an influence over maintenance, should also be communicated to the client. In this regard, the designer should take into account the potential loadings that may be applied to the structure during maintenance and thus provide notification as to safe working loads for various parts of the structure.

The sufficient design information ideally should be communicated before other related designs are completed and certainly before construction work commences. The distribution by the principal designer of the design assumptions at an early stage should be encouraged so that all designers are working from the same starting point.

The designer has to take all reasonable steps to provide the information. This will include editing and presenting the design data so that the information provided can be easily understood. A designer should strive to present the information, whether by BIM or otherwise, in a format that is brief, clear and precise. Where BIM has been adopted, the information can easily be communicated to all the parties. When providing the information, it should ideally be part of a dialogue resulting in a confirmation, preferably in written form, from the recipients that the information has been received. The use of notes on drawings, including information on the design and suggested construction sequences, will ensure that sufficient information is communicated to the construction workers on site.

The duty of cooperation imposed upon all duty holders by virtue of regulation 8(4) and the principal designer's duty to coordinate the pre-construction phase compels designers to cooperate with the client, other designers and contractors. It is only by this means that any incompatibilities or inconsistencies between designs can be identified and resolved before the commencement of construction work.

Designs prepared or modified outside of Great Britain

In the global marketplace it is not uncommon for the location where a design is prepared or modified to be on the other side of the world. The effect of the Regulations would be undermined if designs that have been prepared or modified overseas could be imported into Great Britain as the basis for construction work to be executed within England, Wales or Scotland without having to comply with the Regulations. For that reason, the Regulations impose requirements to ensure that such designs are prepared in compliance with the designer's duties in regulation 9. The relevant provisions are set out in regulation 10(1), which states that

> Where a design is prepared or modified outside Great Britain for use in construction work to which these Regulations apply—
> (a) the person who commissions it, if established within Great Britain; or
> (b) if that person is not so established, the client for the project,
> must ensure that regulation 9 is complied with.

The Regulations place the responsibility upon the person who commissions the design if they are established within Great Britain. This raises two issues that need to be tested. The first test is, 'who commissions the design?' Can commissioning a design be no more than a mere request that a design is prepared or modified? If the purpose of the Regulations is to provide for improvements in design and management, it is very difficult to foresee how some person commissioning a design should escape any liability, otherwise there would be a gap in the overall scheme for design.

The second test relates to the extent to which a person commissioning the design is 'established within Great Britain'. One might have expected the test to be related to having a place of business in Great Britain, but the concept of 'being established' has a much wider connotation. This may include key personnel of the person commissioning the design having a place of residence in Great Britain. Alternatively, the person commissioning the design may have assets within Great Britain but unconnected with their business interests. In either case, it means that a person can be served with proceedings within Great Britain or assets can be seized subject to a court order.

In the event that the person commissioning a design is not established within Great Britain, it becomes the responsibility of the client to ensure that the design complies with regulation 9. A domestic client is not subject to regulation 10(1) by reason of paragraph (2), which states that

> This regulation does not apply to a domestic client.

Checklist

A checklist for designers has been included in Appendix 1.

CDM Regulations 2015 Explained
ISBN 978-0-7277-6009-8

http://dx.doi.org/10.1680/cdmre.60098.115

Chapter 11
The principal contractor

- **Introduction**
- **Definition**
- **Selecting a principal contractor**
- **Duties of the principal contractor**
- **Consultation and engagement with workers**
- **Powers of the principal contractor**

Introduction

Accidents do not happen in the client's boardroom or in the design office – when the planning and design are completed it is the principal contractor, if there is more than one contractor, who is responsible for the safe execution of the construction works.

The Health and Safety Executive has recognised that there is a disproportionate incidence of accidents on small construction sites. This can be explained by the fact that large national contractors have continued to invest in health and safety management commensurate with a general improvement in the recognition by boards of directors of the need to improve corporate governance. However, the large contractors are not immune from prosecution, and constant attention to avoid complacency is a continuing challenge.

Definition

The principal contractor is defined in regulation 2(1) of the CDM Regulations as meaning

> the contractor appointed under regulation 5(1)(b) to perform specified duties in regulations 12 to 14.

The appointment of a person in the role of principal contractor is mandatory on all projects where there is more than one contractor, or it is reasonably foreseeable there will be more than one contractor. The principal contractor has to be appointed by the client in writing as provided by regulation 5(1)(b), which states

> Where there is more than one contractor, or if it is reasonably foreseeable that more than one contractor will be working on a project at any time, the client must appoint in writing a contractor as principal contractor.

If the client has not made an appointment in writing, they will be deemed to have assumed the role of principal contractor by virtue of regulation 5(4).

Ideally, the client should be advised by a contractor if they intend to use sub-contractors at any time during the construction phase, which will inevitably mean that the client has to appoint a principal designer and a principal contractor. However, there is no express requirement on a contractor to advise the client of the need for compliance with the Regulations. A contractor only has to satisfy themselves, in accordance with regulation 15(1), that the client is aware of the client duties under the Regulations.

The principal contractor's primary obligations are to plan, manage, monitor and coordinate, which does not include carrying out any of the construction work. Thus, a client is able to appoint a contractor who will not carry out any construction work but merely provide a management service as a management contractor.

Selecting a principal contractor

A client who is required to appoint a principal contractor has to ensure compliance with regulation 8 and consider if the contractor's proposed allocation of time and other resources will satisfy the overall arrangements that the client has to make at the start of a project. The client has to satisfy themselves as to the skills, knowledge and experience of the principal contractor in executing similar construction work and whether they have the appropriate organisational capability.

The principal contractor should expect to be asked by the client to provide evidence as to their skills, knowledge and relevant experience in addition to their organisational capability and sufficiency of time and other resources that they plan to allocate to the project. In the discharge of their responsibilities, the client will want to be satisfied that the contractor's offer to carry out the role of principal contractor is supported and evidenced by appropriately detailed health and safety policies and procedures

- past relevant project experience
- programming of activities
- manpower planning
- procurement strategy
- management procedures
- relevant industry body approvals and certification.

The enquiries that might be made by a client, whether by the pre- or post-tender stage, certainly before the award of the contract, are listed below.

Stage 1 – the pre-qualification stage prior to tendering.

- Ascertain the existence of the principal contractor's health and safety policy and arrangements for accounting to the board of directors. The policy should include a review procedure to take into account the entire organisation, and be signed off by the managing director or equivalent. The client should check that the health and safety policy is relevant to the nature and scale of the work undertaken by the principal contractor.
- What arrangements does the principal contractor have in place to manage health and safety, both at the head office and on site? In particular, there should be procedures explaining how the principal contractor shall discharge their duties under the Regulations. Evidence that the duties under the Regulations are communicated to the workforce should be expected.
- What resources and expertise does the principal contractor have for access to competent health and safety advice? The health and safety adviser can be an employee, although there is no reason why such an adviser cannot be an independent organisation. The health and safety adviser must be able to provide general health and safety advice in addition to advice specific to construction health and safety issues.
- What arrangements does the principal contractor have for training employees to ensure that they have the skills and understanding required to comply with and discharge their duties under the Regulations? The arrangements should include induction training, refresher training and general updating. Persons employed by the principal contractor at all levels should have appropriate training and information.
- What are the individual training qualifications and experience of key staff who will be responsible for the control and supervision of construction work?
- Does the principal contractor have a system for monitoring their health and safety procedures and for implementing changes as a result of feedback from the monitoring procedures?
- Does the principal contractor have an established means of consulting with their workforce on health and safety matters?
- Does the principal contractor have records of all reportable events for at least the last 3 years?
- Does the principal contractor have in place a system for reviewing all incidents and recording the action taken as a result, including the updating of procedures?
- What arrangements does the principal contractor have for appointing sub-contractors and consultants?

- Is there a procedure capable of being audited to ensure that sub-contractors will also have appropriate arrangements for appointing contractors and sub-consultants?
- What procedures does the principal contractor have in place for monitoring sub-contractor performance?
- What convictions, if any, does the principal contractor have in respect of health and safety legislation over the last 3 years?

Stage 2 – the post-qualification stage.

- By what means will the principal contractor cooperate and coordinate with the other parties identified in the project, including procedures to involve the workforce in drawing up statements and systems of work?
- What proposals does the principal contractor have to ensure that appropriate welfare facilities will be in place before persons start work on site?
- What is the principal contractor's experience on similar projects?
- What procedures will the principal contractor adopt for carrying out risk assessments and developing safe systems of work/method statements for the hazards and risks identified by the client, designers and other contractors?
- What procedures will the principal contractor adopt for preparing the construction phase plan for the particular project?

There are no duty holders under the Regulations who have an express duty to advise the client in respect of the discharge of their liabilities. The client is expected to rely on the advice they can obtain from a competent adviser as provided for in regulation 7(1) of the Management of Health and Safety at Work Regulations 1999. Although the other duty holders under the CDM Regulations do not have an express duty to advise, the client can ask the principal designer, if one has been appointed, for such advice and should be able to rely on the principal designer's cooperation pursuant to regulation 8(4).

Duties of the principal contractor

The duties to which the principal contractor is subject, and their powers, are established by regulations 13 and 14. Regulation 13 sets out the general duties of the principal contractor, in addition to their duties as a contractor as set out in regulations 15. Regulation 13 specifically deals with the principal contractor's duties with respect to the construction phase and regulation 14 deals with consultation with workers engaged by them and other contractors.

Plan, manage, monitor and coordinate

The fundamental duty of the principal contractor is at the head of the list of duties in regulation 13, which emphasises the management and coordination role of the principal contractor. Regulation 13(1) imposes the general duty upon the principal contractor to plan, manage, monitor and coordinate the construction work as follows:

> The principal contractor must plan, manage and monitor the construction phase and coordinate matters relating to health and safety during the construction phase to ensure that, so far as is reasonably practicable, construction work is carried out without risks to health or safety.

The extent of this general duty will depend on the scope and complexity of the project, but will always be a challenge for the principal contractor, irrespective of the size of a project. The principal contractor has to ensure that every person engaged in the construction work not only has the necessary skills, knowledge, training and experience at the start of the project but is also committed to cooperation and is aware of all the site rules, and the construction phase plan, and is committed to the sharing of knowledge for risk assessments and coordinating their work accordingly. The task can be summarised as ensuring that all duty holders and persons engaged in construction work have total commitment to improving health and safety.

The duty in paragraph (1) is also qualified in one very important aspect – the principal contractor is required to have particular regard to the general principles of prevention as provided for in regulation 13(2) as follows:

> In fulfilling the duties in paragraph (1), and in particular when—
> (a) design, technical and organisational aspects are being decided in order to plan the various items or stages of work which are to take place simultaneously or in succession; and
> (b) estimating the period of time required to complete the work or work stages;
> the principal contractor must take into account the general principles of prevention.

The benefits of applying general principles of prevention can only be maximised if the principles are applied by all parties to a project. Thus, in respect of the construction phase, the principal contractor has the duty to ensure that all employers (used in its natural sense) involved in construction work on the project apply the general principles of prevention as provided for by regulation 13(3)(c)(i), which states that

> The principal contractor must ensure that employers and, if necessary for the protection of workers, self-employed persons, apply the general principles of prevention in a consistent manner, and in particular when complying with the provisions of Part 4.

The general principles of prevention are discussed in detail in Chapter 4 of this book. The discharge of the principal contractor's duties under regulation 13(2) is made considerably easier than it might otherwise be by the mutual duties on all the other persons who will be subject to the principal contractor's planning, managing, monitoring and coordination. The principal contractor can expect other contractors to cooperate with them in communicating any legal requirements that relate to specialist construction work. However, the principal contractor is directed to take particular regard of the principles and activities set out in Part 4 of the Regulations, and should make enquiries and give directions to ensure that the Part 4 principles are implemented by all contractors coordinating their respective activities.

The Regulations recognise the importance of the organisational aspects at the planning stage that are the principal contractor's responsibility, in particular programming the work activities concurrently or sequentially during the construction phase and the allocation of time to complete each activity or stage of the construction work. Regulation 13(3) requires the principal contractor to organise cooperation and to coordinate implementation as follows:

> The principal contractor must—
> (a) organise cooperation between contractors (including successive contractors on the same construction site);
> (b) coordinate implementation by the contractors of applicable legal requirements for health and safety.

The principal contractor is under the general duty in regulation 8(3) to ensure that all the contractors they engage on the project have the necessary skills, knowledge, experience and organisational capability. However, on some projects the principal contractor will not be responsible for engaging all the contractors, in which case they should assist other appointers in the task of engaging contractors, as part of their management duty to organise cooperation and coordination.

The principal contractor is assisted in the discharge of their management duty by the implied authority given to him/her to give directions to contractors on the site with which they have to comply, as provided for in regulation 15(3)(a), which states that

> Where there is more than one contractor working on a project, a contractor must comply with any directions given by the principal designer or the principal contractor.

The principal contractor's directions should not be unreasonable and only be for the purposes connected with organising cooperation and implementing coordination. The contractors, who are required to comply with those directions, are not necessarily in any contractual relationship with the principal contractor, but are bound by the duty to comply as provided for in regulation 15(3)(a).

In regulation 13(3)(b), one of the relevant legal requirements referred to requires implementation of regulation 3 of the Management of Health and Safety at Work Regulations 1999, which requires every contractor to prepare a risk assessment. The risk assessment should address risks to employees and to other persons who may be affected by their activities. Therefore, as an important aspect of the principal contractor's duty to coordinate the construction work, they should prepare a risk assessment based on the risk assessments prepared by every other contractor. Three aspects of the risk assessments prepared by the other contractors in a project will influence the role of principal contractor. These are

- The seriousness of the risk.
- The nature of the assessment. The risk assessments prepared by other contractors are likely to comprise two parts. According to the normal activities of the contractor, there is likely to be a generic risk assessment that will not require any amendment from project to project. However, for each individual project the second part of the risk assessment will need to be tailored to the particular risks for each project.
- The principal contractor will be concerned to examine the interrelationships between the risk assessments produced by the other contractors, including their own. Some activities of a contractor will have no effect on other contractors working on the project whereas in certain circumstances, activities of a contractor will affect one or more contractors to a greater or lesser extent.

In coordinating the construction work of other contractors, the principal contractor should take account of the fact that the scope of the relevant legal requirements for health and safety is far wider than the Regulations and includes all the other regulations made under the Health and Safety at Work etc. Act 1974.

The construction phase plan

The principal contractor's responsibility for the health and safety management on the construction site is underlined by their duty to ensure that there is a construction phase plan before setting up a construction site as provided for by regulation 12(1), which states that

> During the pre-construction phase, and before setting up a construction site, the principal contractor must draw up a construction phase plan, or make arrangements for a construction phase plan to be drawn up.

The construction phase plan is considered in detail in Chapter 13 of this book.

The principal contractor is not required to draw up the construction phase plan themselves, so long as the construction plan has been arranged to be drawn up: thus, drawing up the construction phase plan can be sub-contracted. The initial content of the construction phase plan must be relevant and sufficient to cover the construction activities that will start the site work. More importantly, the timing of the construction phase plan is vital because setting up a construction site can be an activity that involves construction work. The principal contractor can expect to receive all the pre-construction information obtained from the client and relevant information from the designers working on the project because the principal designer is under a duty to assist the principal contractor during the preparation of the construction phase plan by reason of regulation 12(3).

The construction phase plan cannot be expected to cover all the construction activities in detail at the outset on larger projects, but there should, as a minimum, be a framework that is then capable of being updated and revised as the construction work progresses as required by regulation 12(4). The principal contractor is required by regulation 13(3)(c)(ii) to ensure that the construction phase plan is followed, which states that

> The principal contractor must ensure that employers and, if necessary for the protection of workers, self-employed persons, where required, follow the construction phase plan.

As part of the obligation to monitor adherence to the construction phase plan and coordinate its implementation by the other contractors, and to keep the construction phase plan under review, the principal contractor could consider regular meetings with the interested parties at which the construction phase plan is a regular agenda item.

Site rules

The site rules are an important and essential means of regulating activity and behaviour on a site. The principal contractor is required by reason of regulation 12(2) to include in the construction phase plan the health and safety arrangements and site rules as follows:

> The construction phase plan must set out the health and safety arrangements and site rules taking account, where necessary, of the industrial activities taking place on the construction site and, where applicable, must include specific measures concerning work which falls within one or more of the categories set out in Schedule 3.

The principal contractor has to ensure that the site rules take into consideration the activities of all the other contractors on the construction site. The principal contractor must coordinate the implementation of the site rules to ensure that they are adopted by and adhered to by all contractors and employees and workers on the site. All contractors must comply with the site rules as provided for by regulation 15(3)(b), which states that

> Where there is more than one contractor working on a project, a contractor must comply with the parts of the construction phase plan that are relevant to that contractor's work on the project.

The site rules will cover all aspects of the construction work where there are risks, including access to parts of the site, traffic arrangements, hot work and so on. The site rules are the basis of communicating to the workers the means of avoiding risks.

The site rules should be in writing, and the principal contractor should pay due attention to the languages and nationalities of the persons employed on the site. The site rules are important, and therefore must be brought to the attention of all persons who are on the site. There should be a system of reporting breaches of site rules, and all persons should be aware of the appropriate sanctions for such breaches, which at the most severe should include removal from the site and the project.

Site induction

In accordance with regulation 13(4)(a), the principal contractor has also to ensure that

> a suitable site induction is provided.

A site induction is for the construction workers rather than contractors, as required by regulation 15(9). Unless the principal contractor takes it upon themselves to provide the site induction, they should coordinate the efforts of the other contractors to ensure that workers have had the benefit of a site induction. It is not good enough for site induction to take place after workers have started work. Although the Regulations do not provide that the site induction should be delivered before commencing construction work, it is implicit in so far as the definition of 'induct' is 'to introduce'.

The principal contractor can only ensure that regulation 13(4)(a) is satisfied if they maintain a regular system of monitoring as to the deployment of workers employed by other contractors. For large construction sites, the principal contractor should consider maintaining a central register of all workers on the site, identifying the particular work that each worker is employed to undertake and that the site induction, relevant information and instruction have been delivered. The principal contractor cannot say as a defence, when in fact no such induction or training took place, that it was the responsibility of a contractor to have provided such training for their own workers.

Prevention of unauthorised access

All the contractors on a site have a responsibility to prevent access by unauthorised persons to the construction site. However, the principal contractor is given the overall and ultimate responsibility to ensure that the necessary steps are taken. This overarching duty is set out in regulation 13(4)(b) as follows:

> The principal contractor must ensure that the necessary steps are taken to prevent access by unauthorised persons to the construction site.

Keeping trespassers safe by preventing access to the site is a priority because the steps are referred to as 'necessary steps'. The requirement to provide the necessary steps is not qualified by a test of so far as is reasonably practicable, presumably on the basis that the potential danger sets a very high threshold for a proportionate response. The principal contractor has to ensure that the setting up of a construction site includes the prevention of access to unauthorised persons. The danger that is posed by the construction site and the activities has to be matched by the appropriate response, which could include high security fencing, inner and outer fencing, CCTV monitoring and security guards.

Provision of welfare facilities

The welfare arrangements and facilities on a construction site are ultimately the responsibility of the principal contractor as set out in regulation 13(4)(c), which provides that

> The principal contractor must ensure that facilities that comply with the requirements of Schedule 2 are provided throughout the construction phase.

The requirements of Schedule 2 are explained in detail in Chapter 5 of this book.

Liaison with the principal designer

The principal contractor has a duty to liaise with the principal designer. This duty is set out in regulation 13(5) as follows:

> The principal contractor must liaise with the principal designer for the duration of the principal designer's appointment and share with the principal designer information relevant to the planning, management and monitoring of the pre-construction phase and the coordination of health and safety matters during the pre-construction phase.

In compliance with this duty, the principal contractor has to cooperate with the principal designer. The extent and degree of the cooperation is not limited to the information that affects the planning and management of the pre-construction phase or is needed for the health and safety file at the end of the construction phase. If the principal designer is of the reasonable opinion that other information is required from the principal contractor, and is appropriate, the principal contractor is duty bound to cooperate in accordance with their duty under regulation 8(4).

Health and safety file

The principal contractor will have an important contribution to make to the health and safety file, not least because the principal contractor will have been responsible for the execution of all the construction work and possess the knowledge of the site above and below ground. Regulation 12(7) requires the principal contractor to give information to the principal designer, so that they can prepare the health and safety plan as follows:

> During the project, the principal contractor must provide the principal designer with any information in the principal contractor's possession relevant to the health and safety file, for inclusion in the health and safety file.

But the principal contractor's responsibility goes further if the principal designer's appointment concludes before the end of the project, because the principal contractor will take possession of the draft health and safety file pursuant to regulation 12(8). In those circumstances the principal contractor acquires the responsibility for ensuring the accuracy and completeness of the health and safety file by reason of regulation 12(9), which states that

> Where the health and safety file is passed to the principal contractor under paragraph (8), the principal contractor must ensure that the health and safety file is appropriately reviewed, updated and revised from time to time to take account of the work and any changes that have occurred.

At the end of the project the principal contractor must pass the health and safety file to the client in accordance with regulation 12(10).

Consultation and engagement with workers

Making and maintaining arrangements

The principal contractor is required to introduce arrangements that affect all workers on a construction site. Regulation 14(a) requires that

> The principal contractor must make and maintain arrangements which will enable the principal contractor and workers engaged in construction work to cooperate effectively in developing, promoting and checking the effectiveness of measures to ensure the health, safety and welfare of the workers.

The principal contractor will need the cooperation of the other contractors and the workers' representatives to make the arrangements in such a manner that the arrangements satisfy the requirements of the Regulations. The arrangements must be workable and encourage persons to make to use of the arrangements to achieve the outcomes referred to in regulation 14(a). The extent and nature of the arrangements will vary according to the nature of each project, to take account of the size and complexity of the construction work, the extent of hazards and the associated risks and the number of workers and contractual arrangements.

The principal contractor can rely on regulation 8(4) to persuade, if not coerce, the contractors and the workers to contribute to the effectiveness of the arrangements. Irrespective of the particular aspects of the project, each of the other contractors and workers' representatives are required to assist and actively promote cooperation for and on behalf of their own employees and workers. On the basis that the arrangements are for the benefit of the workers, it should be a joint commitment, based on mutual interests, to cooperate with their own employers and the principal contractor.

The principal contractor cannot afford to leave the arrangements for cooperation to chance. The arrangements should be planned and recorded in writing and, moreover, represent the outcome of the consultation, which is also required by regulation 14(b).

The arrangements should not just be one of the activities resulting in a completed tick box at the start of the construction phase. The arrangements must be maintained by the principal contractor, which will mean monitoring the health and safety record on the site and the suitability of the welfare facilities. The principal contractor should want to inspect the Reporting of Injuries, Diseases and Dangerous Occurrences Regulations 2013 (RIDDOR) reports kept by the contractors and be notified of accidents and incidents as when they occur. The principal contractor should be particularly vigilant about dangerous occurrences that in practice are often overlooked as being matters that should be entered into the 'accident book'.

Ultimately, the client cannot stand by if they have reason to believe that the principal contractor's arrangements are not effective. The client's duty, as set out in regulation 4(3), is to keep under review and maintain their own general arrangements for ensuring that the construction work is carried out without risk to the health and safety of any person, thus reviewing the health and safety record during the construction phase is a vital contribution that a client makes to the improvement in health, safety and welfare standards.

Consultation

The principal contractor's duty to consult extends to all workers involved on a project. The duty is set out in regulation 14(b) as follows:

> The principal contractor must consult those workers or their representatives in good time on matters connected with the project which may affect their health, safety or welfare, in so far as they or their representatives have not been similarly consulted by their employer.

Consultation implies a dialogue that is opened by the principal contractor. The principal contractor has to listen and take account of what workers say, at all stages of the construction work and all aspects of the health and safety environment. On large sites, where the principal contractor may have a substantial number of employees, the consultation can be done through worker representatives. In the case of sites where there is trade union representation, the workers' representatives may be appointed by the recognised trade unions under the Safety Representatives and Safety Committees Regulations 1977. Alternatively, the workforce can nominate and elect their own representatives under the Health and Safety (Consultation with Employees) Regulations 1996. While it may be appropriate to consult with representatives, no worker should ever be prevented from having an opportunity to make their own representations. There is a natural resistance for workers to report defects or examples of poor management, and the principal contractor should be sympathetic to making arrangements for confidential consultation if appropriate. Employees now have the benefit of protection in making such representations by the protected disclosure provisions of the Employment Rights Act 1996 (as amended).

Information

The identification of hazards, the assessment of risks, method statements and systems of work, management–worker cooperation and consultation, notices, changes to the project and accident reporting all generate information. All persons on a site are entitled to such information by virtue of regulation 14(c), which states that

> The principal contractor must ensure that those workers or their representatives can inspect and take copies of any information which the principal contractor has, or which these Regulations require to be provided to the principal contractor, which relate to the health, safety or welfare of workers at the site ...

The principal contractor's administrative burden should not be underestimated, and the need for an effective document management system cannot be overstated. A principal contractor could justifiable be criticised in the event that such information was not provided promptly.

There are some exclusions from categories of information that a principal contractor has to make available, and these are set out as the remaining part of regulation 14(c) as follows:

> . . . except any information—
> (i) the disclosure of which would be against the interests of national security;
> (ii) which the principal contractor could not disclose without contravening a prohibition imposed by or under an enactment;
> (iii) relating specifically to an individual, unless that individual has consented to its being disclosed;
> (iv) the disclosure of which would, for reasons other than its effect on health, safety or welfare at work, cause substantial injury to the principal contractor's undertaking or, where the information was supplied to the principal contractor by some other person, to the undertaking of that other person;
> (v) obtained by the principal contractor for the purpose of bringing, prosecuting or defending any legal proceedings.

Powers of the principal contractor

The principal contractor's responsibility to discharge their duties relies upon the cooperation of the other contractors and the principal designer and commitment to coordination of their respective construction activities. While cooperation and coordination between all the parties engaged in a project is unarguably a laudable aspiration, and is better if cultivated in a mutually supportive environment, the Regulations aid the principal contractor by compelling other persons to comply with their directions as provided for by regulation 15(3)(a), which states that

> Where there is more than one contractor working on a project, a contractor must comply with any directions given by . . . the principal contractor.

The principal contractor's remedies will depend on whether there is a contractual relationship between the principal contractor and a contractor who does not comply with such instructions. In either situation the principal contractor can advise, in writing, the contractor that it is breach of their obligations under the Regulations and that such a breach is an offence. If such written advice does not remedy the principal contractor's problem, the contractor's continued presence on the site would be potentially a risk to health and safety to other persons, in which case the principal contractor should take steps to have the contractor suspended or removed from the site.

In the situation where the contractor in breach is in a direct contractual relationship with the principal contractor, the contractual remedy may be suspension of the contractor's work or termination of the contract. If, however, the contractor is appointed by the client or a third party, not being in the ladder of sub-contracts where the principal contractor is at the top of the ladder, the principal contractor can advise the client and third party, if appropriate, of the circumstances. The client would be bound to take some action to bring about a resolution of the principal contractor's dilemma. The risk that the client would be taking if the principal contractor was not assured that it had the cooperation of all contractors on the site would be its potential breach of contract with the principal contractor, leading variously to suspension of all the construction work, termination by the principal contractor of their contract with the client and claims for damages.

The principal contractor also has the option of reporting a contractor who refuses to comply with their directions to the Health and Safety Executive for breach of the Regulations.

Checklist

A checklist for principal contractors has been included in Appendix 1.

CDM Regulations 2015 Explained
ISBN 978-0-7277-6009-8

http://dx.doi.org/10.1680/cdmre.60098.131

Chapter 12
The contractor

- **Definition**
- **Selecting a contractor**
- **Duties of contractors**

Definition
A contractor is defined in regulation 2(1) in the CDM Regulations as meaning:

> any person (including a non-domestic client) who, in the course or furtherance of a business, carries out, manages or controls construction work.

A contractor is concerned with construction work, the definition and scope of which has been reviewed in Chapter 3 of this book.

Selecting a contractor
By virtue of regulation 8(1), a person arranging for a contractor to carry out work on a construction project has a general duty to ensure that the contractor has

> the skills, knowledge and experience, and, if they are an organisation, the organisational capability, necessary to fulfil the role that they are appointed to undertake, in a manner that secures the health and safety of any person affected by the project.

The person appointing a contractor has to comply with regulation 8(3) which requires the appointer to take reasonable steps to establish the contractor's suitability in the following terms:

> A person who is responsible for appointing a … contractor to carry out work on a project must take reasonable steps to satisfy themselves that the … contractor fulfils the conditions in paragraph (1).

A contractor should be prepared to produce evidence of being in possession of the relevant attributes to the appointer on request. More importantly, the contractor should satisfy themselves, before they accept an appointment, that they can fulfil the conditions in paragraph (1), otherwise they will be in breach of regulation 8(2), which states that

> A ... contractor must not accept an appointment to a project unless they fulfil the conditions in paragraph (1).

Duties of contractors

The duties of contractors set out in regulation 15 apply to all construction work on all projects irrespective of any need of notification pursuant to regulation 6.

Client awareness

Regulation 15(1) imposes on a contractor the duty not to proceed with any construction work unless they are satisfied that the client is aware of the client duties under the Regulations as follows:

> A contractor must not carry out construction work in relation to a project unless satisfied that the client is aware of the duties owed by the client under these Regulations.

The contractor is not under a duty to make enquiries but merely to know that the client is aware of their duties under the Regulations. The contractor does not have to be satisfied as to the extent that the client is aware of the Regulation beyond the client's duties.

On a large project, where the contractor may be at the bottom of a long contract chain, the contractor can be satisfied that the client is aware of their duties if notification has been given by the client under regulation 6(2) or (4), in which case the notice will clearly be displayed as required by regulation 6(3)(b). On small projects, however, the situation may not be quite so obvious. The small project may not be notifiable, and a contractor, appointed as a sub-contractor, may have suspicions that the client for the project is unaware of the Regulations, further compounded by the fact that their employing contractor is unable to give any suitable assurances. In those circumstances, irrespective of the contractual relationships and obligations, the sub-contractor should make it their business to be satisfied that the client is aware of their duties under the Regulations.

Domestic clients often will have only one contractor undertaking the construction work. A contractor working for a domestic client will assume the duties of the client set out in regulations 4(1) to (7) pursuant to regulation 7(1)(a) and the obligation to notify the Health and Safety Executive, if appropriate, pursuant to regulation 6.

Carrying out, managing and controlling construction work

The definition of a contractor refers to carrying out, managing or controlling construction work, although a contractor can be engaged solely in any one of the activities provided that it is in the course or furtherance of a business. Sub-contractors and suppliers are all deemed to be contractors if they are involved to any extent in carrying out, managing or controlling construction work.

The activity of controlling construction work is noteworthy because none of the other duty holders are defined by their involvement in a project by 'controlling' construction work. To what extent is the activity of 'controlling' different from 'managing', 'monitoring', 'coordinating' or 'making arrangements'? Regulation 15(2) establishes that the primary duty of a contractor is to 'plan, manage and monitor', as follows:

> A contractor must plan, manage and monitor construction work carried out either by the contractor or by workers under the contractor's control, to ensure that, so far as is reasonably practicable, it is carried out without risks to health and safety.

The element of control in paragraph (2) expressly refers to the chain of command where a worker, being an individual, takes instruction from a contractor either in an employer–employee relationship or as a self-employed individual contracted to work for the contractor. By comparison, planning, managing and monitoring does not necessarily involve giving instructions to workers. It is the workers who actually carry out construction work, and, therefore, it becomes imperative that the contractor has to have control over the workers if the construction work is to be carried out at all. Except for the additional element of control, in the fundamental duty for a contractor to carry out their tasks so as to ensure the risks to health and safety are eliminated or mitigated, the contractor shares the same obligation as the principal contractor.

The extent to which the contractor plans, manages and monitors the construction work will only need to be proportionate to the characteristics of the project, including its size, complexity, hazards and commensurate risks, because the contractor's tasks are limited to those that are reasonable and practicable as referred to in regulation 15(2).

The construction phase plan

Unlike previous CDM Regulations, even if there is no principal contractor, the 2015 Regulations require that there must always be a construction phase plan. Thus, a sole contractor has a duty in respect of the construction phase plan as provided for in regulation 15(5), which states that

> If there is only one contractor working on the project, the contractor must draw up a construction phase plan, or make arrangements for a construction phase plan to be drawn up, as soon as is practicable prior to setting up a construction site.

The scope and content of a construction phase plan must comply with regulation 12(2) as provided for by regulation 15(6), which states that

> The construction phase plan must fulfil the requirements of regulation 12(2).

Note that the sole contractor does not necessarily have to draw up the construction phase plan themselves because regulation 15(5) allows the contractor to make arrangements for it to be drawn up. If a contractor sub-contracts the drawing up of the construction phase plan, they will be responsible for its content and efficacy.

No construction work or work involved in setting up the construction site should start until the construction phase plan has been drawn up. Note, however, that there is no requirement for an independent review of the construction phase plan except that the client must be sure that there is a construction phase plan before the construction phase begins, to comply with regulation 4(5)(a). Therefore, provided that the contractor is satisfied with the construction phase plan and subject to the requirements of the construction contract, the commencement of setting up the site is at the sole discretion of the contractor.

During the construction phase the contractor should keep the construction phase plan under review, although there is no express duty to do so commensurate with the principal contractor's duty under regulation 12(4).

Where a contractor is carrying out construction work and there is a principal contractor, the construction phase plan will be the responsibility of the principal contractor under regulation 12(1). The arrangements that the principal contractor makes to have the construction phase plan drawn up may include requesting contributions from contractors for their respective parts of the project. There is no express obligation for a contractor to make a contribution to the principal contractor's construction phase plan, but the obligations to cooperate under regulation 8(4) and to comply with their directions under regulation 15(3)(a) will mean, in practice, that the contractor will be contributing to the construction phase plan.

During the construction phase, and where there is a principal contractor, the contractor has a duty to comply with the construction phase plan in accordance with regulation 15(3)(b), which provides that

> Where there is more than one contractor working on a project, a contractor must comply with the parts of the construction phase plan that are relevant to that contractor's work on the project.

The contractor will rely on the construction phase plan for the purposes of planning, managing and monitoring of their own construction work, which is likely to have contractual consequences for the principal contractor if the construction phase plan is incomplete, in error or no longer up to date.

General principles of prevention

If there is no principal contractor, the sole contractor is required to take account of the general principles of prevention, in the same manner as a principal contractor, by reason of regulation 15(4), which states that

> If there is only one contractor working on the project, the contractor must take account of the general principles of prevention when—
> (a) design, technical and organisational aspects are being decided in order to plan the various items or stages of work which are to take place simultaneously or in succession; and
> (b) estimating the period of time required to complete the work or work stages.

To the extent that a contractor is a designer, they will also be under a duty to take the general principles of prevention into account by reason of regulation 9(2) when preparing or modifying a design.

Competent workers

It is the workers who are at most risk of harm, and therefore it is the workers who need to have the capability of working without risk to themselves or others by adhering to safe practices. Regulation 15(7) recognises that the capability of a worker is dependent upon having the appropriate skills, knowledge, training and experience, in the following terms:

> A contractor must not employ or appoint a person to work on a construction site unless that person has, or is in the process of obtaining, the necessary skills, knowledge, training and experience to carry out the tasks allocated to that person in a manner that secures the health and safety of any person working on the construction site.

In the first instance, the contractor is required to ascertain whether a person has the necessary skills, knowledge, training and experience. If the person has the necessary attributes, there is no obstacle to employing or appointing the worker. However, if the worker does not meet the criteria for skills, knowledge, training and experience, the contractor has the discretion to assess if the worker is sufficiently engaged in a process that will lead to the acquisition of the necessary attributes. A contractor who uses their discretion in appointing a person without the necessary skills, knowledge, training and experience has a further duty to ensure that the person will not be allocated any tasks that will expose any person working on the construction site to the avoidable risk of harm.

The evidence upon which a contractor relies in ascertaining the competence of a person should not be limited to the production of training certificates because the criteria that will determine if the person has all the attributes, will include demonstrable skills and experience. Ideally, a person should be capable of demonstrating possession of the necessary attributes in a practical-based interview process within a construction site environment.

Supervision, information and instruction

The contractor's duties to their workers and those of other contractors or self-employed tradesmen subject to the contractor's control are set out in regulation 15(8). The emphasis is upon supervising and instructing their employees and other workers and ensuring that there is an effective means of communicating relevant information. Regulation 15(8) states that

> A contractor must provide each worker under their control with appropriate supervision, instructions and information so that construction work can be carried out, so far as is reasonable practicable, without risks to health and safety.

Supervision is a means by which a contractor is able to satisfy themselves that a worker has the necessary skills, knowledge, training and experience to perform the allocated tasks. The contractor will also identify any further training needs that they will be obliged to provide if the worker is to continue performing the same tasks. The extent of supervision is also related to the competence of the worker. Less experienced workers will require more supervision. It is in the commercial interest of a contractor to have competent workers, which will mitigate the need for close supervision and the costs of further training. Contracts of employment or terms of engagement for self-employed workers can include probationary periods and the acquisition or maintenance of essential skills as pre-conditions to allow a worker to continue working on a construction site.

The contractor is under an obligation to have provided appropriate instructions for each worker. Instructions given by the contractor should be clear and unambiguous. Verbal instructions can often be 'lost in translation', especially at the place of work, which can be noisy and generally distracting. Subject to the comments below, a contractor should give instructions in writing to avoid the problems of verbal instructions, not least because the evidence of having given the instruction is irrefutable. Written instructions can also be filed so that the worker can access the instruction at any time.

The requirements for providing information and instructions are set out in regulation 15(9), although it should be noted that the requirements are not exhaustive:

The information provided must include—

(a) a suitable site induction, where not already provided by the principal contractor;
(b) the procedures to be followed in the event of serious and imminent danger to health and safety;
(c) information on risks to health and safety—
   (i) identified by the risk assessment under regulation 3 of the Management Regulations; or
   (ii) arising out of the conduct of another contractor's undertaking and of which the contractor in control of the worker ought reasonably to be aware; and
(d) any other information necessary to enable the worker to comply with the relevant statutory provisions.

Paragraphs (a) to (d) can be treated either as an agenda for a face-to-face meeting with the employees or workers, or alternatively information can be provided in written form. Contractors should not assume that employees are sufficiently literate to be able to understand written instructions, and, ideally, therefore, the training should be a combination of a face-to-face presentation and written materials that the employee or worker can retain.

What should be included in a site induction session, which is not included in paragraphs (b) to (d), is not obvious. However, it would be a good idea to provide background information on the construction works. This would include the name of the project, the identity of responsible persons in the management team, the purpose of the completed project, the programme for construction and completion, the site rules, basic statistics such as the number of workers on the site, arrangements for first aid and the reporting of incidents, training opportunities, supervision and personal responsibility for health and safety, before progressing to the more prescriptive requirements in paragraphs (b) to (d).

The planning for evacuation to a safe place is an essential part of planning for health and safety. A contractor is required to have planned for emergency procedures, routes and exits in accordance with regulations 30 and 31. The information and any relevant instructions concerning emergencies must be communicated as required by regulation 15(9)(b).

Serious and imminent danger means that the risk to health and safety is unacceptable such that the risk arises as soon as work starts or becomes obvious or measurable while construction work is in progress. The contractor should recognise that the client may become involved in contributing to the arrangements if the construction site is only part of a larger site that is still occupied by the client. Regulation 8 of the Management Regulations 1999 requires employers to establish and give effect to appropriate procedures to be followed in the event of serious and imminent danger to persons at work. The contractor is bound by regulation 8(1)(b) of the Management Regulations to nominate a sufficient number of competent persons to implement the procedures.

It would be best practice to inform workers and employees of the identity of fire marshals, security staff, first aiders and any other persons, all of whom should have been appropriately trained to meet the requirements of competence under the Management Regulations.

The contractor is also required under paragraph (c) to provide information to every worker who is going to carry our construction work, which states that

> The information provided must include information on risks to health and safety—
> (i) identified by the risk assessment under regulation 3 of the Management Regulations; or
> (ii) arising out of the conduct of another contractor's undertaking and of which the contractor in control of the worker ought reasonably to be aware.

It is axiomatic that a contractor cannot comply with paragraph (c) unless they have carried out the risk assessments under regulation 3 of the Management Regulations and communicated those to the workers and employees. The conduct of another contractor in carrying out their construction work is unlikely to be known to the contractor unless they have been informed by a principal contractor or designer, or the client. In addition to the information provided to the contractor, they would also want to be aware of the activities of other contractors. Even if another contractor is working on the other side of the site, that contractor's activities may still represent risks for the contractor's own workers. Such examples include: traffic movement, laying of power cables and so on.

Paragraph (c) requires the contractor to monitor the risk assessment, and, to the extent that there is any change in those risks, communicate them without delay to their workers.

Following the requirements of paragraphs (a) to (c) does not absolve the contractor from exercising judgement about any other information that a worker should need to know. Paragraph (d) acts as a 'sweep up', requiring the contractor to identify, on a day-to-day basis, any circumstances that have changed, or are likely to change, that a worker will need to know to comply with the relevant statutory provisions.

Health and safety training for employees

The Regulations do not impose an express duty on a contractor to provide training, although the duty to provide instruction and information can be construed as a training obligation. In particular, the need for instruction and information is tailored to each worker, and is required to be kept under review, by regulation 15(8). In any event, a contractor has a duty under regulation 13(2)(b) of the Management Regulations in the following terms:

> Every employer shall ensure that his employees are provided with adequate health and safety training—
> (a) on their being recruited into the employer's undertaking; and
> (b) on their being exposed to new or increased risks because of—
>   (i) their being transferred or given a change of responsibilities within the employer's undertaking,
>   (ii) the introduction of new work equipment into or a change respecting work equipment already in use within the employer's undertaking,
>   (iii) the introduction of new technology into the employer's undertaking, or
>   (iv) the introduction of a new system of work into or a change respecting system of work already in use within the employer's undertaking.

The contractor has to keep under review the health and safety training status of their employees and consider in the event of new equipment or changes in systems of work as to whether their employees need further training.

Visitors to the site

Protection of the public and unauthorised visitors to the site is an important responsibility of a contractor. Regulation 15(10) provides that

> A contractor must not begin work on a construction site unless reasonable steps have been taken to prevent access by unauthorised persons to that site.

The perimeter and delineation of a construction site need to be ascertained by the contractor. There is the construction site for the project, and within the overall construction site there are likely to be discrete areas or zones.

Unauthorised persons will include members of the public, but will also include other workers or employees on the construction site who do not have the necessary permits or competence to enter a part of the construction site where particularly hazardous operations may be in progress.

A contractor, therefore, has to consider the security of the entire site, and if, for good reasons, the contractor is unsatisfied that the site is secure against unauthorised persons, the contractor should not begin work. In such circumstances a contractor would be well advised to inform the principal contractor. It will be a bold contractor who, not being the principal contractor, refuses to begin work because the site is not secured against unauthorised persons. However, any claim brought by a principal contractor or other contractor against such a contractor for delay could be defended on the grounds that the principal contractor or other contractor was in breach of their statutory duty and thus would have put the contractor in breach of their own statutory duties.

Where a contractor is to undertake their own work within a defined area or zone, they should take steps to ensure that only authorised persons are permitted to enter.

Whether the steps to prevent unauthorised persons to enter upon a site are reasonable or not will depend upon the potential hazards and risks. Where the hazard and risks have been assessed as very low, the reasonable steps may consist merely of some temporary barrier. Where the hazard and risks have been assessed to be high, the barrier should be of such a design as to be continuous and secure against determined action to enter. The physical barrier should also, in a high-risk environment, be kept under surveillance by CCTV or patrolling security staff.

The risk to a contractor of an unauthorised person entering a site and suffering harm is of a potential prosecution under the Regulations and a claim from such an injured person under the Occupiers Liability Acts 1957 and 1984.

The onus on a contractor to satisfy themselves that the construction site is secure, to the appropriate extent proportionate to the hazard and risks, cannot be overstated.

Welfare facilities

Every contractor should provide welfare facilities for their employees or any other worker under their control. Regulation 15(11) states that

> A contractor must ensure, so far as is reasonably practicable, that the requirements of Schedule 2 are complied with so far as they affect the contractor or any worker under that contractor's control.

The contractor can make arrangements for the use of the welfare facilities provided by another contractor on the construction site or even provide such facilities outside the boundaries of the construction site. A contractor may not be able to achieve full compliance with Schedule 2 because it is not reasonably practicable to do so, but there cannot be any defence for a contractor who fails to achieve the minimum compliance with

Schedule 2 commensurate with the basic requirements of public health and public order.

Relationship with the principal designer and the principal contractor

The primacy of the principal designer and the principal contractor with respect to health and safety at the pre-construction phase and the construction phase, respectively, is reinforced by regulation 15(3)(a), which states that

> Where there is more than one contractor working on a project, a contractor must comply with any directions given by the principal designer or the principal contractor.

Provided that the directions of the principal designer and the principal contractor are limited to ensuring that their respective duties under the Regulations can be performed, a contractor is bound, by virtue of this regulation, to comply with such directions. This will be so regardless of any contractual relationship or otherwise that might exist between the principal designer, the principal contractor and the contractor.

Checklist

A checklist for contractors has been included in Appendix 1.

CDM Regulations 2015 Explained
ISBN 978-0-7277-6009-8

http://dx.doi.org/10.1680/cdmre.60098.143

Chapter 13
The construction phase plan

- **Definition**
- **Background**
- **The duty to prepare and monitor the construction phase plan**
- **The client's involvement in the construction phase plan**
- **Content within a construction phase plan**
- **Checklist of matters for inclusion in a construction phase plan**

Definition

The construction phase plan is defined in regulation 2(1) in the CDM Regulations as meaning

> a plan drawn up under regulations 12 or 15.

The construction phase plan is a document, and therefore must be kept in a form that is reproducible and secure as required by regulation 2(2), which states that

> Any reference in these Regulations to a plan, rule, document, report or copy includes a copy or electronic version which is—
> (a) capable of being retrieved or reproduced when required; and
> (b) secure from loss or unauthorised interference.

Background

The principal contractor takes the primary responsibility for the management of health and safety on a construction site where there is more than one contractor, and the Regulations ensure that the principal contractor has the sole responsibility for the preparation of the construction phase plan. The success in improving the management of health and safety in construction will rely heavily on the effectiveness of the construction phase plan drafted for the project. Where there is only one contractor on a site, the sole contractor is responsible for the construction phase plan. The 'transparency' of the construction phase plan and its effectiveness will also be one of the measures that the Health and Safety Executive ('the Executive') will be able to use as part of monitoring and investigating any accidents. It will undoubtedly be the first source of information that any health and safety inspector would wish to see on visiting a site or investigating an accident. The construction phase plan is likely to be vital evidence in the Executive's decision-making process when considering enforcement action or prosecution. Equally, in the pursuance of any civil proceedings for injury or death, the construction phase plan will be important evidence.

The duty to prepare and monitor the construction phase plan

Regulation 12(1) establishes that the construction phase plan is the responsibility of the principal contractor, and therefore is only required to take account of the construction phase, which includes all the construction work, as follows:

> During the pre-construction phase, and before setting up a construction site, the principal contractor must draw up a construction phase plan, or make arrangements for a construction phase plan to be drawn up.

Regulation 12(1) supplements the principal contractor's duties included in regulation 13, because regulation 13 does not include any reference to the construction phase plan, although there are duties to plan and manage the construction phase. In the case of a sole contractor, however, regulation 15(5) expressly directs the contractor to prepare a construction phase plan as follows:

> If there is only one contractor working on the project, the contractor must draw up a construction phase plan, or make arrangements for a construction phase plan to be drawn up, as soon as is practicable prior to setting up a construction site.

Thus, the principal contractor, or the sole contractor, has the responsibility to prepare, or have prepared by a third party, a construction phase plan for all their projects, including projects for domestic clients. The construction phase plan is a mandatory obligation as part of the overriding duty on a principal contractor or sole contractor to plan, manage and monitor the construction phase.

A construction phase plan is required to be 'drawn up' before setting up a construction site, which is prior to the start of construction work. On large projects especially, it is unlikely that a construction phase plan can be completed before setting up a construction site. The use of the indefinite article points to the possibility that there can be more than one construction phase plan for a project. Additionally, the use of the expression 'drawn up' does not conclusively require the construction phase plan to be complete. This is supported by regulation 12(4), which imposes on the principal contractor a duty to ensure that

> Throughout the project the principal contractor must ensure that the construction phase plan is appropriately reviewed, updated and revised from time to time so that it continues to be sufficient to ensure that construction work is carried out, so far as is reasonably practicable, without risks to health or safety.

A construction phase plan should therefore be complete as possible and address activities that are still subject to completion of the design process or decisions concerning construction methods, at least in outline, and, for this reason, the monitoring of the plan is an important consideration for complying with regulation 12(4).

A sole contractor is not under the same duty as a principal contractor set out in regulation 12(4), possibly because it has been assumed that projects where there is only one contractor, are likely to be of limited scope and size so that the drawing up of a complete construction phase plan is not unreasonable. In any event, a sole contractor is under the general duty to monitor the way construction work is carried out, which may lead to necessary amendments to the construction phase plan – thus 'monitor' becomes synonymous with 'review'.

The construction phase plan is a management tool, and therefore should be a changing and dynamic document. The need for revising and monitoring the construction phase plan is essential when the planned construction work has yet to be designed for later phases at the start of construction work. In any event, the construction phase plan should be routinely reviewed, revised and refined by the principal contractor or sole contractor as the construction work proceeds. Any change in the design, alternative construction techniques, unusual environmental factors and accidents should all be reasons for a principal contractor, or the sole contractor, to consider the adequacy and effectiveness of the construction phase plan.

The construction phase plan is at the heart of the principal contractor's obligation to coordinate its implementation, which will involve communication to the other parties and duty holders involved in the project as required by paragraph 13(3)(c)(ii):

> The principal contractor must ensure that employers and, if necessary for the protection of workers, self-employed persons where required, follow the construction phase plan.

The distribution of relevant contents of the construction phase plan to the employers for the purposes of protecting their workers and self-employed persons should be a starting point for implementation. Contractors on a site where there is a principal contractor have a duty under regulations 15(8) and (9) to provide their employees or persons working under their control with information and instructions so that construction work can be carried out safely. The information is likely to be contained in the construction phase plan, but not necessarily so. The principal contractor should monitor that the contractors are discharging this duty and must take appropriate action when necessary.

The client's involvement in the construction phase plan

There is no requirement on the principal contractor or the sole contractor to have the construction phase plan checked by any other duty holder other than obtaining the consent of the client to proceed with construction work. The client is not required to check the details of the plan but must in compliance with regulation 4(5) ensure that the principal contractor or sole contractor has prepared a construction phase plan. However, the client is not required to check the construction phase plan for compliance with regulation 12 or any details that the principal contractor proposes for implementing the construction phase plan and its subsequent monitoring and review. In other words, the principal contractor or sole contractor takes responsibility for the sufficiency of the construction phase plan. A client is under a separate duty in regulation 4(6) to take reasonable steps to ensure that the principal contractor and principal designer comply with their duties under regulation 12. On a large or complex project it would be inadvisable for a client not to make some enquiry into or inspection of the construction phase plan before construction work begins. As a minimum, a client should inspect the construction phase plan before construction begins to check if specific measures have been included for the construction site activities that are specifically identified in regulations 17 to 35 and that there will be adequate welfare facilities in accordance with Schedule 2. Such an inspection of the construction phase plan does not require any special expertise, and a failure to do so will be an easily provable breach of the client's duty.

The timing of the preparation of the construction phase plan underpins its importance to the contribution to the health and safety management. The principal contractor or the sole contractor, if relevant, must start preparing the construction phase plan before setting up the construction site. The client is directed by regulation 4(5)(a) to ensure that the construction phase does not begin until a construction phase plan has been prepared in the following terms:

> A client must ensure that before the construction phase begins, a construction phase plan is drawn up by the contractor if there is only one contractor, or by the principal contractor.

Accidents associated with construction work cannot occur on a project until construction work commences. This duty on the client to prevent the start of construction work until the construction phase plan has been prepared is arguably the most important duty of the client in exerting influence over the management of health and safety during construction work.

Content within a construction phase plan

Regulation 12(2) directs what should be included in a construction phase plan as follows:

> The construction phase plan must set out the health and safety arrangements and site rules taking account, where necessary, of the industrial activities taking place on the construction site and, where applicable, must include specific measures concerning work which falls within one or more of the categories set out in Schedule 3.

The Executive made it known to the construction industry before the 2015 Regulations came into force, through its consultation procedure, reports, statements at conferences, seminars and workshops, that the CDM Regulations had generated an unnecessary burden of bureaucracy. The Approved Code of Practice for the 2007 Regulations stressed that the construction phase plan should not be a collection of generic risk assessments, records of how decisions were reached or detailed method statements. The construction phase plan must be proportionate to the scale and complexity of the project and the known hazards and risks. Regulation 12(2) refers to health and safety arrangements that will include the management structure and various parties involved in the project and must be focused on the particular hazards and risks connected with the project.

The 2007 Regulations were more prescriptive with regard to the content of the construction phase plan when compared with Schedule 3 to the 2015 Regulations. There is no longer an express requirement to identify specific risks to health and safety, although the categories of particular risks listed 1 to 10 will require special consideration. There is also no requirement to include sufficient and suitable means of mitigating such risks, but it is unthinkable that a principal contractor or sole contractor should interpret this as a call for brevity for brevity's sake. The task of drafting a construction phase plan requires a sound understanding of design principles. During preparation of the construction phase plan the principal designer must assist the principal contractor as required by regulation 12(3), which states that

> The principal designer must assist the principal contractor in preparing the construction phase plan by providing to the principal contractor all information the principal designer holds that is relevant to the construction phase plan including—
> (a) pre-construction information obtained from the client;
> (b) any information obtained from designers under regulation 9(3)(b).

The skills, knowledge and experience that a principal contractor or sole contractor should possess by reason of regulation 8(1) will be vital in understanding the implications of the design information received from the principal designer. The construction phase plan will be evidence of the principal contractor's appreciation of the risks to health and safety to workers and all other persons at risk and their commitment to a management plan that facilitates coordination and cooperation. The construction phase plan is a method of communication, and should not be confined to long written narratives but can benefit from photographs, sketches, tables and graphs. Ideally, the organisation of the construction phase plan should be such that the relevant parts can be easily distributed to other contractors and to the designers as required.

The construction phase plan is arguably the most difficult document to draft and the most critical document to ensure the delivery of improvements in the health, safety and welfare of workers in the construction industry.

Checklist of matters for inclusion in a construction phase plan

Project particulars

1 Name and address of the client.
2 Name and address of the principal designer.
3 Names and addresses of the designers.
4 Names and addresses of the contractors.
5 Description of the project and identification of specific structures.
6 Project programme with key dates.
7 Statement of the principal/sole contractor's health and safety policy.

Health and safety management

8 Management structure of the principal/sole contractor and all other participants in the management structure, and for the project, identifying responsibilities generally but, in particular, with regard to health and safety.
9 Guidelines for monitoring and review of health and safety performance and health and safety targets.
10 Arrangements for
   (a) meetings and other means to promote cooperation and coordination between parties on the site
   (b) consultation with employees and workers
   (c) disseminating design information required by regulation 9(4)
   (d) implementation and communication of design changes during the project
   (e) selection and supervision of contractors
   (f) the implementation of relevant legal requirements for health and safety information between all affected parties
   (g) site security
   (h) site induction training
   (i) specific training

(j) welfare facilities, as required by Schedule 2, and first aid
(k) reporting and investigation of accidents and other incidents including near misses
(l) production and approval of risk assessments and method statements and systems of work
(m) site rules
(n) fire and emergency procedures.

Identification of significant site risks and the elimination or mitigation of such risks

11 Particular risks.
Risks listed 1 to 10 in Schedule 3.

CDM Regulations 2015 Explained
ISBN 978-0-7277-6009-8

http://dx.doi.org/10.1680/cdmre.60098.151

Chapter 14
The health and safety file

- **Definition**
- **What information should be included in a health and safety file?**
- **Who takes responsibility for the health and safety file?**
- **What happens to the health and safety file on completion of the construction work?**

Definition

The health and safety file is defined in regulation 2(1) of the CDM Regulations as meaning

> a file prepared under regulation 12(5).

What information should be included in a health and safety file?

The content of the health and safety file is prescribed in regulation 12(5), which provides that it must contain

> information relating to the project which is likely to be needed during any subsequent project to ensure the health and safety of any person.

What is likely to be needed for future construction work will be based on the judgement of the principal designer after the construction work has been completed, their detailed knowledge of the project and the receipt of information from the principal contractor as required by regulation 12(7). Information that will not be needed in the health and safety file includes commercial construction management details, which would typically include

- the construction phase plan
- information provided to the contractors at the tender stage
- information provided by tenderers
- construction costing
- contract documentation

- method statements
- records, notes and minutes of meetings
- health and safety statistics and Reporting of Injuries, Diseases and Dangerous Occurrences Regulations (RIDDOR) reports
- notices to the Health and Safety Executive and utilities.

It will not always be necessary to include all design information and 'as-built' records if such information is unlikely to have any consequences for ensuring the health and safety of any persons engaged in future construction work. Information in the health and safety file is not needed for the benefit of the occupants or persons using the facilities created by the project. The purpose of creating the health and safety file is for the benefit of designing and managing future projects involving construction work. For that reason, there should be a distinction in the documentation between the health and safety file and manuals or instructions for operational and maintenance matters.

When a new construction team has to plan and become involved in subsequent construction for a new project, risks to health and safety from the prior project will be such risks as are evident from a visual inspection and unquantifiable or unseen hazards. However, the information that will not be evident and should be included in the health and safety file will not only assist in identifying hazards for the new project but will contribute to saving costs. A non-exhaustive checklist of the items of information that should ideally be included in the health and safety file is set out below:

1. A brief description of the work.
2. Historic site data.
3. Ground investigation reports and records, site survey information, pre- and post-construction phase and any residual hazards.
4. Investigation reports and records.
5. Photographic records of essential site elements.
6. Statement of the design philosophy, structural principles, loads, calculations and applicable design standards.
7. Drawings and plans used throughout the construction process, including drawings prepared for tender purposes.
8. Record drawings and plans of the completed structure showing, where appropriate, means of safe access to service voids.
9. Health and safety information about maintenance and cleaning operations.
10. Instructions on the handling and/or operation of equipment together with the relevant maintenance manuals, with particular regard to removal or dismantling of installed plant and equipment.
11. The results of proofing or load tests.
12. The commissioning test results.

13 Materials used in the structure identifying, in particular, hazardous materials, including data sheets prepared and supplied by suppliers and information provided by the client as specified in regulation 4(9)(c) of the Control of Asbestos Regulations 2012.
14 Identification and specification of in-built safety features, for example emergency and fire-fighting systems and fail-safe devices (see also item 9 above).
15 Nature and location of services, particularly gas and fuel pipelines and electricity cables.

Who takes responsibility for the health and safety file?

A client's duties under the Regulations only apply to managing projects, thus there are no direct duties on a client as to the creation, maintenance or storage of the health and safety file, which, by contrast, are express duties of the principal designer. However, the client is the first person to have a duty in relation to the health and safety file, which is to comply with regulation 4(5)(b), which states that

> A client must ensure that the principal designer prepares a health and safety file for the project, which—
> (i) complies with the requirements of regulation 12(5);
> (ii) is revised from time to time as appropriate to incorporate any relevant new information: and
> (iii) is kept available for inspection by any person who may need it to comply with the relevant legal requirements.

The client is entitled to rely upon the principal designer to ensure that the health and safety file will comply with regulation 12(5), whose duty is expressed as follows:

> During the pre-construction phase, the principal designer must prepare a health and safety file appropriate to the characteristics of the project which must contain information relating to the project which is likely to be needed during any subsequent project to ensure the health and safety of any person.

Indeed, there is no express duty on the principal designer, or the principal contractor, to advise the client on the content of the health and safety file. A prudent client will require a warranty from the principal designer, or principal contractor if appropriate, that the health and safety file will comply with regulation 12(5).

The client must ensure that the principal designer revises the health and safety file as appropriate during the project. The client will derive comfort from the duty on the principal designer to keep the health and safety file under review in accordance with regulation 12(6), which states that

> The principal designer must ensure that the health and safety file is appropriately reviewed, updated and revised from time to time to take account of the work and any changes that have occurred.

There is no express duty on the principal designer to revise or maintain the health and safety file after completion of the project, which is evident from regulation 12(10) which provides that

> At the end of the project, the principal designer, or where there is no principal designer the principal contractor, must pass the health and safety file to the client.

A designer's duty in respect of the health and safety file supports the principal designer's obligations in regulation 9(3)(c) as follows:

> If it is not possible to eliminate these risks, the designer must, so far as is reasonably practicable, ensure appropriate information is included in the health and safety file.

The risks referred to in paragraph (3) are substantially similar to those that apply to the principal designer in regulation 11(3), but the scope of the designer's duty does not extend to identifying them, although this must be implicit within the scope of the designers' work.

In addition to the general duty to liaise with the principal designer and share information with the principal designer relevant to the planning, management and monitoring of the pre-construction phase in regulation 13(5), the principal contractor has an express duty in respect of the health and safety file at regulation 12(7), which states that

> During the project, the principal contractor must provide the principal designer with any information in the principal contractor's possession relevant to the health and safety file, for inclusion in the health and safety file.

The principal contractor, however, will by default, in the event of the principal designer's appointment terminating before the end of the project, take possession of the health and safety file and full responsibility for the completeness of the health and safety file in accordance with regulations 12(8) and (9):

> (8) If the principal designer's appointment concludes before the end of the project, the principal designer must pass the health and safety file to the principal contractor.

> (9) Where the health and safety file is passed to the principal contractor under paragraph (8), the principal contractor must ensure that the health and safety file is appropriately reviewed, updated and revised from time to time to take account of the work and any changes that have occurred.

A contractor, not being the principal contractor, does not have any express obligations to provide to the principal contractor information for inclusion in the health and safety file, although a contractor is under a duty pursuant to regulation 15(3) to comply with

> any directions given by the principal designer or the principal contractor

which could include the provision of information for inclusion in the health and safety file. A principal contractor should consider including a sub-contract requirement that would govern the nature and type of information that would be needed for the health and safety file and any requirements governing the period of time the information should be delivered.

What happens to the health and safety file on completion of the construction work?

The client must ensure that the principal designer revises the health and safety file as appropriate during the project. There is no express duty on the principal designer, or the principal contractor, to revise or maintain the health and safety file after completion of the project, which is evident from regulation 12(10), which provides that

> At the end of the project, the principal designer, or where there is no principal designer the principal contractor, must pass the health and safety file to the client.

On receipt by the client of the health and safety file, the client's duties are provided for in regulation 4(7) as follows:

> If a client disposes of the client's interest in the structure, the client complies with the duty in paragraph (5)(b)(iii) by providing the health and safety file to the person who acquires the client's interest in the structure and ensuring that that person is aware of the nature and purpose of the file.

The client's duty to comply with paragraph (5)(b)(iii) is not a duty on the client to keep possession of the health and safety file but merely to ensure that it is available for inspection.

A person who makes a request of the client to inspect the health and safety file cannot be refused, provided that it is a request to comply with the relevant legal requirements for that person's own purposes such as a new project that will be influenced by or will influence the existing structure. A request to inspect the health and safety file cannot therefore be without some proper purpose. There is no indication as to the time frame within which the client should produce the health and safety file. However, a period of reasonable notice will be implied, depending upon all the circumstances.

A client who disposes of something less than the entire interest in the structure should ensure that a copy of the whole or a relevant part of the health and safety file is provided to the acquirer: typically, tenants under leases and part purchasers. It is important when disposing or acquiring interests in structures that the appropriate warranties and indemnities are put in place by the respective legal advisers with respect to the completeness and accuracy of the health and safety file.

The health and safety file must be kept under review and revised whenever there is a principal designer appointed for a related or new project. The information in the health and safety file will be a significant contribution to the discharge of the client's duty under regulation 4(4) to provide pre-construction information as soon as practicable to every designer and contractor.

CDM Regulations 2015 Explained
ISBN 978-0-7277-6009-8

http://dx.doi.org/10.1680/cdmre.60098.157

Chapter 15
Contract documentation

- Introduction
- Clients and agreement
- The professional appointments – duty of care
- Terms of engagement of the principal designer
- Terms of engagement of designers
- Contractors' tender documentation
- Construction contracts

Introduction

There is no need to include in a contract, as between the parties to a project, the precise obligations and duties that are set out fully in the CDM Regulations. The requirements and prohibitions as they affect the roles of contracting parties according to the Regulations apply regardless of any contractual arrangement. However, for the sake of clarity and avoiding confusion, there are various matters that should be considered when preparing documentation for projects to which the Regulations apply.

If a party to a project has a contractual obligation to perform the role of a duty holder or comply with other obligations imposed by the Regulations, then failure to comply becomes a breach of contract for which there is a remedy in damages.

The unplanned benefit of the 1994 and 2007 Regulations, which compelled the different parties to a project to communicate with each other, had been to import an improved understanding and clarity among the parties of each other's intentions and expectations. The Regulations have probably done as much, if not more, for an improvement in contractual relationships on projects as they did for improvements in health and safety.

Some of the relevant matters for consideration to be included in the project documentation are dealt with below according to the various roles under the Regulations.

Clients and agreement

It is not uncommon for any number of persons to be associated with the inception of a project, any of whom could be identified as a client. These persons may include lenders, landowners, developers, joint venture members, future purchasers or tenants. Accordingly, the documentation that will record the agreement between the various persons will range from funding agreements to agreements for a lease. To avoid any doubt as to which person will fulfil the role of client for the purposes of the Regulations, the person chosen as the client should be identified in the relevant documentation. The person who agrees to act as client should record their agreement to the agreement in writing in accordance with regulation 4(8)(a).

The person appointed to act as the client should consider whether they want an indemnity from the other persons who could have been the client should any claim arise from a breach of the Regulations, including failure to provide pre-construction information or to cooperate with other parties to the project. Conversely, the other persons may wish to have a cause of action against the agreed client for any claim flowing from their breach of the Regulations. The party with the benefit of an indemnity is able to recover their losses and costs, although an indemnity cannot provide protection against the risk of a criminal prosecution.

The other parties who agreed to one of their number becoming the client should give some consideration to the consequences of an event, such as insolvency, that would interrupt or disable the agreed client from discharging their duties.

Changing the client during the course of a project is not prohibited, although it should be remembered that unless there is a fresh written agreement in accordance with regulation 5(8)(a) and all parties to the project have been notified, the original person who agreed to act as the client retains all the duties of the client under the Regulations.

In the event that there is not an agreement by one of the parties to act as the client under the Regulations, all the parties fulfilling some of or sharing the client's duties are likely to be treated as clients with joint and several liability.

The professional appointments – duty of care

The principal designer and designers are obliged to perform their respective duties in accordance with the Regulations to avoid the risk of a criminal prosecution. The duties imposed on the principal designer and designers are mandatory and cannot be avoided. What this means is that the Health and Safety Executive does not have to demonstrate any loss, and there is no possibility of a defence that relies on demonstrating that they had performed at least as well as any other person reasonably skilled in their particular field of expertise. However, principal designers and designers are likely to be subject to terms of engagement with the client, or others involved in a project, which create an additional and completely independent liability of the criminal liability under the Regulations.

Professional indemnity insurers will not, in most if not all cases, provide cover for obligations owed to clients by professionals that go beyond the duty of care established in the case of *Bolam* v. *Friern Hospital Management Committee* [1957] 2 All ER 118, which was:

> Where you get a situation which involves the use of some special skill or competence, then the test as to whether there has been negligence or not is ... the standard of the ordinary skilled man exercising and professing to have that special skill.

Thus, most clients will have to accept that the contractual obligation owed by principal designers or designers will be limited to a duty of care expected of a professional in the same field of expertise as the one in which they are practising. The consequences for a principal designer or designer arise from two concurrent liabilities, one of which is criminal and uninsurable and the other a contractual duty of care that is insurable.

A breach of the Regulations may result in a criminal conviction without any consequences arising from a breach of contract if there has been no loss to the client. Conversely, it is possible that a failure to perform the requirements and observe the prohibitions under the Regulations may not lead to a criminal conviction (at the discretion of the Health and Safety Executive), although the client may have suffered a loss for which damages are recoverable in civil proceedings.

At the present time, standard forms of contract, which require the contractor to design and build, limit the contractor's liability for design to the duty of care expected of a professional in the relevant discipline. When collateral warranties are required from the professionals and contractors, they will incorporate the new obligations under the Regulations, in the same terms as the main appointments. However, even if collateral warranties are not required, by virtue of the Contracts (Rights of Third Parties) Act 1999, unless the rights of third parties have been excluded expressly in the professional appointments, a person who has suffered harm as a result of the design, planning, management, monitoring, coordination and carrying out of construction work may be able to bring a claim against the professional or contractor who is at fault in having breached the Regulations.

Terms of engagement of the principal designer

The client has to appoint a principal designer to comply with regulation 5(1)(a). A written agreement in accordance with regulation 5(1)(a) incorporating the terms of engagement for the appointment of a principal designer will be evidence of the appointment.

The terms of engagement should state expressly that the person is appointed as the principal designer in accordance with the Regulations. The duties of the principal designer set out in regulation 11 cannot be varied by contract and are deemed to be incorporated, although it is good practice to include the duties by including regulation 11 in a written appointment so that there is no doubt that the duties are also contractual.

In negotiating the terms of engagement of the principal designer, some of the matters that might be considered include the following:

- Warranties as to allocation of sufficient time and other resources that the conditions in regulation 8(1) are fulfilled and in compliance with regulation 11.
- The timing and manner of the provision of assistance to the client to assist in the provision of pre-construction information.
- Identification of arrangements for implementing the planning, management, monitoring and coordination of the pre-construction phase.
- Arrangements and timing of requests for advice by the client.
- Identification of arrangements for establishing coordination and circulating pre-construction information to the relevant parties.
- Obligations of cooperation with other parties to the project.
- The preparation, timing and manner of the handing over of the health and safety file.
- Provisions for terminating the appointment of the principal designer, with particular regard to the hand-over information and access to the successor principal designer.
- Reporting regime by the principal designer of information to the client.
- Fee arrangements.

Terms of engagement of designers

The designer is bound at all times by the relevant duties and obligations contained within the Regulations. Accordingly, there is no requirement to set out in any terms of engagement the detailed requirements of regulation 9, although including regulation 9 is good practice for the same reasons that apply to the principal designer. In many cases, a person will be appointed as the principal designer and designer.

There are certain matters that it would be advisable to include in the terms of engagement of a designer. These include

- the identity of the principal designer and a provision for a change and subsequent appointment of a successor principal designer
- the identities of any other designers known at the time
- the identity of the principal contractor if known at the time, and a provision for a change and subsequent appointment of a successor principal contractor
- arrangements for cooperation and coordination

- details of any notices pursuant to regulation 6 if appropriate
- warranty by the designer as to the allocation of sufficient time and other resources.

Contractors' tender documentation

All documentation sent to the principal contractor, contractors and sub-contractors inviting them to submit tenders for projects, in addition to the conditions of contract, bills of quantities and specification or employer's requirements (as appropriate), should include the following information relevant to the Regulations:

- confirmation, or otherwise, that the project is notifiable
- a copy of the notice complying with regulation 6(3), together with
  - the identity of the principal designer
  - the identity of the designer(s)
  - the identity of the principal contractor (if appointed), or confirmation that the award of the contract will include the appointment as the principal contractor in accordance with regulation 5(1)(b).

The tender documentation should include all the relevant pre-construction information gathered by the principal designer, which does not necessarily include information required solely to carry out the construction work. The invitation to tender should request the tenderers to submit information to enable the client, or other appointer, to assess the sufficiency of time and allocation of adequate resources. In particular, it is a demonstration of a client's discharge of their duties if the tenderers are requested to submit a statement or programme illustrating how time and other resources will be allocated for the management of health and safety.

Construction contracts

Organisations responsible for publishing their own standard conditions of contract for construction projects usually issue amendments to incorporate the requirements of the Regulations, which will suffice to fulfil regulation 5(1)(b). However, not all construction contracts are required to be in writing for the purposes of the Regulations or the Housing Grants, Construction and Regeneration Act 1996 (as amended). In view of the written appointment required by regulation 5(1)(b) for the principal contractor, the only appointments that are an exception to the requirement in writing are those construction contracts where the principal contractor is deemed to have been appointed in accordance with regulation 7(2)(b) for domestic clients. Thus, it follows that in respect of all projects for non-domestic clients there must be a written appointment for the principal contractor that provides a remedy in contract by the client against the principal contractor for breach of the Regulations.

CDM Regulations 2015 Explained
ISBN 978-0-7277-6009-8

http://dx.doi.org/10.1680/cdmre.60098.163

Chapter 16
Criminal and civil liability and enforcement

- **Health and safety and the public debate**
- **Enforcement**
- **Criminal proceedings**
- **Civil liability**

Health and safety and the public debate

The public's perception of the health and safety management of large companies is probably based upon the notion that, whenever possible, the profit motive overcomes the need to spend enough on health and safety measures. The Southall, Paddington and Hatfield rail disasters, and various other rail crashes, the *Herald of Free Enterprise* disaster, the King's Cross fire and the *Marchioness* sinking on the Thames all received wide press coverage and stimulated a debate that has created a powerful lobby to employ the full force of the criminal law against companies and management executives where death or injury is caused by negligence.

Parliament responded to the public's sense of outrage that there should be greater accountability for health and safety, to create the offence of corporate manslaughter (corporate homicide in Scotland) by passing the Corporate Manslaughter and Corporate Homicide Act 2007. The introduction of this act provides a basis for penalising organisations that have breached a duty of care and caused a person's death. There is, however, no personal liability imposed on directors. Due to the potential severe financial impact on a business due its negligence, which will include breach of health and safety legislation, directors are required to implement, monitor and review good health and safety management practices as part of any corporate governance measures.

The offence of corporate manslaughter is committed where the manner by which an organisation managed or organised its activities is found to be a 'substantial element' of the breach of a duty of care, and causes a person's death. The maximum penalty is an unlimited fine, and the court may in addition make a publicity order requiring the organisation to publish details of the conviction and fine.

The message is clear enough: health and safety is a management responsibility and there is now a full suite of remedies available to bring individuals, including directors, and companies to account. By putting more onus onto directors to take health and safety management seriously, by the threat of corporate criminal proceedings, hopefully an improved culture will deliver greater awareness among all employees of the need to comply with health and safety legislation.

Enforcement

Generally

The CDM Regulations are enforced by the Health and Safety Executive ('the Executive') in all cases where construction work is being carried out, subject always to the enforcement powers of local authorities allocated to them by the Health and Safety (Enforcing Authority) Regulations 1998, or the Office of Rail Regulation for projects where there are any works associated with railways or tramways. The Executive issued an Enforcement Policy Statement (HSE41) in 2009, which states that the purpose of enforcement is to

- ensure that dutyholders take action to deal immediately with serious risks;
- promote and achieve sustained compliance with the law;
- ensure that dutyholders who breach health and safety requirements, and directors or managers who fail in their responsibilities, may be held to account, which may include bringing alleged offenders before the courts in England and Wales, or recommending prosecution in Scotland, in the circumstances set out later in this policy.

The activities in respect of which the Executive is the enforcing authority at Schedule 2 to the Health and Safety (Enforcing Authority) Regulations 1998 (HSE Enforcement Guide (England and Wales), www.hse.gov.uk/enforce/enforcementguide) together with guidance provided by the Executive to its own inspectors and local authorities are set out in detail in Appendix 5.

The Executive's inspectors have wide-ranging powers enabling them, for example, to enter any premises, including construction sites, where the inspector is of the opinion that there is or likely to be danger. Frequently used powers also include requiring the production of documents, their inspection and having copies taken of such documents. The full extent of an inspector's powers is set out in section 20 of the Health and Safety at Work etc. Act (HASWA) 1974.

The Executive's enforcement powers, if a statutory provision has been contravened, include the service of an improvement notice (requiring a contravention to be remedied within a certain time period) under section 21 of the HASWA or a prohibition notice (requiring that the activity in question be stopped until the contravention is remedied) under section 22 of the HASWA.

The Executive's inspector's visit to a site is likely to lead to a request for the production of relevant documents, including statutory notices and the construction phase plan, as one of the first actions as part of the initial fact finding. The inspector will want to see that the management system on site has implemented the intentions developed in the construction phase plan and is complying with the CDM Regulations and other relevant statutory provisions. However, now that the principal designer has responsibility for the planning and coordination of the pre-construction phase, which is recognised as being very influential on the management of health and safety during the construction phase, visits to the offices of clients and designers can be expected. At the pre-construction phase the inspector may be concerned to see how the client has satisfied themselves with regard to the performance of their appointees, including the principal designer and other designers and the principal contractor and other contractors. Principal designers should be prepared to demonstrate that there is a strategy or framework being followed for designing, managing, monitoring and coordinating all the elements of the pre-construction phase work. If the principal designer is the appointed Building Information Modelling (BIM) manager for a project, many aspects of the principal designer's duties under the CDM Regulations will be discharged in the ordinary course of pursuing sound BIM principles.

In respect of fire

The enforcing authority, following a fire on a construction site, will be determined by the Regulatory Reform (Fire Safety) Order 2005. The Executive will be the enforcing authority in accordance with article 25(b)(iv) of the Order, which confirms that

> For the purposes of this Order, "enforcing authority" means the Health and Safety Executive in relation to any workplace which is or is on a construction site within the meaning of regulation 2(1) of the Construction (Health, Safety and Welfare) Regulations 1996 and to which those Regulations apply, other than construction sites referred to in regulation 33 of those Regulations.

However, there are exceptions. The allocation of responsibility for enforcement with respect to fire as between the Executive and the fire and rescue authority for the area in which the construction site exists, applies in respect of emergency procedures and emergency routes and exits to the extent provided by regulation 36 of the CDM Regulations as follows:

> The enforcing authority for regulations 30 and 31 (so far as those regulations relate to fire) and regulation 32, in respect of a construction site which is

contained within or forms part of premises occupied by persons other than those carrying out construction work, or any activity related to this work, is—

(a) in England and Wales, the enforcing authority within the meaning of article 25 of the Regulatory Reform (Fire Safety) Order 2005 in respect of premises to which that Order applies; or
(b) in Scotland, the enforcing authority within the meaning of section 61 of the Fire (Scotland) Act 2005 in respect of premises to which Part 3 of that Act applies.

The first test to ascertain the identity of the enforcing authority is to determine if the premises are occupied by non-construction workers. However, even if there are only persons occupying the premises carrying out construction work, for a construction site that is within a defence establishment that comes within the meaning of article 25(c) of the Regulatory Reform (Fire Safety) Order 2005 or section 61(9)(zb) of the Fire (Scotland) Act 2005, the enforcing authority will be the fire service maintained by the Secretary of State for Defence. In respect of sports grounds that require a safety certificate or a regulated stand at a sports ground, the enforcing authority will be the relevant local authority for regulations 30 and 31.

Criminal proceedings

Section 33 of the HASWA lists 15 separate offences, which include the contravention of any health and safety regulations or any requirement or prohibition imposed under any such regulations. The parties to a project are also liable to a criminal prosecution if they fail to comply with the requirements of the Executive's inspectors, which might, for example, involve the production of the health and safety file, the construction phase plan and/or the design documentation. Most importantly, directors, managers and other officers of corporate organisations can be prosecuted personally where it is shown that they have consented to, or connived at, the commission of any offence or where an offence has been committed by neglect on their part. Many breaches of health and safety legislation will attract no more than a warning or, in ascending seriousness, improvement and prohibition notices, but the Executive has shown in recent years a greater willingness to prosecute individuals, which has led to large fines and terms of imprisonment. There can be no doubt that the trend of prosecuting individuals will continue.

The Health and Safety Offences Act 2008 increased the sentencing powers such that the magistrates' courts now have jurisdiction, according to the nature of the offence, to impose fines not exceeding £20 000 and a term of up to 12 months imprisonment, or both. Alternatively, if the offence is sufficiently serious to be tried in the Crown Court by a jury on indictment, the maximum fine is unlimited, and imprisonment for a term not exceeding 2 years can be imposed, or both. In extreme cases a fine might be imposed in addition to a term of imprisonment.

Guidelines on sentencing

The Court of Appeal in *R.* v. *F. Howe and Son (Engineers) Limited* [1999] 2 All ER 249 established guidelines on sentencing for health and safety offences. The Executive has noted that the Lord Chancellor said that someone injured by a breach of health and safety legislation is no less a victim than someone who is assaulted. The court stressed that every case would have to be decided on its own facts, and it avoided laying down any tariff or rule relating to the size of the fine to turnover or net profit. Nonetheless, in general terms, the following criteria were said to be relevant to sentencing:

- How far short of the appropriate standard was the defendant's conduct in failing to reach the reasonably practicable test?
- Death is to be treated as an aggravating feature of an offence, and public disquiet should be reflected in the penalty.
- What was the degree of risk and the extent of the danger created?
- What was the extent of the breach/breaches (e.g. an isolated incident or continuous over a period)?
- What are the defendant's resources and what effect will a fine have on their business?
- Failure to heed warnings will be a particularly aggravating feature.
- Any financial profit that the defendant has deliberately made from failing to take the necessary health and safety steps, or being prepared to run the risk of not taking them to save money, will be a particularly aggravating feature.

Mitigating factors that a court will take into account will include

- prompt admission of liability
- a timely plea of guilty
- steps taken to remedy deficiencies after the defendant became aware of them
- the defendant's good safety record.

In the later Court of Appeal case of *R.* v. *Friskies Petcare Limited* it was recommended, based on the Howe guidelines, that the prosecution should present to the court any aggravating features in addition to the facts.

Under the Company Directors Disqualification Act 1986, a person can be disqualified from holding the office of director of a company after conviction of an indictable offence connected with the management of a company. This may extend to the management of health and safety matters. This extension of the concept of the management of a company was supported by Viscount Ullswater speaking for the government in the House of Lords, who said (Hansard 28/11/91 Col. 1429):

> in our view, section 2 of the Company Directors Disqualification Act 1986 is capable of applying to health and safety matters. That Act provides for the court to make a disqualification order against a person connected with the promotion, formation, management or liquidation of a company. We believe that the potential scope of section 2(1) of that Act is very broad and that 'management' includes the management of health and safety.

The courts are likely to use their powers under section 2(1) of the Company Directors Disqualification Act 1986 more readily in a climate of improving standards in corporate governance.

A conviction under the HASWA, or for any other crime, by virtue of section 11 of the Civil Evidence Act 1968, is admissible as evidence in any subsequent civil proceedings, subject to such evidence being relevant to any issue in those proceedings. In civil proceedings, discussed below, a conviction constitutes the basic fact of a presumption. The defendant would have the uphill task of persuading the court that the verdict reached beyond reasonable doubt was wrong.

Failure to comply with an approved code of practice is not in itself an offence, although it may be taken as proof that a person has contravened the relevant regulation (section 17 of the HASWA). It would, however, be open to the accused to prove that compliance with the CDM Regulations had been achieved in some other way.

The role of guidelines published by the Executive on its own or together with the construction industry does not provide an authorative statement or interpretation of the CDM Regulations or a definitive approach to ensure compliance. The benefit of guidance is to provide some help by obtaining the opinions of organisations whose experience and knowledge is respected, but it remains the responsibility of each person who is required to comply with the Regulations to form their own opinion and proceed accordingly.

Under the 2007 CDM Regulations nearly all the prosecutions were connected with accidents or other incidents, particularly where children and public safety were an issue. In other words, the Executive has not been proactive in prosecuting as a deterrent but is being reactive to what has already manifested itself as a failure in the management of health and safety. The number of prosecutions under the 2007 Regulations were

- 44 in 2010
- 39 in 2011
- 45 in 2012
- 47 in 2013
- 27 in 2014.

Civil liability

Breach of statutory duty

The Enterprise and Regulatory Reform Act 2013 (Health and Safety) (Consequential Amendments) Order 2013 omitted regulation 45 of the 2007 CDM Regulations, thus removing the right to bring civil proceedings for breach of the Regulations. Generally, in respect of any health and safety regulations, section 69 of the Enterprise and Regulatory Reform Act 2013 provides that a

> Breach of a duty imposed by a statutory instrument containing (whether alone or with other provision) health and safety regulations shall not be actionable except to the extent that regulations under this section so provide.

There are no exclusions or exceptions in the 2015 CDM Regulations for bringing an action for breach of statutory duty, unlike the previous 1994 and 2007 Regulations. Therefore, it will not be possible for a person who has been injured as a result of a breach of the Regulations to bring a claim for breach of statutory duty.

Negligence

The CDM Regulations do not prevent an injured person from pursuing a claim in negligence. The essential elements of negligence are

- a duty owed by the defendant to the claimant
- breach of the duty owed by the defendant
- breach of the duty that caused damage.

The duty owed by an employer to their employees was summed up in the leading case of *Wilsons and Clyde Coal Co. Ltd* v *English* [1938] AC 57 as

> A duty which rests on the employer and which is personal to the employer, to take reasonable care for the safety of his workmen, whether the employer be an individual, a firm, or a company, and whether or not the employer takes any share in the conduct of the operations.

The duty owed by employers has been categorised by the courts as a duty to provide

- a safe workplace
- safe equipment
- competent staff and fellow workers
- a safe system of work.

The entire philosophy behind the CDM Regulations is to provide a safer workplace on site, together with a safer system of work, or method of construction, and that the principal designer, designers, the principal contractor and contractors are required to be appropriately resourced and experienced. There will be overlap with other regulations, particularly the Provision and Use of Work Equipment Regulations 1998, in respect of the requirement to provide safe equipment, and the Management of Health and Safety at Work Regulations 1999, which deal with general principles of risk assessment.

In respect of a personal injury the causation of which can be attributed to a breach of the CDM Regulations, such failure to comply with the Regulations or take account of any approved code of practice or industry guidance will be persuasive evidence to prove negligence.

Contributory negligence

Many personal injury claims arising from industrial accidents, whether based on breach of statutory duty or negligence, often have to overcome an allegation of contributory negligence. Contributory negligence is proved when

- the injury of which the claimant complains results from that particular risk to which the negligence of the plaintiff exposed them
- the negligence of the claimant contributed to their injury
- there was fault or negligence on the part of the claimant.

The extent to which an employee has suffered as a result of contributory negligence will depend on the facts in each case. Section 7 of the HASWA provides that

> It shall be the duty of every employee while at work—
> (a) to take reasonable care for the health and safety of himself and of other persons who may be affected by his acts or omissions at work; and
> (b) as regards any duty or requirement imposed on his employer or any other person by or under any of the relevant statutory provisions, to cooperate with him so far as is necessary to enable that duty or requirement to be performed or complied with.

A discussion on contributory negligence of employees and the statutory duties that they owe to their employers is beyond the scope of this book but is mentioned for the sake of completeness.

CDM Regulations 2015 Explained
ISBN 978-0-7277-6009-8

http://dx.doi.org/10.1680/cdmre.60098.171

Chapter 17
Transitional and saving provisions

- **Introduction**
- **Projects with no existing CDM coordinator or principal contractor**
- **Projects with an existing CDM coordinator**
- **Projects with only one contractor**

Introduction

The CDM Regulations came into force on 6 April 2015, and the transitional and saving provisions recognise and take account of projects that started before and will continue after 6 April 2015 that were subject to the 2007 Regulations. Regulation 37 simply states that

> Schedule 4, which makes transitional and saving provisions has effect.

Schedule 4 is divided according to the status of a project under the 2007 Regulations that had started before 6 April 2015 as follows:

- projects with no existing CDM coordinator or principal contractor (paragraph 3)
- projects with an existing CDM coordinator (paragraphs 4 to 6)
- projects with only one contractor (paragraph 7).

Projects with no existing CDM coordinator or principal contractor

For projects with no existing CDM coordinator or principal contractor, paragraph 3(2) of Schedule 4 provides that regulation 5 will not apply immediately on 6 April 2015 if three conditions are met as required by paragraph 3(1) of Schedule 4 follows:

> This paragraph modifies the application of these Regulations in relation to a relevant project where, immediately before 6 April 2015—
> (a) no CDM coordinator or principal contractor is appointed for the project under the 2007 Regulations;

(b) there is more than one contractor, or it is reasonably foreseeable that more than one contractor will be working on the project; and
(c) the construction phase has started.

Thus, if the construction phase has started, paragraph 3(4) requires that the client must appoint a contractor as the principal contractor as soon as practicable after 6 April 2015 on a project where there is more than one contractor, irrespective of whether a principal designer has been appointed as follows:

> The client must appoint in writing a contractor as principal contractor as soon as is practicable after 6th April 2015.

Once the principal contractor has been appointed, whatever the state of progress of the construction phase, they must comply with paragraph 3(5), which states that

> The principal contractor must draw up a construction phase plan or make arrangements for a construction phase plan to be drawn up under regulation 12(1) and (2) as soon as is practicable after 6th April 2015 and the requirement that the plan must be drawn up during the pre-construction phase and before setting up a construction site is disapplied.

The client must ensure that the appointed principal contractor complies with sub-paragraph (5) by reason of paragraph 3(6), which states that

> The client, other than a domestic client, must ensure that the principal contractor complies with sub-paragraph (5) and the client duty in regulation 4(5)(a) is disapplied.

The client can choose if they want to appoint a designer as the principal designer, but is not bound to do so because paragraph 3(3) states that

> The client may appoint in writing a designer as principal designer.

If the client does not appoint a principal designer, the client must ensure that the principal contractor takes responsibility for the health and safety file in accordance with paragraph 3(7) as follows:

> If the client does not appoint a principal designer, the principal contractor must—
> (a) prepare a health and safety file under regulation 12(5) as soon as is practicable after 6th April 2015 and the requirement for the file to be prepared during the pre-construction phase is disapplied; and

(b) ensure that the health and safety file is reviewed, updated and revised from time to time under regulation 12(6).

If the client does not appoint a principal designer, paragraph 3(8) requires the principal contractor to accept design information about unavoidable risks from the designers, and the client must ensure that the principal contractor prepares the health and safety file, although certain duties of the client and principal contractor do not apply as follows:

> If the client does not appoint a principal designer—
> (a) the references to the principal designer in regulations 4(5)(b) and 9(3)(b) are treated as references to the principal contractor;
> (b) the client duty in regulation 4(6)(a) does not apply; and
> (c) the principal contractor duties in regulations 12(7) and 13(5) do not apply.

If the client fails to appoint a principal contractor as soon as is practicable after 6 April 2015, they are deemed to fulfil the duties of the principal contractor as required by paragraph 3(9) as follows:

> Where a client, other than a domestic client, fails to appoint a principal contractor under sub-paragraph (4) the client must fulfil the duties of the principal contractor specified in these Regulations, as modified by this paragraph.

If the client is a domestic client, the transition should not make any difference to the domestic client, and indeed that is what paragraph 3(10) achieves as follows:

> Where the client is a domestic client—
> (a) regulation 7(2) does not apply; and
> (b) if the client fails to appoint a principal contractor under sub-paragraph (4) the principal contractor for the project is the contractor in control of the construction phase.

Projects with an existing CDM coordinator

Until the CDM coordinator appointed before 6 April 2015 has been replaced, they continue in their duties as provided for in paragraph 4(2):

> Where this paragraph applies, the appointment of the CDM coordinator continues to have effect for the purposes of these Regulations until a principal designer is appointed or the project comes to an end.

A client has 6 months to replace the CDM coordinator with an appointment of a principal designer, being not later than 6 October 2015, as required in paragraph 4(3):

> The client must appoint in writing a principal designer for the project before the 6th October 2015 unless the project comes to an end on or before that date.

The CDM coordinator is not expected to have all the qualities that a principal designer should possess because the roles are fundamentally different. The Regulations recognise what would otherwise be a difficulty for the client and the CDM coordinator, and have modified the duties of the CDM coordinator, until a principal designer is appointed, as provided for in paragraph 4(4)(a) as follows:

> Where the appointment of a CDM coordinator continues to have effect under sub-paragraph (2) the CDM coordinator must comply with the duties in paragraph 5.

The CDM coordinator is bound to comply with the duties in paragraph 5 with effect from 6 April 2015, although they will not apply for longer than 6 months.

All the designers are not relieved of their duties to provide information to the principal designer as required by regulation 9(3)(b), and must immediately treat the CDM coordinator as the principal designer. The same approach applies to the principal contractor, who must provide information to the CDM coordinator for the health and safety file. Paragraphs 4(4)(b) and (c) direct the designers and principal contractor as to how they should treat the CDM coordinator as follows:

> Where the appointment of a CDM coordinator continues to have effect under sub-paragraph (2)—
> (b) the duties in regulations 9(3)(b) and 12(7) to provide information to the principal designer are treated as duties to provide information to the CDM coordinator; and
> (c) the duty in regulation 13(5) to liaise with the principal designer is treated as a duty to liaise with the CDM coordinator.

Some duties of the client are expressly disapplied if the construction phase had started prior to 6 April 2015, notably appointing a principal designer, subject to the requirement to make an appointment as required by paragraph 4(3), as set out in paragraph 6(1) as follows:

> The duties in regulation 5(1)(a) and (3) do not apply to a project referred to in paragraph 4(1).

The client is relieved of certain duties in the interim period from 6 April 2015 until the appointment of a principal designer within six months prior to 6 October 2015 with regard to the health and safety plan, checking compliance with a principal designer's duties (which will not be performed while there is no principal designer) and generally the duties of the principal designer, as provided by paragraph 6(2):

> The following duties do not apply to a project referred to in paragraph 4(1) until the principal designer is appointed—
> (a) the duties in regulations 4(5)(b) and (6)(a);
> (b) the duties of the principal designer in regulations 11 and 12(3), (5), (6), (8) and (10).

If the client does not make an appointment in writing of the principal designer by 6 October 2015, they will be deemed to be fulfilling the principal designer's duties as provided by paragraph 6(3):

> If a client fails to make the appointment required by paragraph 4(3) the client must fulfil the duties of a principal designer in regulations 11 and 12 on and after 6th October 2015.

Projects with only one contractor

A sole contractor carrying out construction work on 6 April 2015 is required to draw up a construction phase plan in accordance with paragraph 7 as follows:

> Where a relevant project has only one contractor and the construction phase has started, the contractor must draw up a construction phase plan, or make arrangements for a construction phase plan to be drawn up, under regulation 15(5) and (6) as soon as is practicable after 6th April 2015 and the requirement that the plan must be drawn up prior to setting up a construction site is disapplied.

If a principal contractor had been appointed prior to 6 April 2015, the client is not required to take any action because the status of the principal contractor will be recognised as the principal contractor under the Regulations as provided for in paragraph 8(1) as follows:

> Where, immediately before 6th April 2015 there is a principal contractor appointed for a relevant project under regulation 14(2) of the 2007 Regulations, for the purposes of these Regulations that principal contractor is treated on and after 6th April 2015 as having been appointed under regulation 5(1)(b) of these Regulations.

Paragraph 8(2) avoids duplication by providing that the documents and information required by the 2007 Regulations are also recognised as being the documents and information required by the 2015 Regulations as follows:

For the purposes of these Regulations, on and after 6th April 2015—

(a) a health and safety file prepared for a relevant project under regulation 20(2)(e) of the 2007 Regulations is treated as a health and safety file prepared under regulation 12(5) of these Regulations;
(b) a construction phase plan drawn up for a relevant project under regulation 23 of the 2007 Regulations is treated as a construction phase plan drawn up under regulation 12(1) or 15(5) of these Regulations;
(c) pre-construction information provided for a relevant project under regulation 10 of the 2007 Regulations is treated as pre-construction information provided under regulation 4(4) of these Regulations;
(d) notice given for a relevant project under regulation 21 of the 2007 Regulations is treated as notice given under regulation 6 of these Regulations.

CDM Regulations 2015 Explained
ISBN 978-0-7277-6009-8

http://dx.doi.org/10.1680/cdmre.60098.177

Bibliography

Better Regulation Executive (2015) *Policy: Reducing the Impact of Regulation on Business*. See https://www.gov.uk/government/policies/reducing-the-impact-of-regulation-on-business (accessed 16/02/2015).

Building Research Establishment (2005) *Safer Foundations by Design*. HSE, Sudbury, UK, RR319.

Carpenter C, Lazarus J and Perkins D (2006) *Safer Surfaces to Walk On: Reducing the Risk of Slipping*. CIRIA, London, UK, C652.

Construction (Design and Management) Regulations (2015) See http://www.legislation.gov.uk/uksi/2015/51/contents/made (accessed 09/03/2015).

Fawcett W and Palmer J (2004) *Good Practice Guidance for Refurbishing Occupied Buildings*. CIRIA, London, UK, C621.

Gilbertson A (2007) *Workplace 'In-use' Guidance for Designers*. CIRIA, London, UK, C663.

HM Government (2013) *Construction 2025*. See https://www.gov.uk/government/uploads/system/uploads/attachment_data/file/210099/bis-13-955-construction-2015-industrial-strategy.pdf (accessed 09/03/2015).

HSE (Health and Safety Executive) (1988) *Blackspot Construction: Study of Five Years Fatal Accidents in the Building and Civil Engineering Industries*. HSE, Sudbury, UK, PML22.

HSE (1995, reprinted 2002) *Establishing Exclusion Zones When Using Explosives in Demolition*. HSE, Sudbury, UK, CIS45.

HSE (2002) *Cement*. HSE, Sudbury, UK, CIS26, revision 2.

HSE (2002) *Revitalising Health and Safety in Construction*. HSE, Sudbury, UK, DDE20.

HSE (2003) *Safe Erection, Use and Dismantling of False Work*. HSE, Sudbury, UK, CIS56.

HSE (2003) *Solvents*. HSE, Sudbury, UK, CIS27, revision 2.

HSE (2003) *The High 5: Five Ways to Reduce Risk on Site*. HSE, Sudbury, UK, INDG384.

HSE (2005) *Controlling Noise at Work*. HSE, Sudbury, UK, L108.

HSE (2005) *Handling Kerbs: Reducing the Risks of Musculoskeletal Disorders*. HSE, Sudbury, UK, CIS57.

HSE (2005) *Inspections and Reports*. HSE, Sudbury, UK, CIS47, revision.

HSE (2006) *Health and Safety in Construction*, 3rd edn. HSE, Sudbury, UK, HSG150.

HSE (2006) *Backs for the Future: Safe Manual Handling in Construction*. HSE, Sudbury, UK, HSG149.

HSE (2006) *Construction Site Transport Safety: Safe Use of Site Dumpers*. HSE, Sudbury, UK, CIS52.

HSE (2006) *Portland Cement Dust, Hazard Assessment Document*. HSE, Sudbury, UK, EH75/7.

HSE (2007) *The Absolutely Essential Toolkit for the Smaller Construction Contractor*. HSE, Sudbury, UK, INDG344.

HSE (2009) *Enforcement Policy Statement*. HSE, Sudbury, UK, HSE41.

HSE (2009) *Protecting the Public: Your Next Move*. HSE, Sudbury, UK, HSG151.

HSE (2009) *The Safe Use of Vehicles on Construction Sites*. HSE, Sudbury, UK, HSG144.

HSE (2010) *Asbestos Essentials*. HSE, Sudbury, UK, HSG210.

HSE (2010) *Dust Control on Cut-off Saws Used for Stone or Concrete*. HSE, Sudbury, UK, CIS54.

HSE (2010) *Fire Safety in Construction Work*, 2nd edn. HSE, Sudbury, UK, HSG168.

HSE (2010) *Provision of Welfare Facilities During Construction Work*. HSE, Sudbury, UK, CIS59.

HSE (2011) *Assessment of Current Guidance in Relation to Safe Carriageway Crossing (CIS53) on High Speed Roads*. HSE, Sudbury, UK, RR185.

HSE (2011) *Occupational Exposure Limited*. HSE, Sudbury, UK, EH40.

HSE (2012) *Health and Safety in Roof Work*, 4th edn. HSE, Sudbury, UK, HSG33.

HSE (2012) *Managing Asbestos in Workplace Buildings*. HSE, Sudbury, UK, INDG223.

HSE (2012) *Outline Map on Competence, Training and Certification*. HSE, Sudbury, UK. See http://www.hse.gov.uk/aboutus/furtherinfo/policy/outline.htm (accessed 09/03/2015).

HSE (2013) *Construction Dust*. HSE, Sudbury, UK, CIS36.

HSE (2013) *Upper Limb Disorders: Assessing the Risks*. HSE, Sudbury, UK, INDG171.

HSE (2014) *ALARP 'At a Glance'*. HSE, Sudbury, UK. See http://www.hse.gov.uk/risk/theory/alarpglance.htm (accessed 09/03/2015).

HSE (2014) *Avoiding Danger from Underground Services*, 3rd edn. HSE, Sudbury, UK, HSG47.

HSE (2014) *The Selection, Management and Use of Mobile Elevating Work Platforms*. HSE, Sudbury, UK, GEIS6.

HSE (2014) *Tower Scaffolds*. HSE, Sudbury, UK. See www.hse.gov.uk/construction/safetytopics/scaffold.htm (accessed 16/02/2014).

HSE (2014) *Health and Safety in Construction in Great Britain*. HSE, Sudbury, UK. See http://www.hse.gov.uk/statistics/industry/construction/construction/pdf.

Iddon J and Carpenter J (2004) *Safe Access for Maintenance and Repair*. CIRIA, London, UK, C611.

Joyce R and Houghton D (2014) *ICE Legal Notes Series: BIM and the Law*. Institution of Civil Engineers, London, UK.

Löfstedt RE (2011) *Reclaiming Health and Safety for All: An Independent Review of Health and Safety Legislation*. Department for Work and Pensions, London, UK, Cm 8219.

Mordue S and Finch R (2014) *BIM for Construction Health and Safety*. National Building Specification, Newcastle upon Tyne, UK.

Oloke D and McAleenan C (eds) (2015) *ICE Manual of Health and Safety in Construction*, 2nd edn. Institution of Civil Engineers, London, UK.

Ove Arup and Partners (2007) *Construction Work Sector Guidance for Designers*. CIRIA, London, UK, C662.

Oxford Dictionaries (2006) *Oxford English Dictionary*, 11 revised edn. Oxford University Press, Oxford, UK.

Strategic Forum for Construction (2005) *Respect for People – RfP: Code of Good Working Health and Safety Practices*. Strategic Forum for Construction, London, UK.

CDM Regulations 2015 Explained
ISBN 978-0-7277-5739-5

http://dx.doi.org/10.1680/icsiam.57395.181

Appendix 1
The 'have you done' checklists

The checklists for each of the duty holders are a convenient shorthand means of providing some assurance that you have addressed the relevant duties created by the CDM Regulations. Each of the items in the checklists is cross-referenced to the relevant regulation. There is no substitute for reading each of the regulations, which set out in a comprehensive form every aspect of the relevant duty.

- client
- principal designer
- designer
- principal contractor
- contractor

Client

Pre-project (non-domestic) considerations

- [ ] Have you identified the need for a project that will involve construction work, such that the CDM Regulations will apply? *Reg. 3*
- [ ] Have you decided who will be the client for the purposes of the CDM Regulations if there are other parties who could be identified as possible clients? *Reg. 4(8)*
- [ ] Have you decided if you will fulfil the duties of the principal designer, principal contractor, designer or contractor? If the answer is yes to at least one of the duty holders, go to the relevant checklist.

Making suitable arrangements

- [ ] Have you made suitable arrangements for managing the project, including the allocation of sufficient time and other resources? *Reg. 4(1)*
- [ ] Have you put in place an effective procedure to promote and facilitate communication and cooperation between members of the project team and the duty holders? *Reg. 4(1)*
- [ ] Have you taken reasonable steps to ascertain the skills, knowledge, experience and organisational capability, if appropriate, of any designer or contractor you have appointed or are likely to appoint? *Reg. 8(1), (3)*
- [ ] Have you put in place a procedure to maintain and keep under review all the arrangements and procedures created by you, and others, for the duration of the project? *Reg. 4(3)*

Pre-construction phase

- [ ] Have you assessed if the project is notifiable? *Reg. 6(1)*
- [ ] Have you notified the Health and Safety Executive if the project is notifiable? *Reg. 6(2)*
- [ ] Have you notified the Office of Rail Regulation if the project includes work in respect of which the Office of Rail Regulation is the enforcing authority? *Reg. 6(4)*

- ☐ Have you notified the Office for Nuclear Regulation if the project includes work in respect of any nuclear energy or defence installations? *Reg. 6(5)*
- ☐ Have you appointed in writing a principal designer if there will be, or there is likely to be, more than one contractor? *Reg. 5(1)(a)*
- ☐ Have you collected together or procured the pre-construction information and provided it to every designer and contractor? *Reg. 4(4)*
- ☐ Have you sought the assistance of the principal designer in collecting together or procuring the pre-construction information? *Reg. 11(6)(a)*
- ☐ Have you provided to the principal designer an existing health and safety file? *Reg. 4(4), 4(5)(b)*
- ☐ Have you taken steps to ensure that the principal designer is preparing the health and safety file? *Reg. 4(5)(b)*
- ☐ Have you taken steps to ensure that the principal designer is complying with the duties of a principal designer in the CDM Regulations? *Reg. 4(6)(a)*
- ☐ Have you ensured that the minimum welfare facilities will be provided on the site before the start of construction work? *Reg. 4(2)(b)*
- ☐ Have you ensured that a construction phase plan has been prepared before the start of the construction phase? *Reg. 4(5)(a)*

Construction phase

- ☐ Have you appointed in writing a principal contractor if there will be, or there is likely to be, more than one contractor, not later than the start of the construction phase? *Reg. 5(1)(b), 5(2)*
- ☐ Have you taken steps to ensure that the principal contractor is complying with the duties of a principal contractor in the CDM Regulations? *Reg. 4(6)(b)*
- ☐ Have you ensured that the health and safety file prepared by the principal designer is available for inspection by any person who may need it? *Reg. 4(5)(b)(iii)*

Post-construction

- ☐ Have you received the health and safety file from the principal designer or principal contractor? *Reg. 12(10)*

- ☐ Have you disposed of your interest in the structure and provided the health and safety file to the acquirer? *Reg. 4(7)*

Principal designer

Appointment

- ☐ Have you assessed your skills, knowledge and experience to plan, manage and monitor the pre-construction phase and coordinate matters relating to health and safety during the pre-construction phase, to perform the required duties for the project? *Reg. 8(1), 11(1)*
- ☐ If you employ more than one designer, do you have the organisational capacity to perform the required duties for the project? *Reg. 8(1)*
- ☐ If your answer is no to either 1 or 2 above, you must not accept the appointment. *Reg. 8(2)*
- ☐ If you are performing design work you must also go to the checklist for a designer.
- ☐ Have you checked the skills, knowledge and experience of any sub-designers/contractors working for you and their organisational capabilities if appropriate? *Reg. 8(3)*

Pre-construction design work

- ☐ Have you received the pre-construction information from the client? If the answer is no, you must ask for the pre-construction information from the client and provide assistance to the client in the provision of the pre-construction information designer. *Reg. 4(4), 11(6)(a)*
- ☐ Have you provided the pre-construction information promptly to every appointed designer and contractor and in a convenient form? *Reg. 11(6)(b)*
- ☐ Have you identified all the designers so that you are able to ensure they are all complying with their duties in regulation 9? *Reg. 11(4)*
- ☐ Have you identified the duty holders with whom you must cooperate if they make known a need for your cooperation? *Reg. 8(4)*
- ☐ Have you made arrangements to manage all persons working in relation to the pre-construction phase to cooperate with you, the client and each other? *Reg. 11(5)*

- ☐ Have you assisted the principal contractor in preparing the construction phase plan by providing all the information that is relevant to the construction phase plan? *Reg. 12(3)*
- ☐ Have you prepared a preliminary health and safety file? *Reg. 12(5)*
- ☐ Have you applied the general principles of prevention to the design work, taking into account the health and safety file and the construction phase plan? If the answer is no, refer to Schedule 1 to the Management of Health and Safety at Work Regulations 1999. *Reg. 11(2)*
- ☐ Have you taken account of the general principles of prevention when deciding design, technical and organisational aspects as part of the planning and management of the pre-construction and construction work and estimating the periods of time for completing the items or stages of work? *Reg. 11(2)*
- ☐ Have you identified the foreseeable hazards at the construction site before, during and after the construction phase and, in particular, the associated risks to the health and safety of persons carrying out, or liable to be affected by, construction work, maintaining or cleaning the structure, or using the structure as a workplace? *Reg. 11(3)*
- ☐ Have you eliminated the foreseeable risks in the previous item or taken steps to control the risks? If the answer is no, you must take steps to reduce or control the risks through the design process, and provide the relevant information to the other designers and contractors as appropriate. *Reg. 11(3)*

Construction phase

- ☐ Have you, following the appointment of the principal contractor, established a procedure for liaising with the principal contractor for the duration of your appointment? *Reg. 11(7)*
- ☐ Have you shared the information with the principal contractor which they need for the planning, management and monitoring of the construction phase and the coordination of health and safety matters? *Reg. 11(7)*
- ☐ Have you received information from the principal contractor for inclusion in the health and safety file? *Reg. 12(7)*

☐ Have you ensured that the health and safety file is reviewed, updated and revised to take account of the work and any changes that have occurred, particularly in the construction phase? *Reg. 12(6)*

Post-construction

☐ Have you passed the health and safety file to the client or to the principal contractor, if appropriate? *Reg. 12(10) or 12(8)*

Designer

Appointment

☐ Have you assessed your skills, knowledge and experience to perform the required duties for the project? *Reg. 8(1)*

☐ If you employ more than one designer, do you have the organisational capacity to perform the required duties for the project? *Reg. 8(1)*

☐ If your answer is no to either 1 or 2 above, you must not accept the appointment. *Reg. 8(2)*

☐ Have you checked the skills, knowledge and experience of any sub-designers working for you and their organisational capabilities if appropriate? *Reg. 8(3)*

☐ Is there likely to be more than one contractor? If your answer is yes, are you the designer appointed as the principal designer? *Reg. 5(1)(a)*

☐ If you are the principal designer, go to the checklist for a principal designer.

☐ Have you identified the principal designer if you are not the principal designer?

☐ If the client is a domestic client, has the client appointed you as the principal designer? *Reg. 7(1)(c)*

☐ If the client is a domestic client and has not appointed a principal designer or principal contractor, are you in control of the pre-construction phase of the project? If the answer is yes, go to the checklist for a principal designer.

Pre-construction design work

- ☐ Have you satisfied yourself that the client is aware if their duties under the CDM Regulations? You must only start the design work on the project if you are satisfied that the client is aware of their duties. *Reg. 9(1)*

- ☐ Have you identified the duty holders with whom you must cooperate if they make known a need for your cooperation? *Reg. 8(4)*

- ☐ Have you received the pre-construction information from the principal designer? If the answer is no, you must ask for the pre-construction information from the principal designer. *Reg. 11(6)(b)*

- ☐ Have you applied the general principles of prevention to the design work? If the answer is no, refer to Schedule 1 to the Management of Health and Safety at Work Regulations 1999.

- ☐ Have you identified the foreseeable hazards at the construction site before, during and after the construction phase, and, in particular, the associated risks to the health and safety of persons carrying out, or liable to be affected by, construction work, maintaining or cleaning the structure, or using the structure as a workplace? *Reg. 9(2)*

- ☐ Have you eliminated the foreseeable risks in the previous entry? If the answer is no, you must take steps to reduce or control the risks through the design process, provide the relevant information to the principal designer and ensure that the information is included in the health and safety file. *Reg. 9(3)*

- ☐ Have you provided sufficient information without delay about the design, construction or maintenance of the structure to the following duty holders to assist them in their duties? *Reg. 8(6)*
  - the client
  - the principal designer
  - other designers
  - the principal contractor
  - the contractor.

- ☐ Have you commissioned the preparation or modification of design work outside Great Britain? If the answer is yes, you must ensure that regulation 9 is complied with.

Construction phase

☐ Have you been appointed by a contractor for design? If the answer is yes, you must comply with regulation 9 and provide information to the principal designer for the permanent works to be included in the health and safety file. *Reg. 9(3)(b)*

Post-construction

☐ Have you ensured that the appropriate information about the control of risks that could not be eliminated have been included in the health and safety file? *Reg. 9(3)(c)*

Principal contractor

Appointment

- ☐ Have you assessed your skills, knowledge and experience to plan, manage and monitor the pre-construction phase and coordinate matters relating to health and safety during the construction phase, to perform the required duties for the project? *Reg. 8(1), 13(1)*
- ☐ If you employ more than one worker, do you have the organisational capacity to perform the required duties for the project? *Reg. 8(1)*
- ☐ If your answer is no to either 1 or 2 above, you must not accept the appointment. *Reg. 8(2)*
- ☐ If you are also a contractor carrying out, managing or controlling construction work, go to the checklist for a contractor.

Pre-construction design work

- ☐ Have you an obligation to prepare a design for your own construction work or have you to modify the design work of others? If the answer is yes, go to the checklist for a designer.
- ☐ Have you made arrangements for the planning, management and monitoring of the construction phase and coordinating all matters relating to health and safety? *Reg. 13(1)*
- ☐ Have you applied the general principles of prevention to the planning, management and monitoring of the construction phase? If the answer is no, refer to Schedule 1 to the Management of Health and Safety at Work Regulations 1999. *Reg. 13(2)*
- ☐ Have you taken account of the general principles of prevention when deciding design, technical and organisational aspects as part of the planning, management and monitoring of the construction work and estimating the periods of time for completing the items or stages of work? *Reg. 13(2)*
- ☐ Have you shared with the principal designer the information relevant to the planning, management and coordination of all health and safety matters during the pre-construction phase? *Reg. 13(5)*

☐ Have you identified the duty holders with whom you must cooperate if they make known a need for your cooperation? *Reg. 8(4)*

Construction phase plan

☐ Have you drawn up a construction phase plan, or made arrangements to do so, before setting up the construction site? *Reg. 12(1)*

☐ Have you set out a procedure for cooperation between the contractors and the coordination of their construction work and adherence to the construction phase plan? *Reg. 13(3)(a), (b)*

☐ Have you included all the health and safety arrangements and site rules in the construction phase plan, taking particular account of the categories of work listed in Schedule 3 to the CDM Regulations? *Reg. 12(2)*

☐ Have you received from the principal designer information in their possession relevant to the preparation of the construction phase plan, notably the pre-construction information and design information? *Reg. 12(3)*

Construction phase

☐ Have you implemented the arrangements to review, update and revise the construction phase plan? *Reg. 12(4)*

☐ Have you implemented the organisational arrangements to plan, manage and monitor the construction phase? *Reg. 13(1)*

☐ Have you organised to ensure that the other contractors will apply the general principles of prevention in a consistent manner, particularly when complying with Part 4 of the CDM Regulations? *Reg. 13(3)(c)*

☐ Have you made arrangements to ensure that a suitable site induction is provided for all workers and visitors to the site, that the site is secure and that the minimum welfare facilities are provided throughout the construction phase? *Reg. 13(4)*

☐ Have you, following your appointment, established a procedure for liaising with the principal designer for the duration of the principal designer's appointment? *Reg. 13(5)*

Consultation with workers

- [ ] Have you made arrangements to enable all workers on the site to cooperate with each other and with you to develop, promote and check the effectiveness of the health, safety and welfare procedures for all workers? *Reg. 14(a)*

- [ ] Have you consulted workers, or their representatives, in good time on health, safety and welfare matters connected with the project that may affect them? *Reg. 14(b)*

- [ ] Have you ensured that the workers and their representatives have copies of, or access to, all information in your possession or that you should have received under the CDM Regulations, subject to the exceptions in paragraphs (c)(i) to (v) of regulation 14. *Reg. 14(c)*

Post-construction

- [ ] Have you received the health and safety file from the principal designer before completion of the construction phase? If the answer is yes, you must keep it under review and update it and revise it until the end of the construction phase, when you must complete the health and safety file and pass it to the client. *Reg. 12(9), (10)*

Contractor

Appointment

- ☐ Have you assessed your skills, knowledge and experience to perform the required duties for the project? *Reg. 8(1)*
- ☐ If you employ more than one worker, do you have the organisational capacity to carry out the required duties for the project? *Reg. 8(1)*
- ☐ If your answer is no to either 1 or 2 above, you must not accept the appointment. *Reg. 8(2)*
- ☐ Have you reason to assume that you are the sole contractor who will be carrying out construction work? If you intend to appoint one or more sub-contractors, you will be the principal contractor. If the answer is yes, go to the principal contractor checklist.
- ☐ Have you checked the skills, knowledge and experience of any sub-contractors working for you and their organisational capabilities if appropriate? *Reg. 8(3)*
- ☐ Have you satisfied yourself that the client is aware if their duties under the CDM Regulations? You must only start construction work if you are satisfied that the client is aware of their duties. *Reg. 15(1)*

Pre-construction design and planning work

- ☐ Have you an obligation to prepare a design for your own construction work or have you to modify the design work of others? If the answer is yes, go to the checklist for a designer.
- ☐ Have you planned the construction work to ensure that, so far as is reasonably practicable, it will be carried out without risks to health and safety? *Reg. 15(2)*
- ☐ Have you identified the duty holders with whom you must cooperate if they make known a need for your cooperation? *Reg. 8(4)*

If you are a sole contractor

☐	Have you taken account, as a sole contractor, of the general principles of prevention when deciding design, technical and organisational aspects as part of the planning and management of the construction work and estimating the periods of time for completing the construction phase?	*Reg. 15(4)*
☐	Have you drawn up a construction phase plan, or made arrangements to do so, which complies with regulation 12(2)?	*Reg. 15(5), (6)*
☐	Have you provided or made arrangements for the minimum welfare facilities?	*Reg. 15(11), Schedule 2*

Construction workers

☐	Have you taken steps to ensure that persons working for you are competent, possessing the necessary skills, knowledge, training and experience to carry out the tasks without risk to any person's health and safety?	*Reg. 15(7)*
☐	Have you made arrangements for, and provided to each worker, appropriate supervision, instruction and information so that the tasks can be carried out without risks to health and safety?	*Reg. (8)*
☐	Have you ensured that the information for workers includes a suitable site induction, procedures in the event of serious and imminent danger to health and safety, other contractor's activities that might be a risk to health and safety, risk assessments and any other relevant information?	*Reg. 15(9)*

Construction phase

☐	You must not start work without being satisfied that the client is aware of their duties under the CDM Regulations and that the site has been secured from unauthorised access.	*Reg. 15(1), 15(10)*
☐	Have you made arrangements so that the construction work will be managed and monitored to ensure it will be carried out without risks to health and safety?	*Reg. 15(2), 15(4), if appropriate*
☐	Have you made arrangements for cooperation and coordination of your construction work with others and especially the receipt and processing of directions given by the principal designer and the principal contractor?	*Reg. 15(3)(a)*

☐	Have you planned your construction work such that it complies with the construction phase plan?	*Reg. 15(3)(b)*

Have you

☐	made arrangements for suitable and sufficient safe access to and egress from the construction site?	*Reg. 17(1), (2), (3)*
☐	ensured that there is sufficient working space?	*Reg. 17(4)*
☐	arranged for keeping the site in good order?	*Reg. 18(1)*
☐	provided adequate fencing to the perimeter of the site to make it secure?	*Reg. 18(2)*
☐	prohibited timber or other materials having projecting sharp nails that would be a danger to any person?	*Reg. 18(3)*
☐	ensured that new or existing structures are stable and secure against collapse?	*Reg. 19*
☐	planned and recorded in writing the arrangements for demolition or dismantling?	*Reg. 20*
☐	made arrangements for the safe use, storage and transport of explosives?	*Reg. 21*
☐	taken all practical steps to make safe any excavation and appointed a competent inspector?	*Reg. 22, 24*
☐	designed the cofferdam or caisson to be a safe working environment and appointed a competent inspector?	*Reg. 23, 24*
☐	suitably located energy distribution installations, ensuring that they are safe, periodically checked and clearly indicated?	*Reg. 25*
☐	taken precautions to avoid persons falling into water or other liquids?	*Reg. 26(1)*
☐	made arrangements for safe transport for any person conveyed by water?	*Reg. 26(2), (3)*
☐	organised transport routes so that, so far as is reasonably practicable, pedestrians and vehicles can move without risk to health and safety?	*Reg. 27*
☐	made arrangements to prevent or control the unintended movement of any vehicle?	*Reg. 28*

- ☐ made arrangements to prevent, so far as is reasonably practicable, the risk of injury to any person arising from fire, explosion, flooding or any substance liable to cause asphyxiation? *Reg. 29*
- ☐ provided a sufficient number of suitable emergency routes and exits in the event of any danger? *Reg. 31*
- ☐ provided suitable and sufficient fire-fighting equipment and fire detection and alarm systems? *Reg. 32*
  made arrangements to ensure, so far as is reasonably practicable, that there is a supply of fresh or purified air to every part of the site? *Reg. 33*
- ☐ made arrangements for the protection of workers from adverse weather conditions or a reasonable working temperature if working indoors? *Reg. 34*
- ☐ provided suitable and sufficient lighting at the construction site and its approach and on traffic routes? *Reg. 35*

CDM Regulations 2015 Explained
ISBN 978-0-7277-5739-5

http://dx.doi.org/10.1680/icsiam.57395.197

Appendix 2
Construction (Design and Management) Regulations 2015

PART 1 – Introduction

Regulation 1 Citation and commencement

These Regulations may be cited as the Construction (Design and Management) Regulations 2015 and come into force on 6th April 2015 immediately after the Mines Regulations 2014(**e**).

Regulation 2 Interpretation

(1) In these Regulations—

"the 1974 Act" means the Health and Safety at Work etc. Act 1974;

"the 2007 Regulations" means the Construction (Design and Management) Regulations 2007(**a**);

"the Management Regulations" means the Management of Health and Safety at Work Regulations 1999(**b**);

"business" means a trade, business or other undertaking (whether for profit or not);

"client" means any person for whom a project is carried out;

"construction phase" means the period of time beginning when construction work in a project starts and ending when construction work in that project is completed;

"construction phase plan" means a plan drawn up under regulations 12 or 15;

"construction site" includes any place where construction work is being carried out or to which the workers have access, but does not include a workplace within the site which is set aside for purposes other than construction work;

(**e**) S.I. 2014//3248.

(**a**) S.I. 2007/320, as amended by S.I. 2012/632, 2013/1471, 2013/1666 and 2014/469.

(**b**) S.I. 1999/3242, as amended by S.I. 2003/2457, 2007/320, 2010/93 and 2013/1667. S.I. 2005/1541 amends the instruments in relation to England and Wales and S.S.I. 2006/457 in relation to Scotland.

"construction work" means the carrying out of any building, civil engineering or engineering construction work and includes—

(a) the construction, alteration, conversion, fitting out, commissioning, renovation, repair, upkeep, redecoration or other maintenance (including cleaning which involves the use of water or an abrasive at high pressure, or the use of corrosive or toxic substances), de-commissioning, demolition or dismantling of a structure;

(b) the preparation for an intended structure, including site clearance, exploration, investigation (but not site survey) and excavation (but not pre-construction archaeological investigations), and the clearance or preparation of the site or structure for use or occupation at its conclusion;

(c) the assembly on site of prefabricated elements to form a structure or the disassembly on site of the prefabricated elements which, immediately before such disassembly, formed a structure;

(d) the removal of a structure, or of any product or waste resulting from demolition or dismantling of a structure, or from disassembly of prefabricated elements which immediately before such disassembly formed such a structure;

(e) the installation, commissioning, maintenance, repair or removal of mechanical, electrical, gas, compressed air, hydraulic, telecommunications, computer or similar services which are normally fixed within or to a structure,

but does not include the exploration for, or extraction of, mineral resources, or preparatory activities carried out at a place where such exploration or extraction is carried out;

"contractor" means any person (including a non-domestic client) who, in the course or furtherance of a business, carries out, manages or controls construction work;

"design" includes drawings, design details, specifications and bills of quantities (including specification of articles or substances) relating to a structure, and calculations prepared for the purpose of a design;

"designer" means any person (including a client, contractor or other person referred to in these Regulations) who in the course or furtherance of a business—

(a) prepares or modifies a design; or

(b) arranges for, or instructs, any person under their control to do so,

relating to a structure, or to a product or mechanical or electrical system intended for a particular structure, and a person is deemed to prepare a design where a design is prepared by a person under their control;

"domestic client" means a client for whom a project is being carried out which is not in the course or furtherance of a business of that client;

"excavation" includes any earthwork, trench, well, shaft, tunnel or underground working;

"the general principles of prevention" means the general principles of prevention specified in Schedule 1 to the Management Regulations;

"health and safety file" means a file prepared under regulation 12(5);

"inspector for the Executive" means an inspector within the meaning given in section 53(1) of the 1974 Act(**a**);

"loading bay" means any facility for loading or unloading;

"place of work" means any place which is used by any person at work for the purposes of construction work or for the purposes of any activity arising out of or in connection with construction work;

"pre-construction information" means information in the client's possession or which is reasonably obtainable by or on behalf of the client, which is relevant to the construction work and is of an appropriate level of detail and proportionate to the risks involved, including—

(a) information about—

(i) the project;

(ii) planning and management of the project;

(iii) health and safety hazards, including design and construction hazards and how they will be addressed; and

(b) information in any existing health and safety file;

"pre-construction phase" means any period of time during which design or preparatory work is carried out for a project and may continue during the construction phase;

"principal contractor" means the contractor appointed under regulation 5(1)(b) to perform specified duties in regulations 12 to 14;

"principal designer" means the designer appointed under regulation 5(1)(a) to perform specified duties in regulations 11 and 12;

"project" means a project which includes or is intended to include construction work and includes all planning, design, management or other work involved in a project until the end of the construction phase;

"site rules" means rules which are drawn up for a particular construction site and are necessary for health or safety purposes;

"structure" means—

(a) any building, timber, masonry, metal or reinforced concrete structure, railway line or siding, tramway line, dock, harbour, inland navigation, tunnel, shaft, bridge, viaduct, waterworks, reservoir, pipe or pipeline, cable, aqueduct, sewer, sewage works, gasholder, road, airfield, sea defence works, river works, drainage works, earthworks, lagoon, dam, wall, caisson, mast, tower, pylon,

(**a**) There are amendments to section 53(1) of the 1974 Act but none is relevant.

underground tank, earth retaining structure or structure designed to preserve or alter any natural feature and fixed plant;

(b) any structure similar to anything specified in paragraph (a);

(c) any formwork, falsework, scaffold or other structure designed or used to provide support or means of access during construction work,

and any reference to a structure includes part of a structure;

"traffic route" means a route for pedestrian traffic or for vehicles and includes any doorway, gateway, loading bay or ramp;

"vehicle" includes any mobile work equipment;

"work equipment" means any machinery, appliance, apparatus, tool or installation for use at work (whether exclusively or not);

"working day" means any day on which construction work takes place;

"workplace" means a workplace within the meaning of regulation 2(1) of the Workplace (Health, Safety and Welfare) Regulations 1992(**a**) other than a construction site.

(2) Any reference in these Regulations to a plan, rule, document, report or copy includes a copy or electronic version which is —

(a) capable of being retrieved or reproduced when required; and

(b) secure from loss or unauthorised interference.

Regulation 3 Application in and outside Great Britain

These Regulations apply—

(a) in Great Britain; and

(b) to premises and activities outside Great Britain to which sections 1 to 59 and 80 to 82 of the 1974 Act apply by virtue of articles 9 and 11(1)(a) of the Health and Safety at Work etc. Act 1974 (Application outside Great Britain) Order 2013(**b**).

PART 2 – Client duties

Regulation 4 Client duties in relation to managing projects

(1) A client must make suitable arrangements for managing a project, including the allocation of sufficient time and other resources.

(2) Arrangements are suitable if they ensure that—

(a) the construction work can be carried out, so far as is reasonably practicable, without risks to the health or safety of any person affected by the project; and

---

(**a**) S.I. 1992/3004; the definition of "workplace" in regulation 2(1) was amended by S.I. 2002/2174.

(**b**) S.I. 2013/240.

(b) the facilities required by Schedule 2 are provided in respect of any person carrying out construction work.

(3) A client must ensure that these arrangements are maintained and reviewed throughout the project.

(4) A client must provide pre-construction information as soon as is practicable to every designer and contractor appointed, or being considered for appointment, to the project.

(5) A client must ensure that—

(a) before the construction phase begins, a construction phase plan is drawn up by the contractor if there is only one contractor, or by the principal contractor; and

(b) the principal designer prepares a health and safety file for the project, which—

(i) complies with the requirements of regulation 12(5);

(ii) is revised from time to time as appropriate to incorporate any relevant new information; and

(iii) is kept available for inspection by any person who may need it to comply with the relevant legal requirements.

(6) A client must take reasonable steps to ensure that—

(a) the principal designer complies with any other principal designer duties in regulations 11 and 12; and

(b) the principal contractor complies with any other principal contractor duties in regulations 12 to 14;

(7) If a client disposes of the client's interest in the structure, the client complies with the duty in paragraph (5)(b)(iii) by providing the health and safety file to the person who acquires the client's interest in the structure and ensuring that that person is aware of the nature and purpose of the file.

(8) Where there is more than one client in relation to a project—

(a) one or more of the clients may agree in writing to be treated for the purposes of these Regulations as the only client or clients; and

(b) except for the duties specified in sub-paragraph (c) only the client or clients agreed in paragraph (a) are subject to the duties owed by a client under these Regulations;

(c) the duties in the following provisions are owed by all clients—

(i) regulation 8(4); and

(ii) paragraph (4) and regulation 8(6) to the extent that those duties relate to information in the possession of the client.

Regulation 5 Appointment of the principal designer and the principal contractor

(1) Where there is more than one contractor, or if it is reasonably foreseeable that more than one contractor will be working on a project at any time, the client must appoint in writing—

(a) a designer with control over the pre-construction phase as principal designer; and

(b) a contractor as principal contractor.

(2) The appointments must be made as soon as is practicable, and, in any event, before the construction phase begins.

(3) If the client fails to appoint a principal designer, the client must fulfil the duties of the principal designer in regulations 11 and 12.

(4) If the client fails to appoint a principal contractor, the client must fulfil the duties of the principal contractor in regulations 12 to 14.

Regulation 6 Notification

(1) A project is notifiable if the construction work on a construction site is scheduled to—

(a) last longer than 30 working days and have more than 20 workers working simultaneously at any point in the project; or

(b) exceed 500 person days.

(2) Where a project is notifiable, the client must give notice in writing to the Executive as soon as is practicable before the construction phase begins.

(3) The notice must—

(a) contain the particulars specified in Schedule 1;

(b) be clearly displayed in the construction site office in a comprehensible form where it can be read by any worker engaged in the construction work; and

(c) if necessary, be periodically updated.

(4) Where a project includes construction work of a description for which the Office of Rail Regulation is the enforcing authority by virtue of regulation 3 of the Health and Safety (Enforcing Authority for Railways and Other Guided Transport Systems) Regulations 2006 (**a**), the client must give notice to the Office of Rail Regulation instead of the Executive.

(5) Where a project includes construction work on premises which are or are on—

(a) a GB nuclear site (within the meaning given in section 68 of the Energy Act 2013)(**b**);

(**a**) S.I. 2006/557. Regulation 3 was amended by S.I. 2007/1573 and 2014/469.

(**b**) 2013 c.32.

(b) an authorised defence site (within the meaning given in regulation 2(1) or the Health and Safety (Enforcing Authority) Regulations 1998)(**c**); or

(c) a new nuclear build site (within the meaning given in regulation 2A of those Regulations),

the client must give notice to the Office for Nuclear Regulation instead of the Executive.

Regulation 7 Application to domestic clients

(1) Where the client is a domestic client the duties in regulations 4(1) to (7) and 6 must be carried out by—

(a) the contractor for a project where there is only one contractor;

(b) the principal contractor for a project where there is more than one contractor; or

(c) the principal designer where there is a written agreement that the principal designer will fulfil those duties.

(2) If a domestic client fails to make the appointments required by regulation 5—

(a) the designer in control of the pre-construction phase of the project is the principal designer;

(b) the contractor in control of the construction phase of the project is the principal contractor.

(3) Regulation 5(3) and (4) does not apply to a domestic client.

PART 3 – Health and safety duties and roles

Regulation 8 General duties

(1) A designer (including a principal designer) or contractor (including a principal contractor) appointed to work on a project must have the skills, knowledge and experience, and, if they are an organisation, the organisational capability, necessary to fulfil the role that they are appointed to undertake, in a manner that secures the health and safety of any person affected by the project.

(2) A designer or contractor must not accept an appointment to a project unless they fulfil the conditions in paragraph (1).

(3) A person who is responsible for appointing a designer or contractor to carry out work on a project must take reasonable steps to satisfy themselves that the designer or contractor fulfils the conditions in paragraph (1).

(4) A person with a duty or function under these Regulations must cooperate with any other person working on or in relation to a project, at the same or an

(**c**) S.I. 1998/494. The definition of "authorised defence site" was inserted in regulation 2(1), and new regulation 2A was inserted into the Regulations, by S.I. 2014/469.

adjoining construction site, to the extent necessary to enable any person with a duty or function to fulfil that duty or function.

(5) A person working on a project under the control of another must report to that person anything they are aware of in relation to the project which is likely to endanger their own health or safety or that of others.

(6) Any person who is required by these Regulations to provide information or instruction must ensure the information or instruction is comprehensible and provided as soon as is practicable.

(7) To the extent that they are applicable to a domestic client, the duties in paragraphs (3), (4) and (6) must be carried out by the person specified in regulation 7(1).

Regulation 9 Duties of designers

(1) A designer must not commence work in relation to a project unless satisfied that the client is aware of the duties owed by the client under these Regulations.

(2) When preparing or modifying a design the designer must take into account the general principles of prevention and any pre-construction information to eliminate, so far as is reasonably practicable, foreseeable risks to the health or safety of any person—

(a) carrying out or liable to be affected by construction work;

(b) maintaining or cleaning a structure; or

(c) using a structure designed as a workplace.

(3) If it is not possible to eliminate these risks, the designer must, so far as is reasonably practicable—

(a) take steps to reduce or, if that is not possible, control the risks through the subsequent design process;

(b) provide information about those risks to the principal designer; and

(c) ensure appropriate information is included in the health and safety file.

(4) A designer must take all reasonable steps to provide, with the design, sufficient information about the design, construction or maintenance of the structure, to adequately assist the client, other designers and contractors to comply with their duties under these Regulations.

Regulation 10 Designs prepared or modified outside Great Britain

(1) Where a design is prepared or modified outside Great Britain for use in construction work to which these Regulations apply—

(a) the person who commissions it, if established within Great Britain; or

(b) if that person is not so established, the client for the project,

must ensure that regulation 9 is complied with.

(2) This regulation does not apply to a domestic client.

Regulation 11 Duties of a principal designer in relation to health and safety at the pre-construction phase

(1) The principal designer must plan, manage and monitor the pre-construction phase and coordinate matters relating to health and safety during the pre-construction phase to ensure that, so far as is reasonably practicable, the project is carried out without risks to health or safety.

(2) In fulfilling the duties in paragraph (1), and in particular when—

(a) design, technical and organisational aspects are being decided in order to plan the various items or stages of work which are to take place simultaneously or in succession; and

(b) estimating the period of time required to complete such work or work stages,

the principal designer must take into account the general principles of prevention and, where relevant, the content of any construction phase plan and health and safety file.

(3) In fulfilling the duties in paragraph (1), the principal designer must identify and eliminate or control, so far as is reasonably practicable, foreseeable risks to the health or safety of any person—

(a) carrying out or liable to be affected by construction work;

(b) maintaining or cleaning a structure; or

(c) using a structure designed as a workplace.

(4) In fulfilling the duties in paragraph (1), the principal designer must ensure all designers comply with their duties in regulation 9.

(5) In fulfilling the duty to coordinate health and safety matters in paragraph (1), the principal designer must ensure that all persons working in relation to the pre-construction phase cooperate with the client, the principal designer and each other.

(6) The principal designer must—

(a) assist the client in the provision of the pre-construction information required by regulation 4(4); and

(b) so far as it is within the principal designer's control, provide pre-construction information, promptly and in a convenient form, to every designer and contractor appointed, or being considered for appointment, to the project.

(7) The principal designer must liaise with the principal contractor for the duration of the principal designer's appointment and share with the principal contractor information relevant to the planning, management and monitoring of the construction phase and the coordination of health and safety matters during the construction phase.

Regulation 12 Construction phase plan and health and safety file

(1) During the pre-construction phase, and before setting up a construction site, the principal contractor must draw up a construction phase plan, or make arrangements for a construction phase plan to be drawn up.

(2) The construction phase plan must set out the health and safety arrangements and site rules taking account, where necessary, of the industrial activities taking place on the construction site and, where applicable, must include specific measures concerning work which falls within one or more of the categories set out in Schedule 3.

(3) The principal designer must assist the principal contractor in preparing the construction phase plan by providing to the principal contractor all information the principal designer holds that is relevant to the construction phase plan including—

(a) pre-construction information obtained from the client;

(b) any information obtained from designers under regulation 9(3)(b).

(4) Throughout the project the principal contractor must ensure that the construction phase plan is appropriately reviewed, updated and revised from time to time so that it continues to be sufficient to ensure that construction work is carried out, so far as is reasonably practicable, without risks to health or safety.

(5) During the pre-construction phase, the principal designer must prepare a health and safety file appropriate to the characteristics of the project which must contain information relating to the project which is likely to be needed during any subsequent project to ensure the health and safety of any person.

(6) The principal designer must ensure that the health and safety file is appropriately reviewed, updated and revised from time to time to take account of the work and any changes that have occurred.

(7) During the project, the principal contractor must provide the principal designer with any information in the principal contractor's possession relevant to the health and safety file, for inclusion in the health and safety file.

(8) If the principal designer's appointment concludes before the end of the project, the principal designer must pass the health and safety file to the principal contractor.

(9) Where the health and safety file is passed to the principal contractor under paragraph (8), the principal contractor must ensure that the health and safety file is appropriately reviewed, updated and revised from time to time to take account of the work and any changes that have occurred.

(10) At the end of the project, the principal designer, or where there is no principal designer the principal contractor, must pass the health and safety file to the client.

Regulation 13 Duties of a principal contractor in relation to health and safety at the construction phase

(1) The principal contractor must plan, manage and monitor the construction phase and coordinate matters relating to health and safety during the construction phase to ensure that, so far as is reasonably practicable, construction work is carried out without risks to health or safety.

(2) In fulfilling the duties in paragraph (1), and in particular when—

(a) design, technical and organisational aspects are being decided in order to plan the various items or stages of work which are to take place simultaneously or in succession; and

(b) estimating the period of time required to complete the work or work stages,

the principal contractor must take into account the general principles of prevention.

(3) The principal contractor must—

(a) organise cooperation between contractors (including successive contractors on the same construction site):

(b) coordinate implementation by the contractors of applicable legal requirements for health and safety; and

(c) ensure that employers and, if necessary for the protection of workers, self-employed persons—

(i) apply the general principles of prevention in a consistent manner, and in particular when complying with the provisions of Part 4; and

(ii) where required, follow the construction phase plan.

(4) The principal contractor must ensure that—

(a) a suitable site induction is provided;

(b) the necessary steps are taken to prevent access by unauthorised persons to the construction site; and

(c) facilities that comply with the requirements of Schedule 2 are provided throughout the construction phase.

(5) The principal contractor must liaise with the principal designer for the duration of the principal designer's appointment and share with the principal designer information relevant to the planning, management and monitoring of the pre-construction phase and the coordination of health and safety matters during the pre-construction phase.

Regulation 14 Principal contractor's duties to consult and engage with workers

The principal contractor must—

(a) make and maintain arrangements which will enable the principal contractor and workers engaged in construction work to cooperate effectively in developing, promoting and checking the effectiveness of measures to ensure the health, safety and welfare of the workers;

(b) consult those workers or their representatives in good time on matters connected with the project which may affect their health, safety or welfare, in so far as they or their representatives have not been similarly consulted by their employer;

(c) ensure that those workers or their representatives can inspect and take copies of any information which the principal contractor has, or which these Regulations require to be provided to the principal contractor, which relate to the health, safety or welfare of workers at the site, except any information—

  (i) the disclosure of which would be against the interests of national security;

  (ii) which the principal contractor could not disclose without contravening a prohibition imposed by or under an enactment;

  (iii) relating specifically to an individual, unless that individual has consented to its being disclosed;

  (iv) the disclosure of which would, for reasons other than its effect on health, safety or welfare at work, cause substantial injury to the principal contractor's undertaking or, where the information was supplied to the principal contractor by another person, to the undertaking of that other person;

  (v) obtained by the principal contractor for the purpose of bringing, prosecuting or defending any legal proceedings.

Regulation 15 Duties of contractors

(1) A contractor must not carry out construction work in relation to a project unless satisfied that the client is aware of the duties owed by the client under these Regulations.

(2) A contractor must plan, manage and monitor construction work carried out either by the contractor or by workers under the contractor's control, to ensure that, so far as is reasonably practicable, it is carried out without risks to health and safety.

(3) Where there is more than one contractor working on a project, a contractor must comply with—

  (a) any directions given by the principal designer or the principal contractor; and

  (b) the parts of the construction phase plan that are relevant to that contractor's work on the project.

(4) If there is only one contractor working on the project, the contractor must take account of the general principles of prevention when—

(a) design, technical and organisational aspects are being decided in order to plan the various items or stages of work which are to take place simultaneously or in succession; and

(b) estimating the period of time required to complete the work or work stages.

(5) If there is only one contractor working on the project, the contractor must draw up a construction phase plan, or make arrangements for a construction phase plan to be drawn up, as soon as is practicable prior to setting up a construction site.

(6) The construction phase plan must fulfil the requirements of regulation 12(2).

(7) A contractor must not employ or appoint a person to work on a construction site unless that person has, or is in the process of obtaining, the necessary skills, knowledge, training and experience to carry out the tasks allocated to that person in a manner that secures the health and safety of any person working on the construction site.

(8) A contractor must provide each worker under their control with appropriate supervision, instructions and information so that construction work can be carried out, so far as is reasonably practicable, without risks to health and safety.

(9) The information provided must include—

(a) a suitable site induction, where not already provided by the principal contractor;

(b) the procedures to be followed in the event of serious and imminent danger to health and safety;

(c) information on risks to health and safety—

(i) identified by the risk assessment under regulation 3 of the Management Regulations; or

(ii) arising out of the conduct of another contractor's undertaking and of which the contractor in control of the worker ought reasonably to be aware; and

(d) any other information necessary to enable the worker to comply with the relevant statutory provisions.

(10) A contractor must not begin work on a construction site unless reasonable steps have been taken to prevent access by unauthorised persons to that site.

(11) A contractor must ensure, so far as is reasonably practicable, that the requirements of Schedule 2 are complied with so far as they affect the contractor or any worker under that contractor's control.

PART 4 – General requirements for all construction sites

Regulation 16 Application of Part 4

(1) This Part applies only to a construction site.

(2) A contractor carrying out construction work must comply with the requirements of this Part so far as they affect the contractor or any worker under the control of the contractor or relate to matters within the contractor's control.

(3) A domestic client who controls the way in which any construction work is carried out by a person at work must comply with the requirements of this Part so far as they relate to matters within the client's control.

Regulation 17 Safe places of construction work

(1) There must, so far as is reasonably practicable, be suitable and sufficient safe access and egress from—

  (a) every construction site to every other place provided for the use of any person whilst at work; and

  (b) every place construction work is being carried out to every other place to which workers have access within a construction site.

(2) A construction site must be, so far as is reasonably practicable, made and kept safe for, and without risks to, the health of a person at work there.

(3) Action must be taken to ensure, so far as is reasonably practicable, that no person uses access to or egress from or gains access to any construction site which does not comply with the requirements of paragraph (1) or (2).

(4) A construction site must, so far as is reasonably practicable, have sufficient working space and be arranged so that it is suitable for any person who is working or who is likely to work there, taking account of any necessary work equipment likely to be used there.

Regulation 18 Good order and site security

(1) Each part of a construction site must, so far as is reasonably practicable, be kept in good order and those parts in which construction work is being carried out must be kept in a reasonable state of cleanliness.

(2) Where necessary in the interests of health and safety, a construction site must, so far as is reasonably practicable, and in accordance with the level of risk posed, comply with either or both of the following—

  (a) have its perimeter identified by suitable signs and be arranged so that its extent is readily identifiable; or

  (b) be fenced off.

(3) No timber or other material with projecting nails (or similar sharp object) must—

(a) be used in any construction work; or

(b) be allowed to remain in any place,

if the nails (or similar sharp object) may be a source of danger to any person.

Regulation 19 Stability of structures

(1) All practicable steps must be taken, where necessary to prevent danger to any person, to ensure that any new or existing structure does not collapse if, due to the carrying out of construction work, it—

(a) may become unstable; or

(b) is in a temporary state of weakness or instability.

(2) Any buttress, temporary support or temporary structure must—

(a) be of such design and installed and maintained so as to withstand any foreseeable loads which may be imposed on it; and

(b) only be used for the purposes for which it was designed and installed and is maintained.

(3) A structure must not be so loaded as to render it unsafe to any person.

Regulation 20 Demolition or dismantling

(1) The demolition or dismantling of a structure must be planned and carried out in such a manner as to prevent danger or, where it is not practicable to prevent it, to reduce danger to as low a level as is reasonably practicable.

(2) The arrangements for carrying out such demolition or dismantling must be recorded in writing before the demolition or dismantling work begins.

Regulation 21 Explosives

(1) So far as is reasonably practicable, explosives must be stored, transported and used safely and securely.

(2) An explosive charge may be used or fired only if suitable and sufficient steps have been taken to ensure that no person is exposed to risk of injury from the explosion or from projected or flying material caused by the explosion.

Regulation 22 Excavations

(1) All practicable steps must be taken to prevent danger to any person, including, where necessary, the provision of supports or battering, to ensure that—

(a) no excavation or part of an excavation collapses;

(b) no material forming the walls or roof of, or adjacent to, any excavation is dislodged or falls; and

(c) no person is buried or trapped in an excavation by material which is dislodged or falls.

(2) Suitable and sufficient steps must be taken to prevent any person, work equipment, or any accumulation of material from falling into any excavation.

(3) Suitable and sufficient steps must be taken, where necessary, to prevent any part of an excavation or ground adjacent to it from being overloaded by work equipment or material.

(4) Construction work must not be carried out in an excavation where any supports or battering have been provided in accordance with paragraph (1) unless—

(a) the excavation and any work equipment and materials which may affect its safety have been inspected by a competent person—

(i) at the start of the shift in which the work is to be carried out;

(ii) after any event likely to have affected the strength or stability of the excavation; and

(iii) after any material unintentionally falls or is dislodged; and

(b) the person who carried out the inspection is satisfied that construction work can be safely carried out there.

(5) Where the person carrying out an inspection informs the person on whose behalf the inspection is carried out of any matter about which they are not satisfied (under regulation 24(1)), construction work must not be carried out in the excavation until the matter has been satisfactorily remedied.

Regulation 23 Cofferdams and caissons

(1) A cofferdam or caisson must be—

(a) of suitable design and construction;

(b) appropriately equipped so that workers can gain shelter or escape if water or materials enter it; and

(c) properly maintained.

(2) A cofferdam or caisson must not be used to carry out construction work unless—

(a) the cofferdam or caisson and any work equipment and materials which may affect its safety have been inspected by a competent person—

(i) at the start of the shift in which the work is to be carried out; and

(ii) after any event likely to have affected the strength or stability of the cofferdam or caisson; and

(b) the person who carried out the inspection is satisfied that construction work can be safely carried out there.

(3) Where the person carrying out an inspection informs the person on whose behalf the inspection is carried out of any matter about which they are not satisfied (under regulation 24(1)), construction work must not be carried out in the cofferdam or caisson until the matter has been satisfactorily remedied.

Regulation 24 Reports of inspections

(1) Where a person who carries out an inspection under regulation 22 or 23 is not satisfied that construction work can be carried out safely at the place inspected, that person must—

  (a) inform the person on whose behalf the inspection was carried out, before the end of the shift within which the inspection is completed, of the matters that could give rise to a risk to the safety of any person; and

  (b) prepare a report which must include—

    (i) the name and address of the person on whose behalf the inspection was carried out;

    (ii) the location of the place of construction work inspected;

    (iii) a description of the place of construction work or part of that place inspected (including any work equipment and materials);

    (iv) the date and time of the inspection;

    (v) details of any matter identified that could give rise to a risk to the safety of any person;

    (vi) details of any action taken as a result of any matter identified in sub-paragraph (v);

    (vii) details of any further action considered necessary; and

    (viii) the name and position of the person making the report; and

  (c) provide the report, or a copy of it, to the person on whose behalf the inspection was carried out, within 24 hours of completing the inspection to which the report relates.

(2) Where the person who carries out an inspection works under the control of another (whether as an employee or otherwise) the person in control must ensure the person who carries out the inspection complies with the requirements of paragraph (1).

(3) The person on whose behalf the inspection was carried out must—

  (a) keep the report or a copy of it available for inspection by an inspector for the Executive—

    (i) at the site where the inspection was carried out until the construction work is completed; and

    (ii) after that for 3 months; and

(b) send to the inspector such extracts from or copies of the report as the inspector may from time to time require.

(4) This regulation does not require the preparation of more than one report where more than one inspection is carried out under regulation 22(4)(a)(i) or 23(2)(a)(i) within a 7 day period.

Regulation 25 Energy distribution installations

(1) Where necessary to prevent danger, energy distribution installations must be suitably located, periodically checked and clearly indicated.

(2) Where there is a risk to construction work from overhead electric power cables—

(a) they must be directed away from the area of risk; or

(b) the power must be isolated and, where necessary, earthed.

(3) if it is not reasonably practicable to comply with paragraph (2)(a) or (b), suitable warning notices must be provided together with one or more of the following—

(a) barriers suitable for excluding work equipment which is not needed;

(b) suspended protections where vehicles need to pass beneath the cables; or

(c) measures providing an equivalent level of safety.

(4) Construction work which is liable to create a risk to health or safety from an underground service, or from damage to or disturbance of it, must not be carried out unless suitable and sufficient steps (including any steps required by this regulation) have been taken to prevent the risk, so far as is reasonably practicable.

Regulation 26 Prevention of drowning

(1) Where, in the course of construction work, a person is at risk of falling into water or other liquid with a risk of drowning, suitable and sufficient steps must be taken to—

(a) prevent, so far as is reasonably practicable, the person falling;

(b) minimise the risk of drowning in the event of a fall; and

(c) ensure that suitable rescue equipment is provided, maintained and, when necessary, used so that a person may be promptly rescued in the event of a fall.

(2) Suitable and sufficient steps must be taken to ensure the safe transport of any person conveyed by water to or from a place of work.

(3) Any vessel used to convey any person by water to or from a place of work must not be overcrowded or overloaded.

Regulation 27 Traffic routes

(1) A construction site must be organised in such a way that, so far as is reasonably practicable, pedestrians and vehicles can move without risks to health or safety.

(2) Traffic routes must be suitable for the persons or vehicles using them, sufficient in number, in suitable positions and of sufficient size.

(3) A traffic route does not satisfy paragraph (2) unless suitable and sufficient steps are taken to ensure that—

(a) pedestrians or vehicles may use it without causing danger to the health or safety of persons near it;

(b) any door or gate for pedestrians which leads onto a traffic route is sufficiently separated from that traffic route to enable pedestrians to see any approaching vehicle or plant from a place of safety;

(c) there is sufficient separation between vehicles and pedestrians to ensure safety or, where this is not reasonably practicable—

(i) other means for the protection of pedestrians are provided; and

(ii) effective arrangements are used for warning any person liable to be crushed or trapped by any vehicle of its approach;

(d) any loading bay has at least one exit for the exclusive use of pedestrians; and

(e) where it is unsafe for pedestrians to use a gate intended primarily for vehicles, at least one door for pedestrians is provided in the immediate vicinity of the gate, is clearly marked and is kept free from obstruction.

(4) Each traffic route must be—

(a) indicated by suitable signs where necessary for reasons of health or safety;

(b) regularly checked; and

(c) properly maintained.

(5) No vehicle is to be driven on a traffic route unless, so far as is reasonably practicable, that traffic route is free from obstruction and permits sufficient clearance.

Regulation 28 Vehicles

(1) Suitable and sufficient steps must be taken to prevent or control the unintended movement of any vehicle.

(2) Where a person may be endangered by the movement of a vehicle, suitable and sufficient steps to give warning to any person who is liable to be at risk from the movement of the vehicle must be taken by either or both—

(a) the driver or operator of the vehicle; or

(b) where another person is directing the driver or operator because, due to the nature of the vehicle or task, the driver or operator does not have full visibility, the person providing directions.

(3) A vehicle being used for the purposes of construction work must, when being driven, operated or towed be—

(a) driven, operated or towed in such a manner as is safe in the circumstances; and

(b) loaded in such a way that it can be driven, operated or towed safely.

(4) A person must not ride, or be required or permitted to ride, on any vehicle being used for the purposes of construction work otherwise than in a safe place in that vehicle provided for that purpose.

(5) A person must not remain, or be required or permitted to remain, on any vehicle during the loading or unloading of any loose material unless a safe place of work is provided and maintained for that person.

(6) Suitable and sufficient measures must be taken to prevent a vehicle from falling into any excavation or pit, or into water, or overrunning the edge of any embankment or earthwork.

Regulation 29 Prevention of risk from fire, flooding or asphyxiation

(1) Suitable and sufficient steps must be taken to prevent, so far as is reasonably practicable, the risk of injury to a person during the carrying out of construction work arising from—

(a) fire or explosion;

(b) flooding; or

(c) any substance liable to cause asphyxiation.

Regulation 30 Emergency procedures

(1) Where necessary in the interests of the health or safety of a person on a construction site, suitable and sufficient arrangements for dealing with any foreseeable emergency must be made and, where necessary, implemented, and those arrangements must include procedures for any necessary evacuation of the site or any part of it.

(2) In making arrangements under paragraph (1), account must be taken of—

(a) the type of work for which the construction site is being used;

(b) the characteristics and size of the construction site and the number and location of places of work on that site;

(c) the work equipment being used;

(d) the number of persons likely to be present on the site at any one time; and

(e) the physical and chemical properties of any substances or materials on, or likely to be on, the site.

(3) Where arrangements are made under paragraph (1), suitable and sufficient steps must be taken to ensure that—

(a) each person to whom the arrangements extend is familiar with those arrangements; and

(b) the arrangements are tested by being put into effect at suitable intervals.

Regulation 31 Emergency routes and exits

(1) Where necessary in the interests of the health or safety of a person on a construction site, a sufficient number of suitable emergency routes and exits must be provided to enable any person to reach a place of safety quickly in the event of danger.

(2) The matters in regulation 30(2) must be taken into account when making provision under paragraph (1).

(3) An emergency route or exit must lead as directly as possible to an identified safe area.

(4) An emergency route or exit and any traffic route giving access to it must be kept clear and free from obstruction and, where necessary, provided with emergency lighting so that it may be used at any time.

(5) Each emergency route or exit must be indicated by suitable signs.

Regulation 32 Fire detection and fire-fighting

(1) Where necessary in the interests of the health or safety of a person on a construction site, suitable and sufficient fire-fighting equipment and fire detection and alarm systems must be provided and located in suitable places.

(2) The matters in regulation 30(2) must be taken into account when making provision under paragraph (1).

(3) Fire-fighting equipment or fire detection and alarm systems must be examined and tested at suitable intervals and properly maintained.

(4) Fire-fighting equipment which is not designed to come into use automatically must be easily accessible.

(5) Each person at work on a construction site must, so far as is reasonably practicable, be instructed in the correct use of fire-fighting equipment which it may be necessary for the person to use.

(6) Where a work activity may give rise to a particular risk of fire, a person must not carry out work unless suitably instructed.

(7) Fire-fighting equipment must be indicated by suitable signs.

Regulation 33 Fresh air

(1) Suitable and sufficient steps must be taken to ensure, so far as is reasonably practicable, that each construction site, or approach to a construction site, has sufficient fresh or purified air to ensure that the site or approach is safe and without risks to health or safety.

(2) Any plant used for the purpose of complying with paragraph (1) must, where necessary for reasons of health and safety, include an effective device to give visible or audible warning of any failure of the plant.

Regulation 34 Temperature and weather protection

(1) Suitable and sufficient steps must be taken to ensure, so far as reasonably practicable, that during working hours the temperature at a construction site that is indoors is reasonable having regard to the purpose for which that place is used.

(2) Where necessary to ensure the health or safety of persons at work on a construction site that is outdoors, the construction site must, so far as is reasonably practicable, be arranged to provide protection from adverse weather, having regard to—

 (a) the purpose for which the site is used; and

 (b) any protective clothing or work equipment provided for the use of any person at work there.

Regulation 35 Lighting

(1) Each construction site and approach and traffic route to that site must be provided with suitable and sufficient lighting, which must be, so far as is reasonably practicable, by natural light.

(2) The colour of any artificial lighting provided must not adversely affect or change the perception of any sign or signal provided for the purposes of health or safety.

(3) Suitable and sufficient secondary lighting must be provided in any place where there would be a risk to the health or safety of a person in the event of the failure of primary artificial lighting.

PART 5 – General

Regulation 36 Enforcement in respect of fire

The enforcing authority for regulations 30 and 31 (so far as those regulations relate to fire) and regulation 32, in respect of a construction site which is contained within or forms part of premises occupied by persons other than those carrying out construction work, or any activity related to this work, is—

(a) in England and Wales, the enforcing authority within the meaning of article 25 of the Regulatory Reform (Fire Safety) Order 2005(**a**) in respect of premises to which that Order applies; or

(b) in Scotland, the enforcing authority within the meaning of section 61 of the Fire (Scotland) Act 2005(**b**) in respect of premises to which Part 3 of that Act applies.

Regulation 37 Transitional and saving provisions

Schedule 4, which makes transitional and saving provisions, has effect.

Regulation 38 Revocation and consequential amendments

(1) The 2007 Regulations are revoked.

(2) The amendments in Schedule 5 have effect.

Regulation 39 Review

(1) The Secretary of State must from time to time—

(a) carry out a review of regulations 1 to 36;

(b) set out the conclusions of the review in a report; and

(c) publish the report.

(2) In carrying out the review the Secretary of State must, so far as is reasonable, have regard to how Council Directive 92/57/EEC(**c**) on the implementation of minimum safety and health requirements at temporary or mobile construction sites (which is implemented by means of regulations 1 to 36), is implemented in other Member States.

(**a**) S.I. 2005/1541. Article 25 was amended by paragraphs 87 and 88 of Part 5 of Schedule 12 to the Energy Act 2013 (c.32).

(**b**) 2005 asp 5. Section 61 was amended by section 103(1)(a)(i) and (ii) and (b) and Part 2 of Schedule 8 to the Police and Fire Reform (Scotland) Act 2012 (asp 8); paragraph 86 of Part 5 of Schedule 12 to the Energy Act 2013; S.I. 2005/2060 and S.I. 2008/960. Section 78 which sets out the meaning of "relevant premises" to which Part 3 of the legislation applies was amended by paragraph 23 of Part 1 of Schedule 6 and Schedule 7 to the Housing (Scotland) Act 2006 (asp 1); S.I. 2005/2060 and S.S.I. 2005/352, 2011/211, 2011/369 and 2012/332.

(**c**) OJ No L 245, 26.8.1992, p6–22.

(3) The report must in particular—

(a) set out the objectives intended to be achieved by the regulatory system established by those regulations;

(b) assess the extent to which those objectives are achieved; and

(c) assess whether those objectives remain appropriate and, if so, the extent to which they could be achieved with a system that imposes less regulation.

(4) The first report under this regulation must be published before the end of the period of five years beginning with the day on which these Regulations come into force.

(5) Reports under this regulation are afterwards to be published at intervals not exceeding five years.

Signed by authority of the Secretary of State for Work and Pensions

Freud

Parliamentary Under Secretary of State

22nd January 2015 Department of Work and Pensions

SCHEDULE 1

Regulation 6

Particulars to be notified under regulation 6

1. The date of forwarding the notice.

2. The address of the construction site or precise description of its location.

3. The name of the local authority where the construction site is located.

4. A brief description of the project and the construction work that it entails.

5. The following contact details of the client: name, address, telephone number and (if available) an email address.

6. The following contact details of the principal designer: name, address, telephone number and (if available) an email address.

7. The following contact details of the principal contractor: name, address, telephone number and (if available) an email address.

8. The date planned for the start of the construction phase.

9. The time allocated by the client under regulation 4(1) for the construction work.

10. The planned duration of the construction phase.

11. The estimated maximum number of people at work on the construction site.

12. The planned number of contractors on the construction site.

13. The name and address of any contractor already appointed.

14. The name and address of any designer already appointed.

15. A declaration signed by or on behalf of the client that the client is aware of the client duties under these Regulations.

SCHEDULE 2

Regulation 4(2)(b), 13(4)(c) and 15(11)

Minimum welfare facilities required for construction sites

Sanitary conveniences

1.—(1) Suitable and sufficient sanitary conveniences must be provided or made available at readily accessible places.

(2) So far as is reasonably practicable, rooms containing sanitary conveniences must be adequately ventilated and lit.

(3) So far as is reasonably practicable, sanitary conveniences and the rooms containing them must be kept in a clean and orderly condition.

(4) Separate rooms containing sanitary conveniences must be provided for men and women, except where and so far as each convenience is in a separate room, the door of which is capable of being secured from the inside.

Washing facilities

2.—(1) Suitable and sufficient washing facilities, including showers if required by the nature of the work or for health reasons, must, so far as is reasonably practicable, be provided or made available at readily accessible places.

(2) Washing facilities must be provided—

(a) in the immediate vicinity of every sanitary convenience, whether or not also provided elsewhere; and

(b) in the vicinity of any changing rooms required by paragraph 4, whether or not provided elsewhere.

(3) Washing facilities must include—

(a) a supply of clean hot and cold, or warm, water (which must be running water so far as is reasonably practicable);

(b) soap or other suitable means of cleaning; and

(c) towels or other suitable means of drying.

(4) Rooms containing washing facilities must be sufficiently ventilated and lit.

(5) Washing facilities and the rooms containing them must be kept in a clean and orderly condition.

(6) Subject to sub-paragraph (7), separate washing facilities must be provided for men and women, except where they are provided in a room the door of which is capable of being secured from inside and the facilities in each room are intended to be used by only one person at a time.

(7) Sub-paragraph (6) does not apply to facilities which are provided for washing hands, forearms and the face only.

Drinking water

3.—(1) An adequate supply of wholesome drinking water must be provided or made available at readily accessible and suitable places.

(2) Where necessary for reasons of health or safety, every supply of drinking water must be conspicuously marked by an appropriate sign.

(3) Where a supply of drinking water is provided, a sufficient number of suitable cups or other drinking vessels must also be provided, unless the supply of drinking water is in a jet from which persons can drink easily.

Changing rooms and lockers

4.—(1) Suitable and sufficient changing rooms must be provided or made available at readily accessible places if a worker—

(a) has to wear special clothing for the purposes of construction work; and

(b) cannot, for reasons of health or propriety, be expected to change elsewhere.

(2) Where necessary for reasons of propriety, there must be separate changing rooms for, or separate use of rooms by, men and women.

(3) Changing rooms must—

(a) be provided with seating; and

(b) include, where necessary, facilities to enable a person to dry any special clothing and any personal clothing or effects.

(4) Suitable and sufficient facilities must, where necessary, be provided or made available at readily accessible places to enable persons to lock away—

(a) any special clothing which is not taken home;

(b) their own clothing which is not worn during working hours; and

(c) their personal effects.

Facilities for rest

5.—(1) Suitable and sufficient rest rooms or rest areas must be provided or made available at readily accessible places.

(2) Rest rooms and rest areas must—

(a) be equipped with an adequate number of tables and adequate seating with backs for the number of persons at work likely to use them at any one time;

(b) where necessary, include suitable facilities for any woman at work who is pregnant or who is a nursing mother to rest lying down;

(c) include suitable arrangements to ensure that meals can be prepared and eaten;

(d) include the means for boiling water; and

(e) be maintained at an appropriate temperature.

SCHEDULE 3

Regulation 12(2)

Work involving particular risks

1. Work which puts workers at risk of burial under earthfalls, engulfment in swampland or falling from a height, where the risk is particularly aggravated by the nature of the work or processes used or by the environment at the place of work or site.

2. Work which puts workers at risk from chemical or biological substances constituting a particular danger to the safety or health of workers or involving a legal requirement for health monitoring.

3. Work with ionizing radiation requiring the designation of controlled or supervised areas under regulation 16 of the Ionising Radiations Regulations 1999(**a**).

4. Work near high voltage power lines.

5. Work exposing workers to the risk of drowning.

6. Work on wells, underground earthworks and tunnels.

7. Work carried out by divers having a system of air supply.

8. Work carried out by workers in caissons with a compressed air atmosphere.

9. Work involving the use of explosives.

10. Work involving the assembly or dismantling of heavy prefabricated components.

SCHEDULE 4

Regulation 37

Transitional and saving provisions

1. In this Schedule—

"CDM coordinator" means a person appointed under regulation 14(1) of the 2007 Regulations;

"competent" means competent to perform any requirement and avoid contravening any prohibition imposed on a person by or under any of the relevant statutory provisions;

"relevant project" means a project which began before 6th April 2015.

2. These Regulations apply to a relevant project with the modifications specified in this Schedule.

Projects with no existing CDM coordinator or principal contractor

3.—(1) This paragraph modifies the application of these Regulations in relation to a relevant project where, immediately before 6th April 2015—

(a) no CDM coordinator or principal contractor is appointed for the project under the 2007 Regulations;

(b) there is more than one contractor, or it is reasonably foreseeable that more than one contractor will be working on a project; and

(c) the construction phase has started.

(2) Regulation 5 does not apply to the project.

(3) The client may appoint in writing a designer as principal designer.

(4) The client must appoint in writing a contractor as principal contractor as soon as is practicable after 6th April 2015.

(**a**) S.I. 1999/3232.

(5) The principal contractor must draw up a construction phase plan or make arrangements for a construction phase plan to be drawn up under regulation 12(1) and (2) as soon as is practicable after 6th April 2015 and the requirement that the plan must be drawn up during the pre-construction phase and before setting up a construction site is disapplied.

(6) The client, other than a domestic client, must ensure that the principal contractor complies with sub-paragraph (5) and the client duty in regulation 4(5)(a) is disapplied.

(7) If the client does not appoint a principal designer, the principal contractor must—

(a) prepare a health and safety file under regulation 12(5) as soon as is practicable after 6th April 2015 and the requirement for the file to be prepared during the pre-construction phase is disapplied; and

(b) ensure that the health and safety file is reviewed, updated and revised from time to time under regulation 12(6).

(8) If the client does not appoint a principal designer—

(a) the references to the principal designer in regulations 4(5)(b) and 9(3)(b) are treated as references to the principal contractor;

(b) the client duty in regulation 4(6)(a) does not apply; and

(c) the principal contractor duties in regulations 12(7) and 13(5) do not apply.

(9) Where a client, other than a domestic client, fails to appoint a principal contractor under sub-paragraph (4) the client must fulfil the duties of the principal contractor specified in these Regulations, as modified by this paragraph.

(10) Where the client is a domestic client—

(a) regulation 7(2) does not apply; and

(b) if the client fails to appoint a principal contractor under sub-paragraph (4) the principal contractor for the project is the contractor in control of the construction phase.

Projects with an existing CDM coordinator

4.—(1) This paragraph and paragraphs 5 and 6 apply where, immediately before 6th April 2015, there is a CDM coordinator appointed for a relevant project.

(2) Where this paragraph applies, the appointment of the CDM coordinator continues to have effect for the purposes of these Regulations until a principal designer is appointed or the project comes to an end.

(3) The client must appoint in writing a principal designer for the project before 6th October 2015 unless the project comes to an end on or before that date.

(4) Where the appointment of a CDM coordinator continues to have effect under sub-paragraph (2)—

(a) the CDM coordinator must comply with the duties in paragraph 5;

(b) the duties in regulations 9(3)(b) and 12(7) to provide information to the principal designer are treated as duties to provide information to the CDM coordinator; and

(c) the duty in regulation 13(5) to liaise with the principal designer is treated as a duty to liaise with the CDM coordinator.

Duties of CDM coordinator during transitional period

5.— (1) The CDM coordinator must—

(a) cooperate with any other person working on or in relation to a project at the same or an adjoining construction site, to the extent necessary to enable any person with a duty or function under these Regulations to fulfil that duty or function;

(b) where the CDM coordinator works under the control of another, report to that person anything they are aware of in relation to the project which is likely to endanger their own health or safety or that of others;

(c) ensure that suitable arrangements are made and implemented for the coordination of health and safety measures during the planning and preparation for the construction phase, including facilitating—

(i) cooperation and coordination between all persons working on the pre-construction phase of the project; and

(ii) the application of the general principles of prevention;

(d) liaise with the principal contractor over—

(i) the content of the health and safety file;

(ii) the information which the principal contractor needs to prepare the construction phase plan; and

(iii) any design development which may affect planning and management of the construction work;

(e) where no or partial pre-construction information has been supplied to the CDM coordinator by the client under regulation 10 of the 2007 Regulations, assist the client to comply with regulation 4(4) of these Regulations;

(f) unless the information has already been provided under regulation 20(2)(b) of the 2007 Regulations, provide any pre-construction information that is in the possession or control of the CDM coordinator, promptly and in a convenient form, to every designer and contractor appointed, or being considered for appointment, to the project;

(g) take all reasonable steps to ensure that designers comply with their duties under regulation 9 of these Regulations;

(h) take all reasonable steps to ensure cooperation between designers and the principal contractor during the construction phase in relation to any design or change to a design;

(i) if a health and safety file has not been prepared under regulation 20(2)(e) of the 2007 Regulations, prepare a health and safety file that complies with the requirements of regulation 12(5) of these Regulations;

(j) review, update and revise the health and safety file from time to time to take account of the work and any changes that have occurred;

(k) if the CDM coordinator's appointment continues to have effect immediately before the project ends, pass the health and safety file to the client at the end of the project;

(l) if a principal designer is appointed, pass the health and safety file and all other relevant health and safety information in the CDM coordinator's possession to the principal designer, as soon as is practicable after the appointment.

(2) The CDM coordinator must not arrange for or instruct a worker to carry out or manage design or construction work unless the worker is competent or under the supervision of a competent person.

Duties disapplied pending appointment of principal designer

6.—(1) The duties in regulation 5(1)(a) and (3) do not apply to a project referred to in paragraph 4(1).

(2) The following duties do not apply to a project referred to in paragraph 4(1) until the principal designer is appointed—

(a) the duties in regulations 4(5)(b) and (6)(a);

(b) the duties of the principal designer in regulations 11 and 12(3), (5), (6), (8) and (10).

(3) If a client fails to make the appointment required by paragraph 4(3) the client must fulfil the duties of a principal designer in regulations 11 and 12 on and after 6th October 2015.

Projects with only one contractor

7.—Where a relevant project has only one contractor and the construction phase has started, the contractor must draw up a construction phase plan, or make arrangements for a construction phase plan to be drawn up, under regulation 15(5) and (6) as soon as is practicable after 6th April 2015 and the requirement that the plan must be drawn up prior to setting up a construction site is disapplied.

Savings

8.—(1) Where, immediately before 6th April 2015 there is a principal contractor appointed for a relevant project under regulation 14(2) of the 2007 Regulations, for the purposes of these Regulations that principal contractor is treated on and after 6th April 2015 as having been appointed under regulation 5(1)(b) of these Regulations.

(2) For the purposes of these Regulations, on and after 6th April 2015—

(a) a health and safety file prepared for a relevant project under regulation 20(2)(e) of the 2007 Regulations is treated as a health and safety file prepared under regulation 12(5) of these Regulations;

(b) a construction phase plan drawn up for a relevant project under regulation 23 of the 2007 Regulations is treated as a construction phase plan drawn up under regulation 12(1) or 15(5) of these Regulations;

(c) pre-construction information provided for a relevant project under regulation 10 of the 2007 Regulations is treated as pre-construction information provided under regulation 4(4) of these Regulations;

(d) notice given for a relevant project under regulation 21 of the 2007 Regulations is treated as notice given under regulation 6 of these Regulations.

SCHEDULE 5

Regulation 38

Amendments

Description of instrument	Reference	Extent of amendment
Factories Act 1961	1961 c. 34[a]	In section 176(1) in the definition of "building operation" and "work of engineering construction" for "2007 (S.I. 2007/320)" substitute "2015".
Workplace (Health Safety and Welfare) Regulations 1992	S.I. 1992/3004[b]	In regulation 3(1)(b) for "2007" substitute "2015".
Work in Compressed Air Regulations 1996	S.I. 1996/1656[c]	In regulation 2(1) in the definition of "the 2007 Regulations" substitute "2015" in both places it appears.
		In regulation 3(1) for "2007" substitute "2015" and for "2(3)" substitute "6(1)".
		In regulation 5(3) for "2007" substitute "2015".
		In regulation 13(2)(a) for "39, 40 and 44(3) of the 2007" substitute "30, 31 and 35(3) of the 2015".
		In regulation 13(2)(d) for "39(1) of the 2007" substitute "30(1) of the 2015".

Description of instrument	Reference	Extent of amendment
		In regulation 14(1) for "41 of the 2007" substitute "32 of the 2015".
Railway Safety (Miscellaneous Provisions) Regulations 1997	S.I. 1997/ 553[(d)]	In regulation 2(1) in the definition of "construction work" for "2007" substitute "2015".
Health and Safety (Enforcing Authority) Regulations 1998	S.I. 1998/ 494[(e)]	In regulation 2(1) in the definition of "construction work" and "contractor" for "2007" substitute "2015". In regulation 2A(5)(a) for "2007" substitute "2015". In Schedule 2, paragraph 4(a)(i) for "2(3)" substitute "6(1)" and for "2007" substitute "2015"
Provision and Use of Work Equipment Regulations 1998	S.I. 1998/ 2306[(f)]	In regulation 6(5)(e) for "31(4) or 32(2)" substitute "22(4) or 23(2)" and for "2007" substitute "2015".
Gas Safety (Installation and Use) Regulations 1998	S.I. 1998/ 2451[(g)]	In regulation 2(4)(d) for "2007" substitute "2015".
Work at Height Regulations 2005	S.I. 2005/ 735[(h)]	In regulation 2(1) in the definition of "construction work" for "2007" substitute "2015".
Regulatory Reform (Fire Safety) Order 2005	S.I. 2005/ 1541[(i)]	In article 25(2)(a) for "2007" substitute "2015" and for "46(1)" substitute "36".
Health and Safety (Enforcing Authority for Railways and other Guided Transport Systems) Regulations 2006	S.I. 2006/ 557[(j)]	In regulation 2(1) in the definitions of "construction work" and "contractor" for "2007" substitute "2015".
REACH Enforcement Regulations 2008	S.I. 2008/ 2852	In paragraph 1(d)(i)(aa) of Part 3 of Schedule 3 for "2(3)" substitute "6(1)" and for "2007" substitute "2015".
Reporting of Injuries, Diseases and Dangerous Occurrences Regulations 2013	S.I. 2013/ 1471	In regulation 2(1) in the definition of "construction site" for "2007" substitute "2015".

(a) As amended by S.I. 1996/1592 and S.I. 2007/320.

(b) As amended by S.I. 2007/320 and S.I. 2014/3248 (the latter coming into force on 6th April 2015).

(c) As amended by S.I. 2007/320.

(d) As amended by S.I. 2007/320.

(e) As amended by S.I. 2007/320 and S.I. 2014/469.

(f) As amended by S.I. 2007/320.

(g) As amended by S.I. 2007/320.

(h) As amended by S.I. 2007/320

(i) Article 25(2) was inserted by Part 5 of Schedule 12 to the Energy Act 2013 (c.32).

(j) As amended by S.I. 2007/320 and S.I. 2008/2323.

CDM Regulations 2015 Explained
ISBN 978-0-7277-6009-8

http://dx.doi.org/10.1680/cdmre.60098.231

Appendix 3
Temporary or Mobile Construction Sites Directive

►B **COUNCIL DIRECTIVE 92/57/EEC**

of 24 June 1992

on the implementation of minimum safety and health requirements at temporary or mobile constructions sites (eighth individual Directive within the meaning of Article 16 (1) of Directive 89/391/EEC)

(OJ L 245, 26.8.1992, p. 6)

Amended by:

		Official Journal		
		No.	page	date
►M1	Directive 2007/30/EC of the European Parliament and of the Council of 20 June 2007	L 165	21	27.6.2007

Corrected by:

►C1 Corrigendum, OJ L 15, 23.1.1993, p. 34 (92/57/EEC)

►C2 Corrigendum, OJ L 33, 9.2.1993, p. 18 (92/57/EEC)

▼B

COUNCIL DIRECTIVE 92/57/EEC

of 24 June 1992

on the implementation of minimum safety and health requirements at temporary or mobile constructions sites (eighth individual Directive within the meaning of Article 16 (1) of Directive 89/391/EEC)

THE COUNCIL OF THE EUROPEAN COMMUNITIES,

Having regard to the Treaty establishing the European Economic Community, and in particular Article 118a thereof,

Having regard to the proposal from the Commission ([1]), submitted after consulting the Advisory Committee on Safety, Hygiene and Health Protection at Work,

In cooperation with the European Parliament ([2]),

Having regard to the opinion of the Economic and Social Committee ([3]),

Whereas Article 118 a of the Treaty provides that the Council shall adopt, by means of directives, minimum requirements for encouraging improvements, especially in the working environment, to ensure a better level of protection of the safety and health of workers;

Whereas, under the terms of that Article, those directives are to avoid imposing administrative, financial and legal constraints in a way which would hold back the creation and development of small and medium-sized undertakings;

Whereas the communication from the Commission on its programme concerning safety, hygiene and health at work ([4]) provides for the adoption of a Directive designed to guarantee the safety and health of workers at temporary or mobile construction sites;

Whereas, in its resolution of 21 December 1987 on safety, hygiene and health at work ([5]), the Council took note of the Commission's intention of submitting to the Council in the near future minimum requirements concerning temporary or mobile construction sites;

Whereas temporary or mobile construction sites constitute an area of activity that exposes workers to particularly high levels of risk;

Whereas unsatisfactory architectural and/or organizational options or poor planning of the works at the project preparation stage have played a role in more than

(1) OJ No C 213, 28.8.1990, p. 2 and OJ No C 112, 27.4.1991, p. 4.
(2) OJ No C 78, 18.3.1990, p. 172 and OJ No C 150, 15.6.1992.
(3) OJ No C 120, 6.5.1991, p. 24.
(4) OJ No C 28, 3.2.1988, p. 3.
(5) OJ No C 28, 3.2.1988, p. 1.

▼B

half of the occupational accidents occurring on construction sites in the Community;

Whereas in each Member State the authorities responsible for safety and health at work must be informed, before the beginning of the works, of the execution of works the scale of which exceeds a certain threshold;

Whereas, when a project is being carried out, a large number of occupational accidents may be caused by inadequate coordination, particularly where various undertakings work simultaneously or in succession at the same temporary or mobile construction site;

Whereas it is therefore necessary to improve coordination between the various parties concerned at the project preparation stage and also when the work is being carried out;

Whereas compliance with the minimum requirements designed to guarantee a better standard of safety and health at temporary or mobile construction sites is essential to ensure the safety and health of workers;

Whereas, moreover, self-employed persons and employers, where they are personally engaged in work activity, may, through their activities on a temporary or mobile construction site, jeopardize the safety and health of workers;

Whereas it is therefore necessary to extend to self-employed persons and to employers where they are personally engaged in work activity on the site certain relevant provisions of Council Directive 89/655/EEC of 30 November 1989 concerning the minimum safety and health requirements for the use of work equipment by workers at work (second individual Directive) (1), and of Council Directive 89/656/EEC of 30 November 1989 on the minimum health and safety requirements for the use by workers of personal protective equipment at the workplace (third individual Directive) (2);

Whereas this Directive is an individual Directive within the meaning of Article 16 (1) of Council Directive 89/391/EEC of 12 June 1989 on the introduction of measures to encourage improvements in the safety and health of workers at work (3); whereas, therefore, the provisions of the said Directive are fully applicable to temporary or mobile construction sites, without prejudice to more stringent and/ or specific provisions contained in this Directive;

Whereas this Directive constitutes a practical step towards the achievement of the social dimension of the internal market with special reference to the subject matter of Council Directive 89/106/EEC of 21 December 1988 on the

(1) OJ No L 393, 30.12.1989, p. 13.
(2) OJ No L 393, 30.12.1989, p. 18.
(3) OJ No L 183, 29.6.1989, p. 1.

▼B

approximation of laws, regulations and administrative provisions of the Member States relating to construction products ([4]) and the subject matter covered by Council Directive 89/440/EEC of 18 July 1989 amending Direaive 71/305/EEC concerning coordination of procedures for the award of public work contracts ([5]);

Whereas, pursuant to Council Decision 74/325/EEC ([6]), the Advisory Committee on Safety, Hygiene and Health Protection at Work is consulted by the Commission with a view to drawing up proposals in this field,

HAS ADOPTED THIS DIRECTIVE:

(4) OJ No L 40, 11.2.1989, p. 12.

(5) OJ No L 210, 21.7.1989, p. 1. Amended by Commission Decision 90/380/EEC (OJ No L 187, 19.7.1990, p. 55).

(6) OJ No L 185, 9.7.1974, p. 15. Last amended by the 1985 Act of Accession.

▼B

Article 1

Subject

1. This Directive, which is the eighth individual Directive within the meaning of Article 16 (1) of Directive 89/391/EEC, lays down minimum safety and health requirements for temporary or mobile construction sites, as defined in Article 2 (a).

2. This Directive shall not apply to drilling and extraction in the extractive industries within the meaning of Article 1 (2) of Council Decision 74/326/EEC of 27 June 1974 on the extension of the responsibilities of the Mines Safety and Health Commission to all mineral-extracting industries ([7]).

3. The provisions of Directive 89/391/EEC are fully applicable to the whole scope referred to in paragraph 1, without prejudice to more stringent and/or specific provisions contained in this Directive.

Article 2

Definitions

For the purposes of this Directive:

(a) 'temporary or mobile construction sites' (hereinafter referred to as 'construction sites') means any construction site at which building or civil engineering works are carried out; a non-exhaustive list of such works is given in Annex I;

(b) 'client' means any natural or legal person for whom a project is carried out;

(c) 'project supervisor' means any natural or legal person responsible for the design and/or execution and/or supervision of the execution of a project, acting on behalf of the client;

(d) 'self-employed person' means any person other than those referred to in Article 3 (a) and (b) of Directive 89/391/EEC whose professional activity contributes to the completion of a project;

(e) 'coordinator for safety and health matters at the project preparations stage' means any natural or legal person entrusted by the client and/or project supervisor, ►C1 during the project preparation stage ◄, with performing the duties referred to in Article 5;

(f) 'coordinator for safety and health matters at the project execution stage' means any natural or legal person entrusted by the client and/or project supervisor, during execution of the project, with performing the duties referred to in Article 6.

---

(7) OJ No L 185, 9.7.1974, p. 18.

▼B

Article 3

Appointment of coordinators — Safety and health plan — Prior notice

1. The client or the project supervisor shall appoint one or more coordinators for safety and health matters, as defined in Article 2 (e) and (f), for any construction site on which more than one contractor is present.

2. The client or the project supervisor shall ensure that prior to the setting up of a construction site a safety and health plan is drawn up in accordance with Article 5 (b).

▼C2

The Member States may, after consulting both management and the workforce, allow derogations from the provisions of the first subparagraph, except where it is a question of:

— work involving particular risks as listed in Annex II, or

— work for which prior notice is required pursuant to paragraph 3 of this Article.

▼B

3. In the case of constructions sites:

— on which work is scheduled to last longer than 30 working days and on which more than 20 workers are occupied simultaneously, or

— on which the volume of work is scheduled to exceed 500 person-days,

the client or the project supervisor shall communicate a prior notice drawn up in accordance with Annex III to the competent authorities before work starts.

The prior notice must be clearly displayed on the construction site and, if necessary, periodically updated.

Article 4

Project preparation stage: general principles

The project supervisor, or where appropriate the client, shall take account of the general principles of prevention concerning safety and health referred to in Directive 89/391/EEC during the various stages of designing and preparing the project, in particular:

— when architectural, technical and/or organizational aspects are being decided, in order to plan the various items or stages of work which are to take place simultaneously or in succession,

— when estimating the period required for completing such work or work stages. Account shall also be taken, each time this appears necessary, of all

▼B

safety and health plans and of files drawn up in accordance with Article 5 (b) or (c) or adjusted in accordance with Article 6 (c).

Article 5

Project preparation stage: duties of coordinators

The coordinator(s) for safety and health matters during the project preparation stage appointed in accordance with Article 3 (1) shall:

(a) coordinate implementation of the provisions of Article 4;

(b) draw up, or cause to be draw up, a safety and health plan setting out the rules applicable to the construction site concerned, taking into account where necessary the industrial activities taking place on the site; this plan must also include specific measures concerning work which falls within one or more of the categories of Annex II;

(c) prepare a file appropriate to the characteristics of the project containing relevant safety and health information to be taken into account during any subsequent works.

Article 6

Project execution stage: duties of coordinators

The coordinator(s) for safety and health matters during the project execution stage appointed in accordance with Article 3 (1) shall:

(a) coordinate implementation of the general principles of prevention and safety:

— when technical and/or organizational aspects are being decided, in order to plan the various items or stages of work which are to take place simultaneously or in succession,

— when estimating the period required for completing such work or work stages;

(b) coordinate implementation of the relevant provisions in order to ensure that employers and, if necessary for the protection of workers, self-employed persons:

— apply the principles referred to in Article 8 in a consistent manner,

— where required, follow the safety and health plan referred to in Article 5 (b);

(c) make, or cause to be made, any adjustments required to the safety and health plan referred to in Article 5 (b) and the file referred to in Article 5 (c) to take account of the progress of the work and any changes which have occurred;

▼B

(d) organize cooperation between employers, including successive employers on the same site, coordination of their activities with a view to protecting workers and preventing accidents and occupational health hazards and reciprocal information as provided for in Article 6 (4) of Directive 89/391/EEC, ensuring that self-employed persons are brought into this process where necessary;

(e) coordinate arrangements to check that the working procedures are being implemented correctly;

(f) take the steps necessary to ensure that only ►C1 authorized persons are ◄ allowed onto the construction site.

Article 7

Responsibilities of clients, project supervisors and employers

1. Where a client or project supervisor has appointed a coordinator or coordinators to perform the duties referred to in Articles 5 and 6, this does not relieve the client or project supervisor of his responsibilities in that respect.

2. The implementation of Articles 5 and 6, and of paragraph 1 of this Article shall not affect the principle of employers' responsibility as provided for in Directive 89/391/EEC.

Article 8

Implementation of Article 6 of Directive 89/391/EEC

When the work is being carried out, the principles set out in Article 6 of Directive 89/391/EEC shall be applied, in particular as regards:

(a) keeping the construction site in good order and in a satisfactory state of cleanliness;

(b) choosing the location of workstations bearing in mind how access to these workplaces is obtained, and determining routes or areas for the passage and movement and equiment;

(c) the conditions under which various materials are handled;

(d) technical maintenance, pre-commissioning checks and regular checks on installations and equipment with a view to correcting any faults which might affect the safety and health of workers;

(e) the demarcation and laying-out of areas for the storage of various materials, in particular where dangerous materials or substances are concerned;

(f) the conditions under which the dangerous materials used are removed;

(g) the storage and disposal or removal of waste and debris;

▼B

(h) the adaptation, based on progress made with the site, of the actual period to be allocated for the various types of work or work stages;

(i) cooperation between employers and self-employed persons;

(j) interaction with industrial activities at the place within which or in the vicinity of which the construction site is located.

Article 9

Obligations of employers

In order to preserve safety and health on the construction site, under the conditions set out in Article 6 and 7, employers shall:

(a) in particular when implementing Article 8, take measures that are in line with the minimum requirements set out in Annex IV;

(b) take into account directions from the coordinator(s) for safety and health matters.

Article 10

Obligations of other groups of persons

1. In order to preserve safety and health on the construction site, self-employed persons shall:

(a) comply in particular with the following, *mutatis mutandis:*

(i) the requirements of Article 6 (4) and Article 13 of Directive 89/391/EEC and Article 8 and Annex IV of this Directive;

(ii) Article 4 of Directive 89/655/EEC and the relevant provisions of the Annex thereto;

(iii) Article 3, Article 4 (1) to (4) and (9) and Article 5 of Directive 89/656/EEC;

(b) take into account directions from the coordinator(s) for safety and health matters.

2. In order to preserve safety and health on the site, where employers are personally engaged in work activity on the construction site, they shall:

(a) comply in particular with the following, *mutatis mutandis:*

(i) Article 13 of Directive 89/391/EEC;

(ii) Article 4 of Directive 89/655/EEC and the relevant provisions of the Annex thereto;

(iii) Articles 3,4(1), (2), (3), (4), (9) and 5 of Directive 89/656/EEC;

(b) take account of the comments of the coordinator(s) for safety and health.

▼B

Article 11

Information for workers

1. Without prejudice to Article 10 of Directive 89/391/EEC, workers and/or their representatives shall be informed of all the measures to be taken concerning their safety and health on the construction site.

2. The information must be comprehensible to the workers concerned.

Article 12

Consultation and participation of workers

Consultation and participation of workers and/or of their representatives shall take place in accordance with Article 11 of Directive 89/391/EEC on matters covered by Articles 6, 8 and 9 of this Directive, ensuring whenever necessary proper coordination between workers and/or workers' representatives in undertakings carrying out their activities at the workplace, having regard to the degree of risk and the size of the work site.

Article 13

Amendment of the Annexes

1. Amendments to Annexes I, II and III shall be adopted by the Council in accordance with the procedure laid down in Article 118a of the Treaty.

2. Strictly technical adaptations of Annex IV as a result of:

— the adoption of directives on technical harmonization and standardization regarding temporary or mobile construction sites, and/or

— technical progress, changes in international regulations or specifications or knowledge in the field of temporary or mobile construction sites

shall be adopted in accordance with the procedure laid down in Article 17 of Directive 89/391/EEC.

Article 14

Final Provisions

1. Member States shall bring into force the laws, regulations and administrative provisions necessary to comply with this Directive by 31 December 1993 at the latest.

They shall forthwith inform the Commission thereof.

2. When Member States adopt these measures, they shall contain a reference to this Directive or be accompanied by such reference on the occasion of their

▼B

official publication. The methods of making such a reference shall be laid down by the Member States.

3. Member States shall communicate to the Commission the texts of the provisions of national law which they have already adopted or adopt in the field governed by this Directive.

▼M1

——————

▼B

Article 15

This Directive is addressed to the Member States.

▼B

ANNEX I

NON-EXHAUSTIVE LIST OF BUILDING AND CIVIL ENGINEERING WORKS REFERRED TO IN ARTICLE 2 (a) OF THE DIRECTIVE

1. Excavation
2. Earthworks
3. Construction
4. Assembly and disassembly of prefabricated elements
5. Conversion or fitting-out
6. Alterations
7. Renovation
8. Repairs
9. Dismantling
10. Demolition
11. Upkeep
12. Maintenance — Painting and cleaning work
13. Drainage

▼B

ANNEX II

NON-EXHAUSTIVE LIST OF WORK INVOLVING PARTICULAR RISKS TO THE SAFETY AND HEALTH OF WORKERS REFERRED TO IN ARTICLE 3 (2), SECOND PARAGRAPH OF THE DIRECTIVE

1. Work which puts workers at risk of burial under earthfalls, engulfment in swampland or falling from a height, where the risk is particularly aggravated by the nature of the work or processes used or by the environment at the place of work or site (*).
2. Work which puts workers at risk from chemical or biological substances constituing a particular danger to the safety and health of workers or involving a legal requirement for health monitoring.
3. Work with ionizing radiation requiring the designation of controlled or supervised areas as defined in Article 20 of Directive 80/836/Euratom ([1]).
4. Work near high voltage power lines.
5. Work exposing workers to the risk of drowning.
6. Work on wells, underground earthworks and tunnels.
7. Work carried out ►C1 by divers having ◄ a system of air supply.
8. Work carried out by workers ►C1 in caissons with ◄ a compressed-air atmosphere.
9. Work involving the use of explosives.
10. Work involving the assembly or dismantling of heavy prefabricated components.

(*) In implementing point 1, Member States have the option of setting figures for individual situations.

(1) OJ No L 246, 17.9.1980, p. 1. Last amended by Directive 84/467/Euratom (OJ No L 265, 5.10.1984, p. 4).

▼B

ANNEX III

CONTENT OF THE PRIOR NOTICE REFERRED TO IN ARTICLE 3(3), FIRST PARAGRAPH ►C1 OF THE DIRECTIVE ◄

1. Date of forwarding: ....
2. Exact address of the construction site: ....

   ....
3. Client(s) (name(s) and address(es)): ....

   ....
4. Type of project: ....
5. Project supervisor(s) (name(s) and address(es)): ....

   ....
6. Safety and health coordinators(s) ►[1]during the project ◄ preparation stage (name(s) and address(es)): ....

   ....
7. Coordinator(s) for safety and health matters during the project execution stage (name(s) and address(es)): ....

   ....

   ....
8. Date planned for start of work on the construction site: ....
9. Planned duration of work on the construction site: ....
10. Estimated maximum number of workers on the construction site: ....
11. Planned number of contractors and self-employed persons on the construction site: ....

    ....
12. Details of contractors already chosen: ....

    ....

    ....

    ....

    ....

►[1] C1

▼B

ANNEX IV

MINIMUM SAFETY AND HEALTH REQUIREMENTS FOR CONSTRUCTION SITES

Referred to in Article 9 (a) and Article 10 (1) (a) (i) of the Directive

Preliminary remarks

The obligations laid down in this Annex apply wherever required by the features of the construction site, the activity, the circumstances or a hazard.

For the purposes of this Annex, 'rooms' covers, *inter alia,* hutted accommodation.

PART A

GENERAL MINIMUM REQUIREMENTS FOR ON-SITE WORKPLACES

1. *Stability and solidity*

1.1. Materials, equipment and, more generally, any component which, when moving in any way, may affect the safety and health of workers must be stabilized in an appropriate and safe manner.

1.2. Access to any surface involving insufficiently resistant materials is not authorized unless appropriate equipment or means are provided to enable the work to be carried out safely.

2. *Energy distribution installations*

2.1. The installations must be designed, constructed and used so as not to present a fire or explosion hazard; persons must be adequately protected against the risk of electrocution caused by direct or indirect contact.

2.2. The design, construction and choice of equipment and protection devices must take account of the type and power of the energy distributed, external conditions and the competence of persons with access to parts of the installation.

3. *Emergency routes and exits*

3.1. Emergency routes and exits must remain clear and lead as directly as possible to a safe area.

3.2. In the event of danger, it must be possible for workers to evacuate all workstations quickly and as safely as possible.

3.3. The number, distribution and dimensions of emergency routes and exits depend on the use, equipment and dimensions of the site and of the rooms and the maximum number of persons that may be present.

▼B

3.4. Specific emergency routes and exits must be indicated by signs in accordance with the national regulations implementing Directive 77/576/EEC ([1]).

Such signs must be sufficiently resistant and be placed at appropriate points.

3.5. Emergency routes and exits, and the traffic routes and doors giving access to them, must be free from obstruction so that they can be used at any time without hindrance.

3.6. Emergency routes and exits requiring illumination must be provided with emergency lighting of adequate intensity in case the lighting fails.

4. *Fire detection and fire fighting*

4.1. Depending of the characteristics of the site, the dimensions and use of the rooms, the on-site equipment, the physical and chemical properties of the substances present and the maximum potential number of people present, an adequate number of appropriate fire-fighting devices and, where required, fire detectors and alarm systems must be provided.

4.2. These fire-fighting devices, fire detectors and alarm systems must be regularly checked and maintained.

Appropriate tests and drills must take place at regular intervals.

4.3. Non-automatic fire-fighting equipment be easily accessible and simple to use.

The equipment must be indicated by signs in accordance with the national regulations implementing Directive 77/576/EEC.

Such signs must be sufficiently resistant and placed at appropriate points.

5. *Ventilation*

Steps shall be taken to ensure that there is sufficient fresh air, having regard to the working methods used and the physical demands placed on the workers.

If a forced ventilation system is used, it must be maintained in working order and must not expose workers to draughts which are harmful to health.

Any breakdown must be indicated by a control system where this is necessary for workers' health.

---

(1) OJ No L 229, 7.9.1977, p. 12. Last amended by Directive 79/640/EEC (OJ No L 183, 19.7.1979, p. 1).

▼B

6. *Exposure to particular risks*

6.1. Workers must not be exposed to harmful levels of noise or to harmful external influences (e.g. gases, vapours, dust).

6.2. If workers have to enter an area where the atmosphere is liable to contain a toxic or harmful substance or to have an insufficient oxygen level or to be inflammable, the confined atmosphere must be monitored and appropriate steps taken to prevent any hazards.

6.3. A worker may not in any circumstances be exposed to a high-risk confined atmosphere.

He must at least be watched at all times from outside and all appropriate precautions must be taken to ensure that he can be assisted effectively and immediately.

7. *Temperature*

During working hours, the temperature must be appropriate for human beings, having regard to the working methods used and the physical demands placed on the workers.

8. *Natural and artificial lighting of workstations, rooms and traffic routes on the site*

8.1. Workstations, rooms and traffic routes must as far as possible have sufficient natural lighting and be provided with appropriate and sufficient artificial lighting at night and when natural daylight is inadequate; where necessary, portable light sources that are protected against impact must be used.

The colour of artificial light used must not alter or affect the perception of signals or signposts.

8.2. Lighting installations for rooms, workstations and traffic routes must be placed in such a way that there is no risk of accident to workers as a result of the type of lighting fitted.

8.3. Rooms, workstations and traffic routes where workers are especially exposed to risks ►C1 in the event of failure of artificial lighting ◄ must be provided with emergency lighting of adequate intensity.

9. *Doors and gates*

9.1. Sliding doors must be fitted with a safety device to prevent them from being derailed and falling over.

9.2. Doors and gates opening upwards must be fitted with a mechanism to secure them against falling back.

9.3. Doors and gates along escape routes must be appropriately marked.

▼B

9.4. In the immediate vicinity of gates intended primarily for vehicle traffic, there must be doors for pedestrian traffic unless it is safe for pedestrians to cross; such doors must be clearly marked and kept free at all times.

9.5. Mechanical doors and gates must operate without any risk of accident to workers.

They must be fitted with emergency stop devices which are easily identifiable and accessible and, unless they open automatically in the event of a power-cut, it must be possible for them to be opened manually.

10. *Traffic routes — danger areas*

10.1. Traffic routes, including stairs, fixed ladders and loading bays and ramps, must be calculated, located, laid out and made negotiable to ensure easy, safe and appropriate access in such a way as not to endanger workers employed in the vicinity of these traffic routes.

10.2. Routes used for pedestrian traffic and/or goods traffic including those used for loading and unloading must be dimensioned in accordance with the number of potential users and the type of activity concerned.

If means of transport are used on traffic routes, a sufficient safety clearance or adequate protective devices must be provided for other site users.

Routes must be clearly marked, regularly checked and properly maintained.

10.3. Sufficient clearance must be allowed between vehicle traffic routes and doors, gates, passages for pedestrians, corridors and staircases.

10.4. If the site includes limited-access areas, these must be equipped with devices to prevent unauthorized workers from entering.

Appropriate measures must be taken to protect workers who are authorized to enter the danger areas.

Danger areas must be clearly signposted.

11. *Loading bays and ramps*

11.1. Loading bays and ramps must be suitable for the dimensions of the loads to be transported.

11.2. Loading bays must have at least one exit point.

11.3. Loading ramps must be sufficiently safe to prevent workers from falling off.

12. *Freedom of movement at the workstation*

The floor area at the workstation must be such as to allow workers sufficient freedom of movement to perform their work, taking account of any necessary equipment or applicances present.

▼B

13. *First aid*

13.1. The employer must ensure that first aid can be provided, and that the staff trained to provide it can be called upon, at any time.

Measures must be taken to ensure that workers who have had an accident or have suddenly been taken ill can be removed for medical treatment.

13.2. One or more first-aid rooms must be provided where the scale of the works or the types of activity being carried out so require.

13.3. First-aid rooms must be fitted with essential first-aid installations and equipment and be easily accessible to stretchers.

They must be signposted in accordance with the national regulations implementing Directive 77/576/EEC.

13.4. In addition, first-aid equipment must be available at all places where working conditions so require.

This equipment must be suitably marked and easily accesible.

The address and telephone number of the local emergency service must be clearly displayed.

14. *Sanitary equipment*

14.1. Changing rooms and lockers.

14.1.1. Appropriate changing rooms must be provided for workers if they have to wear special work clothes and if, for reasons of health or propriety, they cannot be expected to change in another area.

Changing rooms must be easily accessible, be of sufficient capacity and be provided with seating.

14.1.2. Changing rooms must be sufficiently large and have facilities to enable each worker, where necessary, to dry his working clothes as well as his own clothing and personal effects and to lock them away.

If circumstances so require (e.g. ►C1 dangerous substances ◄, humidity, dirt), facilities must be provided to enable working clothes to be kept in a place separate from workers' own clothes and personal effects.

14.1.3 ►C1 Provision must be made ◄ for separate changing rooms or separate use of changing rooms for men and women.

14.1.4. If changing rooms are not required as referred to in point 14.1.1, first paragraph, each worker must be provided with a place in which he can lock away his own clothes and personal effects.

14.2. Showers and washbasins

▼B

14.2.1. Suitable showers in sufficient numbers must be provided for workers if required by the nature of the work or for health reasons.

►C1 Provision must be made ◄ for separate shower rooms or separate use of shower rooms for men and women.

14.2.2. The shower rooms must be sufficiently large to permit each worker to wash without hindrance in conditions of an appropriate standard of hygiene.

The showers must be equipped with hot and cold running water.

14.2.3. Where showers are not required under the first paragraph of 14.2.1, a sufficient number of suitable washbasins with running water (hot water if necessary) must be provided in the vicinity of the workstations and the changing rooms.

►C1 Provision must be made ◄ for separate washbasins, or separate use of washbasins for men and women when so required for reasons of propriety.

14.2.4. Where the rooms housing, the showers or washbasins are separate from the changing rooms, there must be easy communication between the two.

14.3. Lavatories and washbasins

Special facilities with an adequate number of lavatories and washbasins must be provided for workers in the vicinity of workstations, rest rooms, changing rooms and rooms housing showers or washbasins.

►C1 Provision must be made ◄ for separate lavatories or separate use of lavatories for mens and women.

15. *Rest rooms and/or accommodation areas*

15.1. Where the safety or health of workers, in particular because of the type of activity carried out or the presence of more than a certain number of employees as well as the remote nature of the site, so require, workers must be provided with easily accessible rest rooms and/or accommodation areas.

15.2. Rest rooms and/or accommodation areas must be large enough and equipped with an adequate number of tables and seats with backs for the number of workers concerned.

15.3. If there are no facilities of this kind, other facilities must be provided in which workers can stay during interruptions in work.

15.4. Fixed accommodation areas unless used only in exceptional cases, must have sufificient sanitary equipment, a rest room and a leisure room.

They must be equipped with beds, cupboards, tables and seats with backs taking account of the number of workers, and be allocated

▼B

taking account, where appropriate, of the presence of workers of both sexes.

15.5. Appropriate measures should be taken for the protection of non-smokers against discomfort caused by tobacco smoke in rest rooms and/or accommodation areas.

16. *Pregnant women and nursing mothers*

Pregnant women and nursing mothers must be able to lie down to rest in appropriate conditions.

17. *Handicapped workers*

Workplaces must be organized to take account of handicapped workers, if necessary.

The provision applies in particular to the doors, passageways, staircases, showers, washbasins, lavatories and workstations used or occupied directly by handicapped persons.

18. *Miscellaneous provisions*

18.1. The surroundings and the perimeter of the site must be signposted and laid out so as to be clearly visible and identifiable.

18.2. Workers must be provided at the site with a sufficient quantity of drinking water and possibly another suitable non-alcoholic beverage both in occupied rooms and in the vicinity of workstations.

18.3. Workers must:

— be provided with facilities enabling them to take their meals in satisfactory conditions,

— where appropriate, be provided with facilities enabling them to prepare their meals in satisfactory conditions.

▼B

PART B

SPECIFIC ►C1 MINIMUM REQUIREMENTS FOR ◄ ON-SITE WORKSTATIONS

Preliminary remark

If special situations so dictate, the classification of these minimum requirements into two sections, as below, should not regarded as binding.

Section I

On-site indoor workstations

1. *Stability and solidity*

Premises must have a structure and stability appropriate to the nature of their use.

2. *Emergency doors*

Emergency doors must open outwards.

Emergency doors must not be so locked or fastened that they cannot be easily and immediately opened by any person who may require to use them in an emergency.

Sliding or revolving doors are not permitted if intended as emergency exits.

3. *Ventilation*

If air-conditioning or mechanical ventilation installations are used, they must operate in such a way that workers are not exposed to draughts which cause discomfort.

Any deposit or dirt likely to create an immediate danger to the health of workers by polluting the atmosphere must be removed without delay.

4. *Temperature*

4.1. The temperature in rest areas, rooms for duty staff, sanitary facilities, canteens and first-aid rooms must be appropriate to the particular purpose of such areas.

4.2. Windows, skylights and glass partitions should allow excessive effects of sunlight to be avoided, having regard to the nature of the work and the use of the room.

5. *Natural and artificial lighting*

Workplaces must as far as possible have sufficient natural light and be equipped with the means of providing artificial lighting which is adequate for the purposes of protecting workers' safety and health.

▼B

6. *Floors, walls, ceilings and roofs of rooms*

6.1. The floors of workplaces must have no dangerous bumps, holes or slopes and must be fixed, stable and not slippery.

6.2. The surfaces of floors, walls and ceilings in rooms must be such that they can be cleaned or refurbished to an appropriate standard of hygiene.

6.3. Transparent or translucent walls, in particular all-glass partitions, in rooms or in the vicinity of workplaces and traffic routes must be clearly indicated and made of safety material or be shielded from such places or traffic routes to prevent workers from coming into contact with walls or being injured should the walls shatter.

7. *Windows and skylights*

7.1. It must be possible for workers to open, close, adjust or secure windows, skylights and ventilators in a safe manner.

When open, they must not be positioned so as to constitute a hazard to workers.

7.2. Windows and skylights must be designed in conjunction with equipment or otherwise fitted with devices allowing them to be cleaned without risk to the workers carrying out this work or to workers present.

8. *Doors and Gates*

8.1. The position, ►C1 number and dimensions ◄ of doors and gates, and the materials used in their construction, are determined by the nature and use of the rooms or areas.

8.2. Transparent doors must be appropriately marked at a conspicious level.

8.3. Swing doors and gates must be transparent or have see-through panels.

8.4. If transparent or translucent surfaces in doors and gates are not made of safety material and if there is a danger that workers may be injured if a door or gate should shatter, the surfaces must be protected against breakage.

9. *Traffic routes*

Where the use and equipment of rooms so requires for the protection of workers, traffic routes must be clearly identified.

10. *Specific measures for escalators and travelators*

Escalators and travelators must function safely.

They must be equipped with any necessary safety devices.

They must be fitted with easily identifiable and accessible emergency shut-down devices.

▼B

11. *Room dimensions and air space in rooms*

Workrooms must have sufficient surface area and height to allow workers to perform their work without risk to their safety, health or well-being.

Section II

On-site outdoor workstations

1. *Stability and solidity*

1.1. High-level or low-level movable or fixed workstations must be solid and stable, taking account of:

— the number of workers occupying them,

— the maximum loads they may have to bear and the weight distribution,

— the outside influcences to which they may be subject.

If the support and the other components of these workstations are not intrinsically stable, their stability will have to be ensured by appropriate and safe methods of fixing to avoid any untimely or spontaneous movement of the whole or of parts of the workstations.

1.2. Checking

Stability and solidity must be checked appropriately and especially after any change ►C1 in the height or depth ◄ of the workstation.

2. *Energy distribution installations*

2.1. On-site energy distribution installations, especially those subject to outside influences, must be regularly checked and maintained.

2.2. Installations existing before the site began must be identified, checked and clearly signposted.

2.3. Whenever possible, where overhead electric power lines exist, either they must be redirected away from the area of the site or else the current must be cut off.

If this is not possible, there will be barriers or notices to ensure that vehicles and installations are kept away.

Suitable warnings and suspended protections must be provided where vehicles have to pass beneath the lines.

3. *Atmospheric influences*

Workers must be protected against atmospheric influences which could affect their health and safety.

▼B

4. *Falling objects*

Wherever technically feasible, workers must be protected by collective methods against falling objects.

Materials and equipment must be laid out or stracked in such a way as to prevent their collapsing or overturning.

Where necessary, there must be covered passageways ►C1 on the site or access ◄ to danger areas must be made impossible.

5. *Falls from a height*

5.1. Falls from a height must be physically prevented in particular by means of solid cradles which are sufficiently high and have at least an end-board, a main handrail and an intermediate handrail or an equivalent alternative.

5.2. In principle, work at a height must be carried out only with appropriate equipment or using collective protection devices such as cradles, platforms or safety nets.

If the use of such equipment is not possible because of the nature of the work, suitable means of access must be provided and safety harnesses or other anchoring safety methods must be used.

6. *Scaffolding and leaders* (*)

6.1. All scaffolding must be properly designed, constructed and maintained to ensure that it does not collapse or move accidentally.

6.2. Work platforms, gangways and scaffolding stairways must be constructed, dimensioned, protected and used in such a way as to prevent people from falling or being exposed to falling objects.

6.3. Scaffolding must be inspected by a competent person:

(a) before being put into service;

(b) subsequently, at periodic intervals;

(c) after any ►C1 modification, period ◄ without use, exposure to bad weather or seismic tremors, or any other circumstance which may have affected its strength or stability.

6.4. Ladders must be sufficiently strong and correctly maintained.

They must be correctly used, in appropriate places and in accordance with their intended purpose.

6.5. Mobile scaffolding must be secured against spontaneous movements.

(*) This point will be specified in the framework of the future Directive amending Directive 89/655/EEC, particularly with a view to supplementing point 3 of the Annex thereto.

▼B

7. *Lifting equipment* (*)

7.1. All lifting devices and accessories, including their component parts, attachments, anchorings and supports, must be:

(a) properly designed and constructed and sufficiently strong for the use to which they are put;

(b) correctly installed and used;

(c) maintained in good working order;

(d) checked and subjected to periodic tests and inspections in accordance with current legislation;

(e) operated by qualified workers who have received appropriate training.

7.2. All lifting devices ►C1 and accessories must ◄ clearly display their maximum load values.

7.3. Lifting equipment and accessories may not be used for other than their intended purposes.

8. *Excavating and materials-handling vehicles and machinery* (*)

8.1. All excavating and materials-handling vehicles and machinery must be:

(a) properly designed and constructed taking account, as far as possible, of the principles of ergonomics;

(a) kept in good working order;

(c) used correctly.

8.2. Drivers and operators of excavating and materials-handling vehicles and machinery must be specially trained.

8.3. Preventive measures must be taken to ensure that excavating and materials-handling vehicles and machinery do not fall into the excavations or into water.

8.4. Where appropriate, excavating machinery and materials-handling machinery must be fitted with structures to protect the driver against being crushed if the machine overturns, and against falling objects.

9. *Installations, machinery, equipment* (*)

9.1. Installations, machinery and equipment, including hand tools whether power-driven or not, must be:

(a) properly designed and constructed ►C1 taking account, as far as ◄ possible, of the principle of ergonomics;

(*) This point will be specified in the framework of the future Directive amending Directive 89/655/EEC, particularly with a view to supplementing point 3 of the Annex thereto.

▼B

(b) kept in good working order;

(c) used solely for the work for which they were designed;

(d) operated by workers who have received appropriate training.

9.2. Installations and equipment under pressure must be checked and subjected to regular tests and inspections in accordance with existing legislation.

10. *Excavations, wells, underground works, tunnels and earthworks*

10.1. Suitable precautions must be taken in an excavation, well, underground, working or tunnel:

(a) using an appropriate support or embankment;

(b) to prevent hazards entailed in the fall of a person, materials or objects, or flooding;

(c) to provide sufficient ventilation at all workstations so as to ensure a breathable atmosphere which is not dangerous or harmful to health;

(d) to enable workers to reach safety in the event of fire or ►C1 inrush of water ◄ or materials.

10.2. Before excavation starts, measures must be taken to identify and reduce to a minimum any hazard due to underground cables and other distribution systems.

10.3. Safe routes into and out of the excavation must be provided.

10.4. Piles of earth, materials and moving vehicles must be kept away from the excavation; appropriate barriers must be built if necessary.

11. *Demolition work*

Where the demolition of a building or construction may present a danger:

(a) appropriate precautions, methods and procedures must be adopted;

(b) the work must be planned and undertaken only under the supervision of a competent person.

12. *Metal or concrete frameworks, shutterings and heavy prefabricated components*

12.1. Metal or concrete frameworks and their components, shutterings, prefabricated components or ►C1 temporary supports, and ◄ buttresses

(*) This point will be specified in the framework of the future Directive amending Directive 89/655/EEC, particularly with a view to supplementing point 3 of the Annex thereto.

▼B

must be erected and dismantled only under the supervision of a competent person.

12.2. Adequate precautions must be taken to protect workers against risks arising from the temporary fragility or instability of a structure.

12.3. Shutterings, temporary supports and buttresses ►C1 must be devised and designed ◄, installed and maintained so as to safely withstand any strains and stresses which may be placed on them.

13. *Cofferdams and caissons*

13.1. All cofferdams and caissons must be:

(a) well constructed, of appropriate, solid materials of adequate strength;

(b) appropriately equipped so that workers can gain shelter in the event of an irruption of water and materials.

13.2. The construction, installation, transformation or dismantling of a cofferdam or caisson must take place only under the supervision of a competent person.

13.3. All cofferdams and caissons must be inspected by a competent person at regular intervals.

14. *Work on roofs*

14.1. Where necessary to avert a risk or where the height or the slope exceed values set by the Member States, collective preventive measures must be taken to prevent workers, and tools or other objects or materials, from falling.

14.2. Where workers have to work on or near a roof or any other surface made of fragile materials through which it is possible to fall, preventive measures must be taken to ensure that they do not inadvertently walk on the surface made of fragile materials, or fall to the ground.

CDM Regulations 2015 Explained
ISBN 978-0-7277-5739-5

http://dx.doi.org/10.1680/icsiam.57395.259

Appendix 4
Pre-construction information

Information collected by a client, with the assistance of the principal designer, should include the categories of information below where the topic is relevant to the work proposed. *The level of detail in the information should be appropriate and proportionate to the risks involved in the project.*

1. Description of the project

(a) The project description and programme details, including
 (i) key dates (including the planned start and finish of the construction phase)
 (ii) the minimum time to be allowed between the appointment of the principal contractor and instruction to commence work on the site.

(b) Details of the client, designers and other consultants.

(c) Whether or not the structure will be used as a workplace (in which case the finished design will need to take account of the relevant requirements of the Workplace (Health, Safety and Welfare) Regulations 1992).

(d) The extent and location of existing records and plans.

2. Client's considerations and management requircments

(a) Arrangements for
 (i) planning for and managing the construction work, including any health and safety goals for the project
 (ii) communication and liaison between the client and others
 (iii) security of the site
 (iv) welfare provisions.

(b) Requirements relating to the health and safety of the client's employees or customers or those involved in the project such as
 (i) site hoarding requirements
 (ii) site transport arrangements or vehicle movement restrictions
 (iii) client permit-to-work systems

(iv) fire precautions
(v) emergency procedures and means of escape
(vi) 'no-go' areas or other authorisation requirements for those involved in the project
(vii) any areas that the client has designated as confined spaces
(viii) smoking and parking restrictions
(ix) the client's workplace details.

3. Environmental restrictions and existing on-site risks

(a) Safety hazards, including
(i) boundaries and access, including temporary access (e.g. narrow streets, or lack of parking, turning or storage space)
(ii) any restrictions on deliveries or waste collection or storage
(iii) adjacent land uses (e.g. schools, railway lines or busy roads)
(iv) the existing storage of hazardous materials
(v) the location of existing services, particularly those that are concealed (e.g. water, electricity or gas)
(vi) ground conditions, underground structures or water courses where this might affect the safe use of plant (e.g. cranes) or the safety of groundworks
(vii) information about existing structures (e.g. stability, structural form, fragile or hazardous materials, or anchorage points for fall arrest systems – particularly where demolition is involved)
(viii) previous structural modifications, including weakening or strengthening of the structure – particularly where demolition is involved
(ix) fire damage, ground shrinkage, movement or poor maintenance that may have adversely affected the structure
(x) any difficulties relating to plant and equipment in the premises, such as overhead gantries whose height restricts access
(xi) health and safety information in earlier design, construction or 'as-built' material such as drawings (e.g. details of pre-stressed or post-tensioned structures).

(b) Health hazards, including
(i) asbestos, including results of surveys (particularly where demolition is involved)
(ii) the existing storage of hazardous materials
(iii) contaminated land, including results of surveys

(iv) existing structures containing hazardous materials
(v) health risks arising from the client's activities.

4. Significant design and construction hazards

(a) Significant design assumptions and suggested work methods, sequences or other control measures.
(b) Arrangements for the coordination of ongoing design work and handling design changes.
(c) Information on significant risks identified during design.
(d) Materials requiring particular precautions.

5. The health and safety file

Description of its format and any conditions relating to its content.

CDM Regulations 2015 Explained
ISBN 978-0-7277-5739-5

http://dx.doi.org/10.1680/icsiam.57395.263

Appendix 5
Health and Safety (Enforcing Authority) Regulations 1998

SCHEDULE 2

Regulation 4(4)(b)

ACTIVITIES IN RESPECT OF WHICH THE HEALTH AND SAFETY EXECUTIVE IS THE ENFORCING AUTHORITY

1. Any activity in a mine or quarry other than a quarry in respect of which notice of abandonment has been given under section 139(2) of the Mines and Quarries Act 1954.

2. Any activity in a fairground.

3. Any activity in premises occupied by a radio, television or film undertaking in which the activity of broadcasting, recording or filming is carried on, and the activity of broadcasting, recording or filming wherever carried on, and for this purpose "film" includes video.

4. The following activities carried on at any premises by persons who do not normally work in the premises—

(a) construction work if—

(i) regulation 7(1) of the Construction (Design and Management) Regulations 1994 (which requires projects which include or are intended to include construction work to be notified to the Executive) applies to the project which includes the work; or

(ii) the whole or part of the work contracted to be undertaken by the contractor at the premises is to the external fabric or other external part of a building or structure; or

(iii) it is carried out in a physically segregated area of the premises, the activities normally carried out in that area have been suspended for the purpose of enabling the construction work to be carried out, the contractor has authority to exclude from that area persons who are not attending in connection with the carrying out of the work and the work is not the maintenance of insulation on pipes, boilers or other parts of heating or water systems or its removal from them;

(b) the installation, maintenance or repair of any gas system, or any work in relation to a gas fitting;

(c) the installation, maintenance or repair of electricity systems;

(d) work with ionising radiations except work in one or more of the categories set out in Schedule 3 to the Ionising Radiations Regulations 1985.

5. The use of ionising radiations for medical exposure (within the meaning of regulation 2(1) of the Ionising Radiations Regulations 1985).

6. Any activity in premises occupied by a radiography undertaking in which there is carried on any work with ionising radiations.

7. Agricultural activities, and any activity at an agricultural show which involves the handling of livestock or the working of agricultural equipment.

8. Any activity on board a sea-going ship.

9. Any activity in relation to a ski slope, ski lift, ski tow or cable car.

10. Fish, maggot and game breeding except in a zoo.

11. Any activity in relation to a pipeline within the meaning of regulation 3 of the Pipelines Safety Regulations 1996(**1**).

12. The operation of a railway.

CDM Regulations 2015 Explained
ISBN 978-0-7277-6009-8

http://dx.doi.org/10.1680/cdmre.60098.265

Index